Cognitive Psycholog

Books ar

Crucial Study Texts for Psychology Degree Courses

Titles in the series

To order, please call our order line 0845 230 9000, or email orders@learningmatters.co.uk, or visit our website www.learningmatters.co.uk

Cognitive Psychology

Eamon Fulcher

Psychology series editor:
Eamon Fulcher

First published in 2003 by Crucial, a division of Learning Matters Ltd.

British Library Cataloguing in Publication Data
A CIP record for this book is available from the British Library.

ISBN 1 903337 13 5

Cover design by Topics – The Creative Partnership
Project management by Deer Park Productions
Text design by Code 5 Design
Typeset by PDQ Typesetting, Newcastle under Lyme
Printed and bound by Bell & Bain Ltd, Glasgow

Learning Matters Ltd
33 Southernhay East
Exeter EX1 1NX
Tel: 01392 215560
Email: info@learningmatters.co.uk
www.learningmatters.co.uk

Contents

Acknowledgements

I would like to thank those who have helped me develop inspiration, insight, and ambition: Pete Sneddon, Igor Aleksander, Alan Baddeley, Andrew Mathews, Bundy Mackintosh, Marianne Hammerl and Roger Cocks. I thank Jonathan and Mandy of Learning Matters for giving me the editorship of this series and the authorship of this title. I thank the other authors of this series for the timely arrival of their manuscripts, especially Meg Barker and Andy Field. Many thanks also to Rosey Phillips for help with compiling the references.

Dedication

This book is dedicated to Simone and Charlotte.

Introduction
Studying cognitive psychology at degree level

In this chapter I will try to convince you that cognitive psychology is not just something you **have** to study for your degree, but is a topic that you can find interesting. I will also try to make clear what your tutors will expect from you, how to study effectively, and how to write good essays and reports.

Why you need to know about human cognition

Cognitive psychology concerns how people perceive, understand, evaluate and think. Cognitive psychologists argue that all or most of our behaviour is determined by cognition. For example, you are reading this text either because you have just enrolled on a psychology degree programme or are thinking about it. A lot of cognitive processes, busily working away in your mind, have led you to the behaviour of picking up this book and reading it. Furthermore, though reading this text may seem almost effortless to you (well, that was the intention, at least!), think about the many processes going on that allow you to transform these printed characters into meaningful information.

Cognitive psychology is everywhere

This is all pretty important stuff, you might agree, but I suspect that you are wondering whether it really connects with why you want to do a psychology degree. Well, whether you become an educational psychologist, an occupational psychologist, a psychotherapist or work in some other field where you will use your knowledge of psychology, you need first to understand how people perceive their world and others in it, how people make sense of the world and the behaviour of other people, how people come to like and dislike things, and how people are constrained by their own thought processes. These are crucial questions.

It is because cognitive psychology is so important for our understanding of human psychology that virtually every psychology degree programme in the UK (especially those accredited by the British Psychological Society) will include its study. For me, one of the biggest impacts that cognitive psychology has had is in our understanding of disorders such as anxiety and depression. Indeed, my research focuses on anxiety from the cognitive perspective, and my current research project examines attention in anxious children.

Many students do find cognitive psychology immediately appealing. Like me, some of these students are interested in how emotion can colour perception (and vice versa). Others seem to like the computer metaphor and so get interested in cognitive science. Those with a scientific background prefer the formal approach taken in cognitive psychology to the more confusing approach in social psychology, which uses a more diverse range of methods.

Methods of learning in higher education

People who have studied successfully for a psychology degree have in common the ability to study independently. This means that they are able to plan their own study time, find out important information for themselves, meet deadlines and produce their own work to a high standard. For most, it also means the ability to adopt a critical approach when discussing a particular theme.

One of the main differences between studying at degree level from any other level, such as A level or Access, is the expectation that students will organise and plan their own studies. It is most likely that previously all or most of your studies were organised for you by a teacher or tutor who nagged you if you didn't do the work. We academics refer to this as 'nannying' and it is what many students want us to do. However, at degree level your tutor will not be looking over your shoulder or nannying you. Your tutor will not nag you for bad or late work – he or she will just give you bad marks. And herein lies the problem: how do you motivate yourself, how much study time should you put in, how should you study, and why can't you just party-party?

How can you motivate yourself?

A couple of techniques you might find useful are:

- **Thinking in the future and looking at the past**. Imagine that you are 20 years older than you are now, or better still imagine that you are a pensioner. I suspect that one or two readers are already pensioners. Higher education welcomes you and you can study safe in the knowledge that pensioners generally do very well indeed. In any case, at some point in the future you will inevitably look at your past. You might wonder how things could have been different. You might wonder why you didn't just put in a few hours a week of private study. It wasn't a lot to ask of yourself. If you had spent more time studying then you might have got that first or that upper second. Instead you squandered your time and your money doing things that you couldn't even remember doing afterwards! Do remember that this is your opportunity to get a good degree. You are unlikely to get a second chance.
- **Go on, impress yourself**. Ask people why they do the things that they do, and ultimately you'll find that they do things to impress others. We try to impress our peer group, our brothers or sisters, our parents or carers, other people we care about, and even our teachers and tutors. However, a better strategy, perhaps, is to try to impress yourself. Do things in such a way that when you look at what you have done you are impressed. If you can impress yourself then others will follow suit. Although I recommend this approach to life in general, in terms of your studies, if you try to write essays to impress yourself then you are quite likely to impress your tutor (provided you adhere to the guidelines here and those of your tutors).

Using primary and secondary sources

Your psychology tutor will expect you to write in your own words, and he or she makes a distinction between primary and secondary resources. Primary resources are articles that are written by a researcher about his or her research, and mostly take the form of journal articles and occasionally a chapter in a multi-authored book. A secondary resource is one where the author has reviewed, for a primarily student audience, the research of other psychologists and takes the form of a book. It follows that if you simply rehashed the review from a chapter in a textbook then you are not presenting ideas in your own words, you are merely restating the interpretation made by the author of the book. However, if you read the original articles on which the chapter is based then you are in a better position to provide your own interpretation. This way, you then write an essay that reflects your own interpretation and one that is clearly in your own words.

Journal articles

Whenever a researcher carries out his or her experiments and wishes to publish the results, they will submit a report of their work to a psychology journal (e.g. *Personality and Individual Differences*). The editor of the journal has the job of deciding whether the report submitted should be published in the journal. This decision is based on a number of factors, such as, suitability of the topic for the journal, importance of the topic area, importance of the results obtained, clarity of the writing and so on. To help the editor decide, the article is peer reviewed. This means that between two and four other psychologists working in a related area will be sent copies of the article to evaluate. The reviewers then submit a brief written evaluation of the report, including a grade that reflects their opinion as to whether the article should be published. The editor collates the reviews and makes the final decision. Often, an editor will find that more than one reviewer has the same concern (e.g. they may think that the method is unclear in places, or they think that another experiment should be done). In this case they will invite the author to resubmit a modified version of the article. The important point about this procedure is that all journal articles have been peer reviewed. This means that their level of quality is high and that the authors are not making claims that are too difficult to substantiate. Books, on the other hand, are not peer reviewed in the same way. Commonly, books are sent out to other psychologists for a review but it is only on general aspects of the book and it is not scrutinised with the same eye for detail as journal articles are.

The internet

It often amazes me when students complain that they can't find anything about the subject they are writing an essay on via the Internet. Typically they have logged on to google.co.uk and have typed in a few key words. Yet, most departments or their libraries subscribe to at least one bibliographic database, such as IDEAL (www.idealibrary.com). You can type the same key words into its search engine and have scores of abstracts on the subject appear in front of you, often many more than you would want to read. The problem with the Internet is that it is rare that full published articles are uploaded onto the Web; instead all you get is someone's lecture notes or some geek's strange view of the world. Only use sites recommended to you by your tutors and by the authors of the Crucial Study series. To research a topic, use a bibliographic database.

Academic writing

When you read psychology books and journals, you will find it quite difficult at times to understand the language used. Psychologists, as students often point out to me, tend to use 'jargon' terminology throughout their writings and they may as well have been written in Portuguese. However, rest assured that it will get easier the more you study psychology.

Psychologists invent and use their own terms for one important reason. Many of the terms used in everyday language have specific meanings (in everyday terms). The terms psychologists invent are there to differentiate between the everyday use of the term and its meaning in psychological terms. Consider a term chosen at random, like **extinction**. This word is used in psychology to refer to a particular kind of 'forgetting' through a particular kind of method. If you were the first psychologist to have discovered the effect, you would have not wanted to simply call it 'forgetting', since that word has many unwanted associations and implications that have nothing to do with the effect you have just discovered. When a psychologist sees the word 'extinction' he or she immediately knows the field of study and the precise method the term refers to. Some of these terms eventually become part of normal language use (such as 'ego' and 'short-term memory').

Notwithstanding the importance of the use of specialist terms that have precise and particular meanings in psychology, in my mind the better journal articles are those that are written clearly, where psychological terms are defined, and where nothing is left to ambiguity. The first paper that comes to mind is Crick and Mitchison's paper on the reverse learning theory of dreaming (which I briefly mention in Chapter 9); another is Searle's paper on whether machines can think (also discussed in Chapter 9). You might not agree with their views, but they are expressed in clear terms and the arguments they present are arranged in a logical order.

As I point out in Chapter 7 when discussing expertise, it probably takes about 10 years to become a master or expert in something, and this includes becoming an expert in some field of psychology. Consider an example of an expert skill such as kicking a football. To do this, cast your mind back to the World Cup qualifying match between England and Greece in April 2002, if you have any recollection of this game. There are three minutes on the clock and England needs to score to be certain of qualifying. England is awarded a free kick and up steps David Beckham. Under immense pressure to score, Beckham's swerving kick hits the top inside corner of the net, leaving the goalkeeper stranded and helpless. The implication of this act was that England had qualified for the World Cup. According to Dr. Keith Hanna, talking to the *Daily Telegraph*:

> [Beckham had carried out] a multi-variable physics calculation in his head to compute the exact kick trajectory required and then execute it perfectly. He had figured out how to balance the kick angle, kick speed, spin imparted, and kick direction to get this optimal turbulent-laminar transition trajectory ... Our computers take several hours to do the same calculations.

How did Beckham acquire such expertise? Did he really pay attention in his physics lessons at school or is this a natural ability? According to his long-time friend and fellow Manchester United player, Gary Neville, Beckham has spent hour upon hour practising this movement – so much so that he can deliver a pass or a shot with almost 'pinpoint accuracy' and, to use the commentator's terminology, this ability is really quite remarkable!

In sum, the more articles and textbooks on psychology you read, the better will be your ability to write psychologically. Needless to say, your tutor will not expect you to write precisely in the same way as a professional psychologist. Very often when students new to psychology try to do just this, it does not read well at all. Instead you should try to present your arguments clearly and in a straightforward manner. Choose meaning over expression, as it is more important that your tutor has evidence that you understand what you are writing about than it is to write in a style you are not used to. However, at the other extreme are everyday terminologies and idioms which you should avoid using. Be assured that it does get easier, as most final-year undergraduates will tell you.

Finally, it is worth mentioning that since psychologists write about theories and the evidence for and against particular theories, the writing style is closer to that used by lawyers than it is to, say, a script used in a documentary. Some students tend to write in a sort of documentary style. By this I mean that a theory will be discussed as though it were a fact. Programmes like the BBC's *Horizon* tend to dramatise science as a series of important and surprising discoveries. You should avoid writing like this. In psychology everything is 'up for grabs' (this is an example of one of those everyday idioms you should avoid using!), which means that we rarely deal with 'facts', we deal with evidence, rather like a lawyer.

You can imagine that your reader is the jury whom you are trying to convince. The claim of the prosecution is the view or theory you are trying to advance and the defendant's account is the theory you are trying to invalidate. You will cite evidence that the defendant's theory is wrong and evidence that your theory is the better one. You may not be able to prove your theory but may be able to persuade the jury through the clever use of argument given the available evidence. Hence you will find phrases in psychology articles that relate to the evidence as 'supporting the theory', 'rendering the theory implausible', 'being consistent with the theory', 'causing us to doubt the theory' or 'increasing our confidence in the theory'.

Writing essays

Two common problems with essays are: (a) the student has chosen a question (say, in an exam) that they perceive to be easy; and (b) the student fails to answer the question. In terms of the former, questions are, as much as possible, equated for their level of difficulty.

An easy-looking question might look easy (because it is general, for example) but it may require a deeper level of analysis than you at first think. In terms of the latter, many students fail to read the question carefully, and ignore key words in the question such as, **compare**, **contrast**, **evaluate**, **discuss**, and so on. Answer the question in the manner asked of you. So if you are asked to **compare** classical and operant conditioning, for example, you do not write half your essay on classical conditioning and then the other half on operant conditioning, you compare features of classical conditioning with features of operant conditioning, taking each feature or aspect in turn.

Although I can't prove this, I suspect that when some students do their essays, they write as they read. This means that they haven't read the full story before they commit pen to paper, or finger to keyboard. You must try to read an overview before you begin your essay and then formulate in note form what your main arguments will be. Next write out a series of bullet points that outline, very briefly, the order in which you want to make your main points. Structure your bullet points by arranging them as a 'to and fro' of the arguments for and against the central issues. You can then take each bullet point in turn and elaborate by filling in the details. Add new bullet points or modify existing ones when required. Remember that your essay should not be a list of points; it should flow well, be structured logically and must answer the question.

One of the main, more general reasons why a low mark is awarded is because the essay reveals too little evidence of reading on the subject. Don't kid yourself into thinking that getting by with little reading will get you a decent mark or even a pass mark – your tutor has extensive knowledge and will see the gaps in your answer and its lack of depth immediately. You must answer the question by drawing on a range of material. You have to show some understanding of the main issues and theories, and you have to be critical, which means evaluating and appraising what you read. Finally, remember that your marker must not need to **infer** the extent of your knowledge and your understanding, your essay has to **provide evidence to the reader** that you understand the issues and that you are knowledgeable on the subject.

Essays must have the following:

- **An introduction**. You begin by saying what your essay is going to be about. Tell your reader how you are going to answer the question.

- **Main body of the essay**. You should define key terms throughout, develop arguments and discuss the evidence. Your essay should read like a debate on the issues.

- **Conclusion**. When you have written the introduction and the main body, you should then summarise your whole essay in two or three paragraphs. A good, unambiguous conclusion finishes an essay off well and gets additional marks. A conclusion is a bit like an abstract to a report, only it is placed at the end not the beginning.

Finally, and I'm sure your course leader will remind you of this, hand in your work on time. Don't leave your work until the last minute. PCs (and photocopiers, apparently) have an in-built last-minute-panic detector and when it lights up creates an access error at location 56720007GC4. It then terminates. Faulty PCs and printers are no excuse for late essays. Most courses only consider ill health (with documentary evidence) as a legitimate reason for a late hand-in, and it matters not whether it was your dog or your printer that ate your essay – it is still considered your fault.

Writing research reports

I have included a section here on writing research reports because many of the topics covered in cognitive psychology form the basis of the lab practical. It is likely that you will have to write a research report on at least one topic in cognitive psychology. See also the example report in Chapter 10.

Title

Be concise and clear. Give the reader a good idea about the research question. A common method is to mention the IV (independent variable) and the DV (dependent variable), e.g. 'The effect of rehearsal on recognition memory' – rehearsal is the IV (whether it was prevented or encouraged) and recognition is the DV (number of items recognised). An alternative is to state the main finding as the title: 'Rehearsal improves recognition memory'. A poor title is one that is too general, e.g. 'An experimental investigation into recognition memory', as it gives no information about the research question. Another poor title is 'Fail to rehearse at your peril!' – first it is too vague, second it makes a value judgement and third it is expressed in non-scientific terms. Another useful method is to have **two** titles, a main title and a sub-title, e.g. 'An everyday application of mnemonic devices: the effect of rehearsal on recognition memory'. This gives extra details about the research question. Avoid redundant terms, such as 'An investigation ...', 'An experiment ...', 'A study to find out ...', and so on.

Abstract

An abstract is a brief summary of the research carried out. Its length should be between 100 and 250 words, depending on the word limit for the whole report, and should certainly be no longer than one side of A4, typed with single-spaced lines. It must contain brief details about:

- the research question or hypothesis under study (you do not have to state the formal hypothesis but you should paraphrase it in a way that is easy to understand);
- the method used and the basic design of the study;
- the main findings, in words;
- one line on the interpretation of the results.

Note that the abstract must not be 'chatty' – do not review the background to the study but offer only one, or at most two, sentences on background. The abstract does not refer to other works by saying 'Baddeley (1986) defines working memory...', for example, but it can be useful to include **one** key reference to locate the general theoretical framework, such as 'This is a replication of French and Saunders (1992)' or 'this study is aimed at testing Brain's (1986) model of memory'. Make the abstract the last section that you write.

Introduction

The introduction should begin with a broad review of the area leading towards a review of the specific question under study. Its main purpose is to provide a rationale for the present study – why is it being done precisely in this way? Outline the key theories relevant to the study, and mention any problems or controversies in the area. The final paragraph should be a clear statement about the hypothesis or hypotheses under study. Please note that the hypothesis must be stated explicitly – it must be a precise prediction not a general statement that there may be differences somewhere between conditions.

You should **not** provide an account of everything you know or have read on the subject, but review **only** studies that **are directly relevant** for the current research question. A useful way to start working on an introduction is to write down the main points you want to make in the introduction as bullet points. An example of such an attempt is:

- Give a real-life example that demonstrates the question: when faced with a threat such as an angry dog, what comes first, feelings or thoughts?
- Briefly outline a theory that feelings come first, then a theory that thoughts come first, then a theory about how the two are inseparable.
- Explain the **first** theory in detail and provide research evidence that supports it.
- Provide evidence that is difficult for the first theory.
- Explain the **second** theory in detail and provide research evidence that supports it.

- Provide evidence that is difficult for the second theory.
- Explain the **third** theory in detail and provide research evidence that supports it.
- Provide evidence that is difficult for the third theory.
- Evaluate which theory accounts for the evidence best, then say why the question is difficult to resolve.
- Say how the study will approach the problem.
- Provide an outline of the method, e.g. **why** this particular method/approach is being used.
- State which theory will be put to the test and **how** this study will achieve that.
- State the experimental or null hypothesis or hypotheses.

Method

The main function of the method section is to tell your reader exactly what you did. It allows your reader to (1) interpret your results in the light of the method used, and (2) do an **exact** replication of your study based **only** on your write-up of the method you used. If there is any ambiguity here then the reader will not be able to do either of these. There are four subsections of the Method:

1. **Design**. This is a very important section as it lets the reader know how the research question was assessed directly. Here the independent variable(s) is (are) mentioned (e.g. 'rehearsal') and what its levels, or groups, consisted of (e.g. a no-rehearsal group when rehearsal is prevented by a backward counting task, and a mnemonic rehearsal group where a task designed to encourage rehearsal is used). The dependent variable is also stated and **how it was measured** (e.g. 'the number of items recognised out of 50 presented'). Students often omit this. Mention whether it was a repeated measures or independent subjects design, or whether it was a correlation (in which case there are no dependent and independent variables, but you must state explicitly what the variables consist of). Indicate how extraneous variables were controlled for (order effects and so on). Having read this section, the reader should be clear about the design of the study, what the variables are and how they are to be measured.

2. **Participants**. You mention the number of participants used, their age range, the mean age, gender, how they were recruited and any other information that might be important. Include information about the participants or the selection criteria that are directly relevant for the study. For example, a test on responding to colours must indicate whether participants were tested for colour blindness.

3. **Materials**. Mention what the materials used were (if this is lengthy then give a couple of examples and put them in full in an appendix), how materials were presented, and which type of responses were obtained and how they were obtained. Do not mention totally obvious items such as a pen if they had to write something down. You **must** explain why each type of item was chosen – could you have chosen better material, or material that is more suitable for testing the hypothesis? For example, if you created faces using a photofit program, indicate in what way the faces were created and how features were selected, and say why pictures from a magazine were not chosen. Do not just provide a list of the materials used.

4. **Procedure**. This describes in chronological order the details of how you gathered the information. You do not have to type the instructions given to the participants word for word but summarise them by giving your reader a flavour of what they were requested to do. You can place actual instructions given to them in the appendices. Describe what the participants did and in chronological order. Say how long each task took to do, approximately.

In any of the above you must **never** say something such as 'The instructions given are in Appendix 2' without giving an indication of what the instructions were in the method section. In other words, do not rely on appendices or let them 'speak for themselves'.

Results

The purpose of this section is to state clearly what the results were. Descriptive statistics can be written within a sentence (e.g. 'the mean recognition score of the no-rehearsal group was 23.6, with a standard deviation of 9.53'). However, if there are a lot of statistics to mention then these can be placed in a table. Note that where tables are used they should be mentioned in the text (don't just place a table in this section without referring to it in the text); further, table columns and rows should be labelled with an indication of the scale used (e.g. 'mean recognition out of 50'). Tables should be numbered so that they can be individually referred to in the text (e.g. 'the mean scores indicate that overall recognition rates were generally high – see Table 1').

With regard to the use of inferential statistics, first translate the experimental hypothesis into a statistical prediction, e.g. 'the experimental hypothesis predicts that the recognition rates for the rehearsal group will be significantly greater than those of the no-rehearsal group'. Then state which test you used and why it is appropriate. The results of the test should be stated in the conventional manner (e.g. $t(34) = 56.67$, $P < 0.05$) and also where significant differences are found, state which direction these are in. For example, the group or condition corresponding to the higher mean should be stated, so that the reader knows that the direction of the difference agrees with the hypothesis. Some tutors will advise students to report the actual computed value of p as well – check the policy followed in your department. Do not place the calculations or computer printouts of any statistical test in the results section but put them in the appendices. Finally, you must mention what the results mean: 'therefore we can reject the null hypothesis and can conclude that rehearsal improves recognition memory'. Your interpretation of the results is restricted to a direct explanation of what the test statistic means for the hypothesis. All other interpretations, e.g. theoretical ones, go in the discussion section.

Please note that raw data is hardly ever put in the Results section, so put them in an appendix instead. Also, a graph of raw scores for each participant should **not** be placed in the results or in the report at all – such graphs have no meaning. However, do create graphs of means or measures of variance, such as a boxplot, histogram and so on, when you think that they would help the reader interpret your data.

Discussion

Here the results are interpreted in the light of the research question and the particular hypothesis under study. Your reader is looking for the appropriateness of the interpretation of the results, given the context of the study, and also the degree to which plausible alternative explanations are offered and evaluated. In addition, in this section you should mention any methodological issues and the reader is looking at the extent to which non-trivial and highly pertinent methodological issues are explored. For example, it is only helpful to mention an otherwise trivial detail, such as room temperature, if for some reason it varied across conditions and could have influenced the outcome (e.g. 'when testing group B, we noticed that there was a dramatic drop in room temperature due to a heating failure'); thus highlight any undesirable environmental differences **between** the groups.

Most importantly, you should appraise your own study critically, i.e. play devil's advocate, and evaluate it in the wider context and in its relation to appropriate theories. If results are significant, you do not have to go on about how the study was a 'success', but rather examine the implications for theory and then find fault with your design and search for alternative explanations. Also, if the results are non-significant do not report this as some sort of 'failure' of the study, but rather examine its implications for theory, and then go on to say how we could test whether this result is a rogue or a valid one.

One important feature of report writing often overlooked by students is being speculative, creative and even attempting to present your own theory, or your own modification of someone else's theory. Use the discussion to develop your own ideas, speculate about human behaviour and mental processes, dream up your own theory but make it sound at least plausible and not completely off the wall! Always finish this section with a conclusion: say what the main interpretation of the study is given the research question.

In sum, the discussion section should answer the following questions:

- What is the main statistical result of your study?
- What does it mean, in terms of support/refutation for your hypothesis?
- How should your results be interpreted in the light of your expectations?
- Do the results support a theory? If so, which one and how do they support it?
- Do the results refute a theory? If so, which one and how do they refute it?
- Given such support or refutation, should we be cautious in making such conclusions, in terms of methodological weaknesses (e.g. were the materials used appropriate, were the instructions clear enough)?
- In what ways could you alter the method in order to test the theory more conclusively?
- Are there any observations you have made that suggest the theory/theories are good or bad ones?
- Is there a better explanation for your observations, e.g. could you think up a theory that could explain your data? If so, can you think of an experiment that would put **your** theory to the test?
- Are there any improvements in the method that could be made for a future study?
- What are the broader implications of this area? Why is it an important area of research?

References

See Steve Ward's guide at http://www.worc.ac.uk/departs/psycho/Teaching/RefGuide. html for citing other work in the text and how to list them in the References section. Note that every work cited in the report must be listed in the References section.

Appendices

Any materials (e.g. lists of words, pictures, etc.) used in the study can be placed as an appendix, as well as any calculations. Always mention in the main body of the report that you have included something in the appendix (e.g. 'The complete set of instructions may be found in Appendix 2').

Study techniques: which ones work?

Many tutors and introductory textbooks will give you all sorts of advice about how to use certain techniques to aid your memory. However, I doubt if they have checked the scientific validity of many of these techniques. I have never advocated the use of mnemonic devices, for example, largely because I never found them to be useful myself. Moreover, they seem to me and to others to be quite inappropriate for the sort of material psychology students have to study. I won't cite the evidence for this assertion but you could read Chapter 17 of Neath (1998) if you need convincing.

So, what does research tell us about how people learn and what the better methods of study are? First, it is worth debunking a few myths:

- Unless you have a specific condition or recognised disability that affects your ability to retain information, you have an excellent memory and your ability to remember things is much better than you think it is.

- The claim that we only ever use 10 per cent of our brains and that we have some vast untapped potential is nonsense and meaningless.

What we do know about good study techniques is as follows:

- Distributed study is better than massed study. If you studied for 1 hour a day for 8 days then you will learn at least twice as much than if you studied for one long 8-hour session. Thus, although the overall amount of time spent studying is the same, doing a little very often is better than doing a lot once.

- Interestingly, recall of material is improved when studying is soon followed by sleep. This works because it reduces the opportunity to forget through interference from new material. So, if it is appropriate, take a short nap at the end of your study session!

- Asking yourself **why?** is the best way to engage with material and to have a deep understanding of issues. Try to think beyond the information presented to you in textbooks or journal articles. Ask yourself why this theory or that theory was developed in the way it was, or ask yourself whether such an explanation is satisfactory or whether a criticism or a claim is justified. You can also ask yourself **how?** when you read about a behavioural phenomenon: How do people do it? What mental processes must or could be at work? If you accept all of what you read you will have a bland academic mental life as a student, so don't regurgitate from textbooks, think about the issues. Furthermore, if you read a paragraph or an explanation that you cannot understand, even though you may have read it over and over, consult another text on the issue or ask your tutor. Don't feel that you are taking up your tutor's time by asking 'silly' questions; it's what we are paid to do and what you pay your fees for. You could also join or establish the student psychological society at your college. Get the society to debate issues and even bring in outside speakers.

- Alcohol destroys brain cells, as do many types of drugs. Although the rate of neuronal damage may be quite low due to alcohol and drugs, binge drinking surely speeds up the process. The next time you have a hangover, imagine how many thousands of your precious brain cells were probably destroyed during the night. Furthermore, recent research shows that regular binge drinking can increase the likelihood of heart disease in middle life. To finish my sermon, I'd add that if you are a binge drinker you are not necessarily an alcoholic, but you have certainly discovered an excellent way of teaching yourself how to become one. One more point: whatever your view is on drugs, they are illegal and every year thousands of young adults find themselves in court for possession of them or for attempting to distribute them. Many are given jail sentences. It will do your career no favours at all to graduate with a criminal record or as a resident of one of Her Majesty's prisons.

Further reading

One of our authors in this series, Meg Barker, has carried out several studies of the student experience and is something of an expert in this field. I would therefore recommend you get yourself a copy of her text *Introductory Psychology: History, Themes and Perspectives* and read her Introduction, which gives useful advice about being a student, as well as containing a superbly written history of psychology that introduces you to the many areas and applications of psychology.

Chapter 1
Foundations of cognitive psychology

Chapter summary

Understanding the foundations of cognitive psychology is essential for gaining a broader perspective on the many theories that have been developed in this approach. The aim of this chapter is to provide you with an understanding of its philosophic roots, the significance of the computer metaphor, its main underlying assumptions and the logic of the experimental method.

Assessment targets

Target 1: Understanding how cognitive psychology emerged as the dominant paradigm
Cognitive psychology has both philosophical roots and roots based on current technology, especially the development of the computer. Understanding these developments is important for appreciating the strengths and limitations of the approach. Question 1 will assess you on this.

Target 2: Appreciating how theories are developed in cognitive psychology and the research methods used
In Section 2, we discuss the main method used by cognitive psychologists, the experiment, and we outline some of the main assumptions cognitive psychologists make about mental activity and its relation with behaviour. The process whereby theories are developed is also described. This section will help you to appreciate the logic of the experiment as used by the cognitive psychologist. Question 2 will assess you on this.

How will you be assessed on this?

In your first year you are likely to be exposed to the history of psychology, in which the development of cognitive psychology plays an essential part. You will be expected to know how cognitive psychology emerged, what its main assumptions are, and what research methods are used. Ways of assessing your knowledge and your views include essay, exam question and seminar presentation.

Section 1

Emergence of a new discipline

In this first section you will be reading about the emergence of cognitive psychology as the dominant approach in psychology. In order to fully appreciate this, you will need to read about approaches that preceded cognitive psychology.

A brief history of the science of psychology

I like to define psychology simply as the scientific study of why people do the things that they do. In some ways we are all psychologists since virtually everyone wants to understand why people do the things that they do, including themselves. One could easily argue that the preoccupation with knowing why people do what they do predates the written word. We know that the ancient Greeks (such as Aristotle and Plato) asked very pertinent questions about human nature and human behaviour but 'modern' psychology is said to have only begun about 130 years ago (although the writings of the British empiricists of the eighteenth century underlie many of the concerns of modern cognitive psychologists).

CRUCIAL CONCEPT

We should always be aware that modern psychology is a young science. When we step back and look at its progress we see that like most sciences, it has not gradually developed down a single path. Instead, psychology has seen dramatic shifts in what are considered important areas of study and which are the most appropriate methods we should use when we study why people do what they do. These dramatic shifts have been referred to as 'paradigm shifts', where the word **paradigm** refers to a unified and accepted method of study.

Historians of science record that the most significant paradigm shift was the change from the view that the earth is the centre of the universe to the contemporary view that the earth is not the centre of the universe but rotates around the sun, which itself is moving in space. This shift is known as the Copernican revolution after the Polish physician and lawyer Copernicus who speculated, using mathematics, that the sun was at the centre of the universe (the heliocentric view). Although praised for his mathematical tables that became widely used by astronomers, the heliocentric hypothesis was rejected. When Gallileo later made observations of the planets, he concluded that the path they followed could only be explained by supposing that the earth was spinning on its axis and rotating around the sun. Eventually after much persecution had taken place by those with such views, the geocentric view was dropped and now seems almost ridiculous, but understandable for primitive minds.

The story of the Copernican revolution has a cautionary message: views that we have today may seem equally ridiculous to societies of the future. So while cognitive psychologists might be content with their approach to psychology, in time their theories may be overturned and their methodologies abandoned.

Introspection as the first scientific method in psychology

During the nineteenth century, Ernst Weber, Gustav Fechner and Hermann von Helmholtz were three German physiologists who pioneered the experimental method in psychology. But the biggest movement in psychology at around the same time was Wilhelm Wundt (1832–1920). He devised a method in an attempt to break down the elements of consciousness and to determine how they were connected. He argued that pure sensations (sweetness, coldness and so on) were the basic elements of consciousness and that they could best be studied through self-observation or introspection. The central problem with this method, of course, is that it is (by definition) subjective, and perception of the same visual stimulus might be different from person to person (one person's rubbish is another person's treasure). However, the value of the approach was in Wundt's insistence on precise measurements and the necessity of being able to replicate a research finding.

CRUCIAL CONCEPT

Tichener, a student of Wundt, took his research to the US and called it **structuralism**, which used similar methods as introspection. However, with the problem of objectivity (how can you verify someone else's introspective observations?), structuralism was soon considered an invalid approach.

Functionalism

During the early twentieth century, William James advocated the functionalist approach in his magnum opus *Principles of Psychology*. The scope of psychology was broadened by this approach into the study of mental processes and behaviour, and practical application of this knowledge was considered important. Apart from some significant work from the Gestalt school (discussed further in Chapter 2), the newly emerging behaviourist school began to dominate psychology.

CRUCIAL CONCEPT

Functionalism is a scientific approach that assumes that everything exists because it serves some function. For example, William James argued that the 'stream of consciousness' serves the function of allowing humans and animals to adapt to their environment.

Behaviourism

The work of Watson, Pavlov and Skinner became the foundations of mainstream psychology up to the 1960s. Watson disliked introspective and functionalist approaches and recommended that mentalistic concepts (thoughts, feelings and so on) be dropped from the study of psychology since they were not objective and could not be studied directly. The most objective and scientific approach, he argued, is to examine behaviour because it is measurable and observable. Watson published his magnum opus in 1913 and 14 years later in 1927 Ivan Pavlov, a Russian physiologist, had his work published in English. This work had a major impact in psychology since (1) the book presented some impressive findings of a long, systematic series of studies, and (2) it used methods that were consistent with what Watson was advocating. But the major proponent of behaviourism became Skinner who considered the relationship between stimuli, responses and reinforcements as the crucial issues of study for psychology. References to internal processes were deemed unnecessary since they could not be directly observed.

Skinner focused mainly on schedules of reinforcement and showed that similar learning curves could be obtained for a variety of different animals, and that the principles of reinforcement could explain aspects of human learning and behaviour. However, it was in explaining more complex forms of learning and behaviour, such as language, that Skinner met his most severe critic, Chomsky. The debate about the extent to which language was an innate ability and how the environment might shape language development left psychologists more in support of Chomksy's position than Skinner's. In addition, several other important research projects were taking place at this time and the pressure to consider internal processes increased.

The cognitive revolution

A number of crucial events and researchers inspired what is known as the 'cognitive revolution'.

Second World War

During the Second World War it became apparent that fighter pilots had difficulty in flying and paying attention to the information on the large number of dials in front of them. Psychologists such as Broadbent were brought in to advise on how the instrument panel could be redesigned to improve the pilot's performance. Thus in an applied setting psychologists began considering more than just overt behaviour.

Information processing

Mathematicians began developing advanced theories of communication. They were concerned with sending and receiving electronic information accurately. One advantage of information processing theory is that it can be developed irrespective of the content of the message. Hence general theories of the sending and receiving of information could be generated. It seemed to many psychologists at the time that human thinking could be described in terms of receiving information through the senses.

Computers

The computer brought with it an interesting metaphor for human mental processes. Perhaps the brain, like the computer, received input, encoded material, stored the material and later retrieved the material. Von Neumann and McCulloch began to write about computational models of the mind and the term **artificial intelligence** was used for the first time in 1956.

CRUCIAL STUDY – GEORGE MILLER (1956)

Miller reported on a series of studies on human short-term memory ability and found what appeared to be a 'law' of short-term memory. Most people could recall between 5 and 9 items ('seven plus or minus two') when they were presented to them once. Miller's work was important in showing that there might be general laws about short-term information storage, and hence mental processes in general too.

CRUCIAL STUDY – KARL LASHLEY (1929, 1963)

Lashley's work on rats was influential in terms of understanding the physiological basis of memory. He wished to know which part of the rat's brain stored the memory for recently learned mazes (the search for the 'engram'). Despite finding a strong correlation between the overall number of lesions made to the brain and the number of errors made in the maze, he failed to find any particular region where memory for the maze might be localised. Lashley concluded that memory for mazes is distributed throughout the brain. Lashley's work was seen as a departure from the behaviourist's reluctance to consider internal processes, such as memory. Lashley argued that stimulus–response models were inadequate.

Much of the work described above was presented at a number of crucial conferences in the US, such as the Hixon Symposium at Caltech in 1948, the MIT Conference at Cambridge, Massachusetts in 1956 and the conference at Dartmouth College, Hanover, New Hampshire, also in 1956.

Ulric Neisser (1967)

Neisser's book *Cognitive Psychology* detailed a method whereby one can infer mental processes through the use of reaction time. He argued that many mental processes occur too rapidly for people to introspect on the process. By presenting visual stimuli in a systematic manner and asking for a rapid response, one can infer the sequence of mental processes involved in making the response (see later Crucial Study).

As interest in mental processes increased so too did interest in the work of Skinner and the behaviourists diminish. In doing so cognitive psychology became the dominant paradigm. However, it would be unwise to say that behaviourism no longer exists, since the work of Pavlov and Skinner is still being extended to this day and this approach is referred to as Learning Theory (see Chapter 4). Indeed, much of our understanding of the neurophysiological basis of learning, for example, relies heavily on classical conditioning procedures. Furthermore, one of the most recent trends in psychology, that of connectionism, is founded on several principles of association that was originated by the behaviourists (see Chapter 4 and Chapter 9).

Quick test

1. What is a paradigm shift?

2. Describe one 'pre-cognitive psychology' approach to the study of psychology.

3. Describe three important influences of the cognitive revolution.

Section 2

Experimental methods

In this section you will be studying answers to the questions: 'Why do we bother with experiments?' and 'Why don't we just ask people how they think?' The rationale behind the use of experiments is explained and the basic assumptions of cognitive psychology are outlined.

A number of years ago I gave a talk to an audience that included non-psychologists. A geography tutor asked me why psychologists bother to carry out experiments at all. It seemed to him that we could save ourselves a great deal of angst by just asking people about their behaviour and their thinking processes. To this I replied that we cannot be sure that people have a direct access into their internal processes. Furthermore, we have no way of verifying that what someone says about his or her internal processes is valid or otherwise. However, to provide the clearest answer to this question we could look at the issue of subliminal perception. Read the Crucial Study below and then ask yourself how we could have obtained these results by asking people to introspect.

CRUCIAL STUDY – SUBLIMINAL PRIMING

Everyday experience tells us that we are more likely to use a word if we have recently heard it. For example, suppose someone uses the word 'smug'. When later describing someone who we are not too happy with, we may find ourselves using the same word. Although this might not be a particularly good example, I am sure you are familiar with the experience. One intuitively plausible reason why this occurs is because the word is made more accessible in memory than other words we may have used, and this is simply because we have recently heard the word. This process is known as **semantic priming**.

It has been shown in experiments that people are quite likely to use words they have been 'primed' with. Perhaps the most convincing method is the use of subliminal primes, in which the priming word is presented too briefly to be consciously detected. Consider the incomplete word _URSE (known as a word stem). Participants are required to complete the word by providing the missing letter. Participants primed with subliminal presentations of the word DOCTOR are more likely to complete the word stem as NURSE than participants who are primed with subliminal presentations of the word MONEY (which promotes the alternative interpretation, PURSE). Jacoby (1991) has further shown that even when participants are aware that a subliminal prime was presented they find it difficult to resist the effect.

These Crucial studies demonstrate that (a) we may be affected by our environment in ways that we are completely unaware of, and (b) we cannot always 'look inside' our minds to know exactly why we behaved in a certain way.

The point being made here is that we need to use methods that allow us to make observations that we could not otherwise make. We do not always have access to our internal processes even though we have the feeling that we do.

Armchair theory development

Greek philosophers believed that knowledge could be acquired by a combination of reason and uninterrupted thought. If you thought about something for long enough and that thinking was done in a logical manner then you could find the answers to extremely difficult questions. While most scientists would agree that periodic moments of reflection are an important part of the research process such reflection is insufficient by itself. Knowledge is gained through systematic observations, i.e. controlled empirical research.

Suppose your partner dumps you and they have not given you a clear idea why. You will have many questions. You will try to find answers by asking their friends and your friends anything they know that could shed light on the reasons why you were jilted. Given answers to just one or two of these questions you will begin to develop a number of plausible hypotheses. To test each hypothesis you seek further information that could support one and refute the other. When you finally get all this information, it may be that only one plausible hypothesis remains (e.g. they felt they weren't good enough for you, obviously!) and that then becomes your explanation.

When faced with a question like this about why someone did what they did, do we in our everyday lives wait until we have the answers to all of our questions? I doubt that we do. Instead we rely on 'hunches' or intuitions, and we may try to imagine ourselves in the same situation. In addition, we may draw on personal experience and try to recall similar events. Often we pass judgement long before we have all the answers. The simple message is that we have to gather sufficient information before we can pass judgement, and this is just what experimental psychologists try to do.

CRUCIAL TIP

Students sometimes use anecdotal evidence in their essays to verify a view or theory (e.g. citing their pet's 'cupboard love' behaviour to support Pavlov's theory of conditioning). For reasons described in this section, the use of anecdotal evidence is not evidence is the scientific sense. Therefore, it should be used for illustrative purposes only, for example describing the everyday observation of 'cupboard love' to **illustrate** one principle of conditioning.

Without carrying out research we could all begin to develop our own theories about why people do what they do and we could have as many theories as there are psychologists. What is needed is some way of discriminating between good and bad theories.

Discriminating between good and bad theories

A theory begins with an observation or series of observations concerning some aspect of behaviour. The observations may come from everyday life, from a news item or from the findings of one or more experiments. From these observations one develops plausible, 'candidate' theories as to the causes of the behaviour. A researcher may, for various reasons, prefer one theory to another. However, the theorist should be able to make a prediction about behaviour if the theory is a good one. If no predictions can be made then the theory has little value.

Based on the predictions of one or more theories, the researcher then conducts one or more experiments to put the theories to the test. So, the main purpose of an experiment is to pit one theory against another. The results of the experiment may support a theory or they may refute a theory. Generally experiments are seldom that clear and we often say that the results are **consistent** with one theory and are **not consistent** with another theory. If the results are consistent with a theory then the theory is supported and we gain confidence in the theory as an explanation. If the results are not consistent with a theory then that theory is either rejected or modified to fit the new findings.

CRUCIAL TIP

Generally, you should not design any of your own studies as 'fact finding missions' (e.g. 'Do men drink more alcohol than women?'). This isn't testing a theory – it's fact finding. Design your own studies on the theories you have read about and want to test.

What is the difference between a theory and a model?

A theory is a set of related statements about a set of observations. The majority of theories in cognitive psychology are stated as verbal descriptions. A model is a more detailed description or analogy that is used to explain a very specific set of observations. Models often rely on metaphors, for example the behaviourists used the switchboard metaphor where incoming signals (stimuli) become connected to (associated with) outgoing signals (responses). The computer metaphor is also prominent in cognitive psychology. Information processing models are described in an algorithmic form (diagrams or flow charts showing the stages involved in some mental process) rather like the way computer programs can be described. More recently connectionist models are used to theorise about mental processes. These can be described as simplified brain circuits whose behaviour can be understood mathematically (see Chapter 9).

Some basic assumptions in cognitive psychology are as follows.

- Mental processes exist and can be the subject of study. Unlike the behaviourists cognitive psychologists make mental processes their subject of study. Mental processes are considered to be lawful in their operation and the goal of cognitive psychology is to identify what these processes are and to characterise them. Cognitive psychologists attempt to use objective and reliable methods in their observations, and this can be achieved by carrying out carefully designed experiments that can be replicated by different cognitive psychologists in different labs.

- Humans are information processors. People are not passive recipients of stimuli nor do they always make responses without some intervening mental event. People actively seek out information, they try to make sense of their environment and the behaviour of others, and they reflect on the consequences of their actions. Things that we perceive through our senses can be considered as information and how we deal with that information can be considered a process. One example of our need for information is that many people now have mobile phones with which they can send and receive text messages. The messages contain information. The information is analysed and comprehended before a message is texted back. Another example of our need for information is when we hear of an important ongoing event in the news: we check out news bulletins on the hour or we ask others if they have heard of any developments and we try to make sense of the information we receive.

- We can infer mental processes from behaviour. Although cognitive psychologists employ a wide range of methods, there are two main measurements they use to infer mental processes. These are reaction time and an analysis of responses. Reaction time can give an indication of the sorts of mental processes being employed. An example is the Stroop effect (after Stroop, 1935), which is described in the Crucial Study in Section 2 of Chapter 3, on attention (read the study now before continuing). An analysis of responses can also provide an insight into mental processes. For example, suppose 9 numbers were read out to you and you had to repeat them back straightaway. An analysis of correct and incorrect responses would reveal good recall for the first few items and the last few items, but poor recall for the middle items (the so-called 'serial position curve'). With this observation we can draw inferences about mental processes and how information is held in memory over a brief period.

The experimental method

To end this discussion, I'd like to cover the issue of statistical significance. It is something that students often fall over or slightly miss the point of. The aim here is to illustrate the use of statistics in the experimental method and to help you avoid common misconceptions.

In an experiment we compare the results of (at least) two groups. The tasks given to the two groups are identical, except on one count. This single difference is known as the independent variable (IV). If a theory is valid then it should predict that a particular IV would produce different results between the two groups. For example, suppose I had the theory that small groups of students learn better than large groups because they are more likely to ask questions. My theory predicts that, regardless of class size, a student is more likely to learn if she asks questions. I then set up an experiment consisting of two groups of seven students to whom I deliver the same lecture (but at different times). Group A are told not to ask questions and group B are told that they can ask questions. The IV here is whether the students can ask questions or not. I predict that in a later test of learning (e.g. a multiple-choice test) group B will score higher marks on average than group A. If the results of the tests confirm my prediction then the experiment provides support for my theory, otherwise I may have to rethink my theory.

However, the average scores between the two groups are unlikely to be exactly the same, even if they differed by 1 point. Indeed, when we compare the data from any two groups it is rare that the scores are exactly the same. So, how does the experimenter know if the difference in the scores is due to the IV (being able to ask questions during a lecture)? I might state that only a large difference in scores is sufficient. But the problem is how large is large? What difference in scores is sufficient to support my theory?

Suppose instead of taking the test, I gave my participants the more meaningless task: choose a number between 10 and 20 (and without conferring). This is a way of obtaining random numbers from my two groups. I then add them up and find the average scores of the two groups. It is likely that some students will choose a number close to 20, some close to 15, and others close to 10. It is also likely that the scores of the two groups will be very similar but different (e.g. 14.5 and 16.7, giving a difference of 2.2). Using the rules of probability I can calculate how likely it is to obtain the difference of 2.2 under these conditions. In fact, I can calculate the probability of any numerical difference between the two groups (and this calculation is based on the number of participants in each group and the possible range of scores). Small differences are more probable than large differences (for example, it would be most unlikely if everyone in group A chose 20 and everyone in group B chose 10). So, if I were to predict a large difference between the scores of two groups then according to probability my prediction is less likely to be correct than if I were to predict a small difference.

Probability is usually measured as a value between 0 and 1. The higher the value the more likely something is to occur. So, if the weather girl says there is a 0.8 chance of rain today then it is more likely to rain than not. As a percentage 0.8 is 80 per cent. Another way of viewing the value 0.8 is that it is 8 out of 10, or an 8 in 10 chance (which is the same as a 4 in 5 chance). Psychologists have adopted a key value of probability in making decisions about the differences between the scores of two groups. This value is 0.05, which is the same as 5 per cent, which is the same as a 5 in 100 chance or a 1 in 20 chance.

When assessing the difference between two groups the decision we make about whether the difference is large enough goes like this:

- We do the calculations and find what the difference is between the scores of the two groups.
- We (our rather our computers) calculate the probability of this difference occurring by chance (e.g. if the scores were generated in a random way).
- If this value is **less than** 0.05 (or less than 5 per cent or less than 1 in 20) then we say that the difference is due to the experiment (i.e. the effect of the IV) and that it supports the theory.

In other words, if the probability of obtaining the difference in scores between the two groups by chance is very small and we have obtained this difference then it is likely to have occurred as a result of what we did in the experiment. This test is known as a test of statistical significance, and the simple reason why we choose 0.05 as a cut-off point is because about over 40 years ago a social scientist thought that it was quite a reasonable value.

Different statistical tests are used depending upon the design of the experiment and the type of measurement taken. So, for example, one might use the related t-test, the independent t-test, the Wilcoxon test, and so on. Each test produces its own 'test statistic'. For example, the t-test produces a value of t. This value is used to calculate the probability of obtaining the difference in scores by chance. So, our statistical package we used to analyse the data will inform us the value of t, the **degrees of freedom** (a calculation based on the number of groups and the number of participants), and the **P** value (the probability value). When we write the result of our test, we use a particular convention. In the case of the t-test it looks something like t (12) = 7.25, P < 0.05. This means that the difference we have obtained is significant (the probability of obtaining the result by chance is less than 0.05). If the difference obtained is not statistically significant then we write something like t (12) = 0.98, P > 0.05 (the probability of obtaining the result by chance is greater than 0.05).

CRUCIAL TIP

When reporting the result of a statistical test, some students write the result on a line by itself as though the values 'speak for themselves'. Results should always be located within a meaningful sentence, such as:

'The results showed that the group allowed to ask questions did better in the multiple-choice test than students who were not allowed to ask questions, t (12) = 7.25, P < 0.05.'

CRUCIAL TIP

A common mistake is to confuse the symbol > with <. An easy way to remember them is to look at the symbol pictorially: A > B means A is greater than B, and if you look at the symbol, the left side of it is broader than the right side of it, meaning that the letter on the left is larger than the letter to the right.

Effect size

Often, the issue of effect sizes is raised at more advanced levels in psychology, such as second- or third-year undergraduate studies. However, the size of an effect is important and journal editors are becoming increasingly aware of its importance.

Returning to our 'choose a number between 10 and 20' exercise, suppose I asked two groups of 2,000 students to do this. Given such large groups, it is likely that the difference between their average scores will be very small (e.g. 14.9 and 15.1, with a difference of 0.2). If we gave them multiple-choice tests then we would have quite a small difference between the scores of the two groups. However, since our statistical test takes account of the number of participants, it may turn out that this small difference is statistically significant. In other words, it may be that the probability of obtaining a difference of, say, 0.9 between two large groups is extremely low, in which case the experimental hypothesis is supported.

We must remember that our experiments are used to support a theory, and that a theory implemented in applied settings can have important social implications. So, the question we ask is, although a small difference might be significant, is such a small difference really that useful? Suppose you are an advisor for a local college and you are asked to evaluate the effectiveness of a new teaching method, such as e-learning. You design an experiment in which one group of students undergo the new e-learning system and a second group are given the traditional method of learning. After comparing the exam results you find that the difference between the two groups is statistically significant. You then conclude that e-learning is better and you recommend that the college invests thousands of pounds of its limited budget in the technology to deliver e-learning. However, on closer inspection of the exam results you find that although the difference between the two groups is statistically significant it only amounts to a couple of percentage points. You then have to ask yourself whether such an investment is worth raising marks by 1 or 2 per cent, and whether there is a more cost-effective way of increasing exam performance by the same amount (e.g. you could probably achieve better results by offering students an amount of money for passing).

The effect size of a comparison of the two groups in an experiment is related to the actual observed difference, regardless of whether that difference is statistically significant. The effect size ranges from 0 to 1, and values of about 0.6 and above are said to indicate strong effects. Hence, when evaluating a psychological study, it is often very useful to consider the size of the effect when inferring about the usefulness of a theory or an experimental demonstration of an effect, and especially when the obtained p value is close to 0.05, such as 0.048 or 0.058.

Sample sizes

A common statement made in the discussion section of student reports is that 'there weren't enough participants to be representative of the population.' Now, the question I always ask myself is, how does the student know this? So, how should the number of participants be determined? How many is enough?

Another use of the effect size is that (when used in conjunction with other statistics) it can be used to help the experimenter identify an appropriate sample size. Given an expected effect size (which is available from similar experiments that have been published), we can calculate the minimum number of participants required in order to obtain statistical significance (should the results fall that way).

Many students and some psychologists do not realise that if an experimenter has a large enough sample size a statistically significant result is **virtually guaranteed**. That number might run into thousands or tens of thousands but eventually a significant result is assured. Because of this it is important that an appropriate and reasonable number of participants is recruited.

In sum, and for these reasons, there is an increasing emphasis in published articles to state the effect size and to state how the number of participants recruited was calculated. Now that you know this, never again will you write that your study could have done with more participants (unless of course you reached this conclusion by calculating the effect size and the number of participants required)!

Quick test

1. What is the significance of subliminal priming for the study of psychology?
2. What are the main functions of an experiment?
3. What is the difference between a theory and a model?
4. List three basic assumptions about psychology?
5. What is meant by the term 'statistical significance'?
6. In what way is the 'effect size' of an experimental result important?

Section 3

End of chapter assessment

Questions

1. What factors led up to the emergence of cognitive psychology as the main paradigm in psychology?
2. Outline the rationale for the experimental method in cognitive psychology.

Answers

1. This is a popular year 1 question. You could begin by discussing what is meant by paradigm since this is a key term mentioned in the question. You can refer to the

Copernican revolution and how our worldview was overturned, then relate this to prevailing views in science and psychology and how they too can be overturned. As evidence of this you could run through the history of psychology (briefly), mentioning the different approaches that have come and gone. Discuss the inadequacies of behaviourism and then lead into the key influences in cognitive psychology. Make the point that there were advances in a number of areas in parallel, such as the development of the computer and its usefulness as a metaphor for the mind, and the experimental work of Miller and Lashley, for example.

2. By using the term rationale, the question is asking you to **justify** the use of the experimental method in cognitive psychology. There are several points you need to make. The first is that we need to be in the position where we can sensibly discriminate between good and bad theories, and the experiment enables us to do this. Second, make the point that since cognitive psychology is about mental processes its study requires a method whereby the operation of these processes can be inferred, and the examination of error rates and reaction times can help us do this. Third, make the point that we may not be able to introspect accurately on our own mental processes (and use the example of subliminal priming as evidence of this).

You can also add a discussion of the role of the model in theory development to your answer. This is relevant because models can help us make precise predictions about cognitive behaviour that we can test experimentally. You can then say how these points are related to the main set of assumptions in cognitive psychology. Finally, it can be worth a few extra marks by outlining the logic of the experiment, such as the statistical comparison of groups (i.e. the concepts of statistical significance and effect sizes).

Section 4

Further reading

For a more detailed history of cognitive psychology have a look at:

Baars, B. J. (1986) *The Cognitive Revolution in Psychology.* New York: Guilford.

For a non-mathematician's guide on the experimental method read:

Dancey, C. P. & Reidy, J. (2002) *Statistics without Maths for Psychology*. Harlow: Prentice Hall.

For a more advanced discussion of cognitive psychology read:

Eysenck, M.W. and Keane, M. T. (2000). *Cognitive Psychology, 4th Edn*. Hove: Psychology Press.

To calculate effect sizes and the number of participants needed for an experiment, visit:

http://www.uccs.edu/~lbecker/psy590/escalc3.htm
http://calculators.stat.ucla.edu/powercalc

Chapter 2
Perception

Chapter summary

Perception mostly concerns how we make sense of our visual world. Since our contact with the world is through our senses, the question which arises is whether we see 'reality' or whether what we see is guided by expectation. Studies on visual illusions make it clear that we often make mistakes when viewing our environment. This chapter focuses on these issues as well as the influence of the environment in the development of the visual system.

Assessment targets

Target 1: Understanding basic visual processes
In order to understand more advanced theories of perception, you need to study basic visual processes, such as the flow of information from the eye to the cortex. We focus on theories of colour perception since this is a popular topic in this field. Question 1 will assess you on this.

Target 2: Understanding how objects are recognised
Object recognition is an area of study that has broad applications such as speech recognition, understanding language and the perception of other people, as well as in the study of visual perception. In Section 2, you will study the main approaches to the question of how we recognise objects. Question 2 will assess you on this.

Target 3: Understanding the two main theoretical approaches to visual perception
The two main approaches are the top-down view (the view that perception is guided by knowledge) and the bottom-up view (the view that there is enough information reaching the retina that we do not overly depend on knowledge to perceive objects). These views are outlined in Section 3 and provide you with the background to this debate. Question 3 will test you on this.

Target 4: Understanding the developmental process of perception
Are perceptual systems fully developed at birth or do they require extensive interaction with the environment to develop properly? There are several views on this important question and we outline them in Section 4. Question 4 will assess your knowledge of these theories.

How will you be assessed on this?

You should expect questions about the visual system in your cognitive psychology course. The topics discussed in this chapter make for good essay and exam questions, and especially lab practicals.

Section 1

Visual processing

In this first section you are introduced to basic visual processes such as visual pathways from the eye to the cortex, sensory adaptation and the processing of colour.

Pathways from the eye to the cortex

- **The eye**. The wavelength of visible light ranges from 380 to 760 nanometers (nm) and different wavelengths are perceived as different colours (e.g. 380 nm looks violet and 760 nm looks red). All other wavelengths are invisible to the eye, such as those corresponding to ultraviolet radiation, X-rays, gamma rays, and TV and radio waves. The lens lies behind the iris and causes images to be focused on the inner surface of the eye known as the retina. The shape of the lens is altered by muscles to obtain a focused image of either nearby or distant objects (a process known as accommodation).

- **The retina**. The retina performs the sensory functions of the eye and consists of over 130 million photoreceptors (specialised neurons that convert light into neural activity). Information from photoreceptors is transmitted along the optic nerve which travels to the brain. The retina consists of two general types of photoreceptors: 125 million rods and 6 million cones. Rods function mainly in dim light, cones function in clear light and respond to colour. The fovea, a small pit in the back of the retina about 1 millimetre in diameter, contains only cones and is responsible for our most detailed vision (the point at which we are looking). Farther away from the fovea, the number of cones decreases and the number of rods increase.

- **Visual pathways**. The optic nerve projects to the lateral geniculate nucleus, a structure that is involved in early processing of movement, colour, fine texture and objects. Neurons then project to the primary visual cortex or V1, which appears to carry out further processing of motion, colour, location and orientation of objects. In terms of the function of the remainder of the visual cortex, the most popular theory is that different parts then become specialised for different visual functions (Zeki, 1992).

Sensory adaptation

The phenomenon of sensory adaptation can be illustrated by what happens when someone turns the light out suddenly. The momentary blindness is caused by the action of photopigments which are two molecules that exist in the photoreceptors on the retina. They react to light by becoming bleached and this action stimulates the photoreceptors. As photopigments become bleached they need to be regenerated before they can respond again to light. When high levels of light strike the retina, the rate of regeneration falls behind the rate of bleaching. With only a small percentage of the photopigments available to respond to light, the rods become insensitive to light. If you enter a dark room after being in a brightly lit room, there are too few photopigments ready to be stimulated by dim light. However, after a while the regeneration of photopigments overcomes the rate of bleaching, and at this point the eye becomes adapted to darkness.

The perception of colour

Young-Helmholtz theory

The Young-Helmholtz theory was inspired by the observation that varying the amounts of red, blue and green can produce any colour. They speculated that the retina might consist of three different types of colour-detecting cells, each sensitive to red, blue or green wavelengths of light. They further speculated that different rates of firing of these cells

23

gives rise to the perception of different colours. There are two phenomena that this theory cannot explain easily:

- **Colour blindness**. This occurs when a person is unable to distinguish between at least two certain wavelengths of light (e.g. shades of red from shades of green). In some cases there is no perception of colour at all. It is difficult to see how a theory based on different types of cone cells for red, blue and green could account for colour blindness.
- **Negative after-effects**. Stare at a red patch for a couple of minutes or so, and then look at a white sheet of paper. An after-effect will appear in the form of green patch of colour. After-effects reflect the opposite of the stimulus to which they have been exposed (the opposite of the pairs red/green, blue/yellow or light/dark). The Young-Helmholtz theory cannot explain after-effects.

Opponent-process theory

An alternative theory of colour perception was suggested by Hering (1878–1964) in an attempt to explain colour blindness and negative after-effects. It is based on the idea that three types of cells in the retina respond to pairs of opposite colours: red/green, blue/yellow and light/dark. In its anabolic phase, a cell processes one colour of the pair it is responsive to and processes the opposite colour in its catabolic phase. Negative after-effects can be explained by assuming that cells become fatigued by prolonged stimulation of the same colour and that they will work in the opposite way as they recover.

De Valois, Abramov and Jacobs (1966) provide support for the opponent-process theory. They found bipolar cells in the second layer of the retina and also in the thalamus. However, MacNichol (1986) found three different types of cells in the retina that respond maximally to one of the three different wavelengths of light as predicted by the Young-Helmholtz theory. It seems then that processes described by both theories are evident in the visual system.

Quick test

1. Outline some important features of the retina.
2. What is the main route from the eye to the cortex?
3. What is sensory adaptation?
4. Describe the Young-Helmholtz theory of colour perception.
5. Describe the opponent-process theory of colour perception.

Pattern recognition

Although our ability to recognise objects seems a fairly effortless affair, it is a very complex process. Key research questions you will read about concern how we recognise objects that are partially hidden, how we recognise the same object at different distances and in different orientations, and how we categorise a diverse range of stimuli as the same object.

Theories of pattern or object recognition

Template-matching theory

Perhaps the most obvious theory of object recognition is that we have internalised 'templates' stored in memory for every pattern or object (e.g. Ullman, 1989). Recognising an object means matching a visual stimulus with the most similar template. Through experience we may acquire a large library of such templates.

Evaluation

This theory explains very little about pattern recognition, since it suggests that all we do is match a visual stimulus with its unique representation in memory. The main problem for this theory is that recognition of even the simplest object (such as the letter **A**) requires us to store a template for every possible **A** we might come across. Given the number of different printing fonts that exist and the large differences in handwriting between people, this theory seems implausible. Furthermore, the theory predicts that the more templates that are stored then the longer it should take to find a matching template. Yet we know that, generally, the more knowledge people have the quicker they respond.

CRUCIAL TIP

Type the letter **A** in a word processing package and run through the different fonts available. Notice how the features of the letter can change between fonts in quite dramatic ways.

Feature detection theories

According to feature detection theory, each object will have critical features that enable it to be recognised. Other features that are less critical may or may not be present. For example, the letter **A** has two diagonal lines and a connecting cross-bar as its critical features (e.g. / - \). If we read a handwritten $\not{A}$ with the cross-bar projecting beyond one or both of the diagonals, then this would be a non-critical feature that could be ignored.

Evaluation

Evidence that supports feature theory has been obtained by Neisser (1964) who compared the time taken to recognise a straight-lined letter (Z) among other straight-lined letters (W, V) or among letters existing of curved lines (O, G). Performance was faster when both the target and the other letters were straight-lined letters. The main problem is that the theory has to stipulate structural relations between the features of the object, otherwise recognition errors would be more commonplace than they are. For example, \-/ and /-\ contain the same features but only the latter could be classified as an **A**.

CRUCIAL STUDY – RECORDINGS OF INDIVIDUAL NEURONS IN THE VISUAL CORTEX

One prediction of feature detection theory is that if a visual stimulus is processed according to its features then it should be possible to find individual neurons that only respond to specific features. Hubel and Wiesel (1968) identified three types of cells that appeared to be specialised for the detection of different visual stimuli:

- Simple cells respond to a dot in one part of the visual field or to a line at one particular angle and no other. Large numbers of these cells cover all of the visual field, collecting simple information about dots and lines.
- Complex cells receive information from many simple cells and combine the information about lines at particular angles in the visual field.
- Hypercomplex cells receive information from complex cells, and these appear to respond to simple figures and shapes.

The behaviour of these cells appears to support feature detection theory. However, more recent research suggests that spatial frequency is more important than individual features in pattern recognition (Sekular and Blake, 1985). Spatial frequency concerns the amount of light–dark contrast between the lines of a particular pattern. While many letters having many features in common (e.g., **K** and **N**) do not get confused when presented very briefly, letters with similar spatial frequencies tend to be confused.

Prototype theories

Another idea is that objects are stored in memory in some prototypical or idealised form (for example, we may have a mental picture of what a chair looks like). Each prototype contains features that are central to the object (e.g. legs), but all features need not be present (e.g. arm rests).

CRUCIAL CONCEPT

A **prototype** represents an 'average' image of the object, abstracted from the many different forms the object can take. For example, the character A represents a prototype of the letter, since it has the essential features. However, each feature can vary to some extent, as in *A*.

Although like template theory, prototype theory is based on the notion of matching a sensory input with stored representations in memory, prototype theory is the more parsimonious of the two. This is because (a) it appears to be a more flexible approach (since prototypes can be updated continuously with new experiences), and (b) fewer representations need to be stored.

CRUCIAL CONCEPT

Psychologists prefer theories that are **parsimonious** or explained using only one or two basic assumptions. A theory that is dependent upon a large number of assumptions or one that has a degree of complexity is low on parsimony. All else being equal, if two theories can account for the same observation then the more parsimonious of the two is preferred.

Evaluation

Prototypes as average images of objects suffer from the problem that they discard too many vital features. For example, by definition, an average image does not have much variability. But the same object (e.g. a chair) can exist in many different varieties.

Face recognition

An example of a model of pattern recognition in a particular domain is the model of face recognition of Bruce and Young (1986). Imagine a face that you know well. You will have seen that face in many different ways, such as with different emotional expressions, at different distances and in different lighting conditions, at different angles and even the same face several years later when it has changed with age. This phenomenon is one example of pattern invariance. Our ability to recognise it often appears to be effortless and automatic. According to Haig (1984), this ability arises not just from the recognition of particular facial features but also from the detection of the way the facial features are combined (for example, the spaces between individual features).

CRUCIAL CONCEPT

Pattern invariance refers to the fact that, despite seeing a pattern in different orientations and in different lighting conditions and so on, we recognise it as the same pattern.

The Bruce and Young (1986) model is based on experimental evidence as well as evidence from individuals with clinical disorders that leave them with an impaired ability to recognise faces. The model has several key assumptions:

- Faces we know are stored as recognition units. When we see a known face, its corresponding recognition unit is activated automatically, bypassing any need to analyse their facial features. However, unknown faces do not have corresponding recognition units, therefore in recognising them their facial features need to be analysed.

- Facial recognition units are associated with information we know about that person (semantic information), but not their name. In the model, person names are stored separately from both recognition units and associated semantic information.

Furthermore, it is claimed that there is no direct link between a name and a face in memory, and that in putting a name to a face we have to draw on semantic information.

Evidence that supports the model comes from Bruce and Valentine (1985) who showed that names are not very good aids for priming the recognition of faces. People can recognise that a presented face is one that has been presented previously, but associating a name with each face neither helped nor hindered the recognition process.

The disorder known as **prosopagnosia** provides clinical evidence for the model. In one study by Bruyer *et al.* (1983), an individual with prosopagnosia could learn to recognise new faces but could not recognise faces of people he knew. Another patient could identify familiar faces but had great difficulty in matching up photographs of unfamiliar ones taken at different angles or with different expressions. The evidence suggests that the difficulties experienced by prosopagnosic patients occur because of brain damage to specific face-processing mechanisms rather than a general inability to make precise discriminations.

Quick test

1. Describe template-matching theory.

2. What are the main assumptions of feature theories of pattern recognition?

3. Describe the model developed by Bruce and Young (1986).

Section 3

Visual perception

You will be studying the main theories of visual perception, such as Gestalt theory, Gibson's theory of direct perception and Gregory's constructivist theory of perception. As you read about these theories, you will also learn about a number of research methodologies and findings in visual perception.

Gestalt theory

In the 1930s the Gestalt psychologists (such as Koffka, Köhler and Wertheimer) investigated how we perceive objects and visual forms. They argued that we constantly search for a 'good fit' between the visual image and stored memories of visual objects. This usually happens very quickly since visual objects naturally have organised patterns and these are only minimally related to an individual's past experience.

CRUCIAL CONCEPT
The word **Gestalt** is German for 'organised whole', and the theory they developed reflects a holistic approach to explaining visual perception.

Several principles of perception were defined, known as the Laws of Prägnanz.

- **Law of proximity**. Stimuli that are close together are seen as forming a group, even if they are not similar (e.g. HHH THT YY XCV).
- **Law of similarity**. Stimuli that are similar tend to be grouped together (e.g. IIISSSIIISSSIII).
- **Law of good continuation**. Stimuli that are simple are preferred to more complex ones (e.g. lines that follow a smooth course are preferred over ones that make a sharp turn).

- **Law of closure**. Figures that can be closed (e.g., [ ][ ][ ]) are given processing priority over figures that are fragmented or unconnected (e.g.]][[]][ ).

Evaluation

Gestalt theory laid much of the groundwork for the study of how we detect object boundaries and how we can separate visual objects from each other and from the background. However, such perception may be dependent upon an individual's past visual experience and the evidence for this is reviewed later in this section.

Gibson's theory of direct perception

Gibson (1979, 1986) argued that perception is a bottom-up process, which means that sensory information is analysed in one direction: from simple analysis of raw sensory data to ever increasing complexity of analysis through the visual system. Gibson attempted to give pilots training in depth perception during the Second World War, and this work led him to the view that our perception of surfaces was more important than depth/space perception. Surfaces contain features sufficient to distinguish different objects from each other. In addition, perception involves identifying the function of the object: whether it can be thrown or grasped, or whether it can be sat on, and so on.

CRUCIAL CONCEPTS

Psychologists distinguish between two types of processes in pattern recognition: bottom-up processing and top-down processing.

- **Bottom-up processing** is also known as data-driven processing, because perception begins with the stimulus itself. Processing is carried out in one direction from the retina to the visual cortex, with each successive stage in the visual pathway carrying out ever more complex analysis of the input.
- **Top-down processing** refers to the use of contextual information in pattern recognition. For example, understanding difficult handwriting is easier when reading complete sentences than when reading single and isolated words. This is because the meanings of the surrounding words provide a context to aid understanding. There are many experimental examples of the influence of top-down processing, such as Palmer (1975) who found higher recognition accuracy scores of cartoon facial features when they were presented together rather than in isolation. Another example is given in McClelland, Rumelhart and Hinton (1986), who point out how easy it would be to read a word if one or two of its letters became partially obscured by an ink blot.

CRUCIAL CONCEPT

Central to Gibson's theory is the concept of **affordances**, and it refers to what the object means to us.

For Gibson our nervous system is perfectly attuned for detecting necessary information in the environment. For example, he understood movement and action to be an integral aspect of perception. In real environments people move their bodies and heads in order to understand their visual environment better. Movement of the perceiver or of the objects helps to clarify the boundaries and textures of objects. In addition, the optic array gives important information about movement, such that we can detect whether an object is moving or whether we are moving. The perception of movement, Gibson argued, is not dependent upon developing a perceptual hypothesis since there is enough information in the optic array.

Research on depth perception may provide some evidence for Gibson's theory. The distances of objects are detected in two main ways.

First, **monocular cues** are cues that operate equally with one or two eyes. These cues are used by artists, who try to indicate distance in a painting.

- One cue is **relative size** and is simply the fact that the same object has a smaller retinal image the further away from the viewer it is.

- Another cue is **shadowing**, which gives rise to an awareness that one object is in front of another object.
- A third cue is **superposition**, which occurs when a close object obscures parts of a more distant object.
- Another important cue is **texture gradient**, which can be observed by comparing the texture details of near and distant objects: objects at a distance appear to be smoother in appearance and more grey in colour, while near objects have clear, sharp colour and are more detailed.
- **Motion parallax** is another important cue to depth and can be observed when looking out of the window on a moving vehicle: objects in the distance appear to move more slowly than do near objects.

Second, **binocular cues** are those that arise from the two retinal images obtained with two eyes.

- The difference between the two retinal images, known as **binocular disparity**, can give rise to distance (this difference can be directly experienced by holding a pencil at arm's length and closing one eye and then the other).
- Another binocular cue is **convergence**, which is the movement of the eye muscles as we focus on near and distant objects.

Such visual cues to depth could be taken as evidence of direct perception, since they do not seem to be dependent upon top-down processes. This approach has been known as the ecological approach because it recognises that stimuli mean something to the perceiver. In this sense perception is said to be a direct decoding of information.

Gregory's theory of perception

Gregory argued that perception is a **constructive process** which relies on top-down processing. For Gregory, perception involves making inferences about what we see and trying to make a best guess. Prior knowledge and past experience, he argued, are crucial in perception. When we look at something, we develop a **perceptual hypothesis**, which is based on prior knowledge. The hypotheses we develop are nearly always correct. However, on rare occasions, perceptual hypotheses can be disconfirmed by the data we perceive.

Several studies using visual illusions provide support for Gregory's theory. The **Müller-Lyer illusion** consists of two equal length parallel lines, which appear to be different in length when one line has inwardly pointing fins and the other has outwardly pointing fins (Figure 2.1). Gregory (1963) argued that the illusion occurs because it brings in cues of our visual knowledge of the world. For example, the left figure can appear to represent the inside corner of a room, and the other the outside corner. In using depth cues, incorrect perceptual hypotheses are created, and in this case the hypothesis is a mismatch between past experience of depth and the raw sensory information.

Figure 2.1 The Müller-Lyer illusion

Object constancy and visual illusions

We can perceive an object as the same despite different viewing conditions, and this is known as object constancy. In shape constancy, the retinal image of a cup being viewed from above and the retinal image of it being viewed on its side are quite different yet it is perceived as the same object. Other constancies concern the object's size (which varies with distance from the perceiver) and the object's colour (which appears to remain constant even in different lighting conditions).

According to Gregory (1963), many visual illusions occur due to misapplied constancy scaling. One example is the **Ponzo illusion**, in which two horizontal lines appear to be of unequal length when enclosed between two converging lines (Figure 2.2). Another example is the **Necker cube**, which is a line drawing of a hollow cube that appears to change its orientation as it is viewed (Figure 2.3). Gregory argued that this object appears to flip between orientations because the brain develops two equally plausible hypotheses and is unable to decide between them. Other types are the **paradoxical illusions** which consist of figures that seem plausible initially but are physically impossible. Examples are the 'impossible triangle' and the paintings by M. C. Escher of which *Waterfall* is probably the best known. Gregory argues that in these illusions the brain develops more than one hypothesis, but these contradict one another. This results in a paradox and gives rise to the illusion.

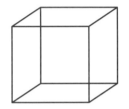

Figure 2.2 The Ponzo illusion   Figure 2.3 The Necker cube

Gibson argued strongly against the idea that perception involves top-down processing and criticises Gregory's discussion of visual illusions on the grounds that they are artificial examples and not images found in our normal visual environments. This is crucial because Gregory accepts that misperceptions are the exception rather than the norm. Illusions may be interesting phenomena, but they might not be that informative about the debate.

--- CRUCIAL STUDY ---

In the experiments by Tulving *et al.* (1964), words had to be identified as quickly and as accurately as possible. Some of the words were presented quite briefly and others were presented for longer durations. Also, on some trials the word appeared after a semantically related sentence (a sentence that related to the meaning of the word) and on other trials the word followed a semantically unrelated sentence. If the word was presented very briefly, then the sentence helped participants to recognise the word accurately. This demonstrates the importance of contextual or top-down influences in perception. However, when the word was presented for a longer duration, the sentence neither helped not hindered recognition accuracy of the word. This implies that when viewing conditions are clear, top-down or contextual processing was not required, and that visual processing can proceed in a bottom-up manner.

There is evidence that what Gibson referred to as affordances can be influenced by top-down processes such as expectation, motivation and emotion.

- **Expectation**. Bruner and Minturn (1955) presented either letters or numbers to their participants, and then showed them an ambiguous figure that was a cross between **B** and **13**. Participants shown letters perceived the figure as **B**, those shown the numbers saw **13**. In addition, when they were later asked to draw it, their drawings of the figure were unambiguous. Thus perception of an ambiguous object can be influenced by what one expects or anticipates.

- **Motivation**. The longer individuals are deprived of food, the more likely they are to perceive ambiguous pictures as food-related (Sandford, 1936). In a similar study, food deprivation was associated with rating pictures of food as being visually brighter than other pictures (Gilchrist and Nesberg, 1952).

- **Emotion**. The Crucial Study on Lazarus and McCleary below demonstrates that emotional associations with stimuli and events can influence our perception of them.

CRUCIAL STUDY – EMOTION AND PERCEPTION

In Lazarus and McCleary (1951), nonsense syllables were shown to participants and some of the syllables were paired with a small electric shock. Their responses to later presentations of the nonsense syllables were monitored by recording their galvanic skin responses (GSR). It was found that participants had increases in GSR when presented with the nonsense syllables that had been paired with a shock. However, and more significantly, when the nonsense syllables were presented subliminally (at presentation rates so brief that people report not seeing them), those previously paired with a shock elicited a marked increase in GSR. This study demonstrates that perception, and especially learning, involves past emotional experiences, even when perception does not involve conscious awareness.

Quick test

1. Describe three laws of Prägnanz.
2. Define top-down and bottom-up processing.
3. According to Gibson what is an 'affordance'?
4. Outline three monocular cues to depth perception.
5. Of what value is the study of visual illusions for Gregory's theory of perception?
6. In what way can perception be influenced by expectation, motivation or emotion?

Section 4

Developmental aspects of perception

You will be studying the question of whether the ability to perceive the world is given at birth or whether it is critically dependent upon exposure to a visual environment. You will encounter a number of theories on this issue. The issue of nature versus nurture appears elsewhere in psychology (and is taken up in Chapter 6 where we focus on whether language ability is innate or not) and hence is one of the major debates.

Perception of patterns

Salapatek (1975) used an eye-tracking device and observed significant changes in the perception of patterns in infants. For example, a one-month-old infant tends to look at the edges of a figure rather than the inside, while at two months the internal features of the object begin to be investigated. However, up to about two years, the infant spends more time looking at the edges and contours of objects rather than the internal features. This is known as the **externality effect** (Bushnell, 1979) and is likely to be due to the fact that processing of contrast, which is necessary for processing features, has yet to be developed in the visual system.

CRUCIAL STUDY – THE VISUAL CLIFF

Infants are placed on a 'visual cliff', which is a transparent platform placed over a checkerboard pattern. Babies between 6 and 12 months of age were reluctant to crawl over the 'cliff' edge, even when called by their mothers (Gibson and Walk, 1960). This suggests that the infants perceived the drop and that depth perception is innate. However, since the infants were six months old, depth perception may have developed in this time.

Other evidence of innate depth perception comes from studies that show that newly born kittens as well as small ducklings refuse to go over the visual cliff. Later studies on infants revealed that depth perception may not be innate for humans. The heart-rate of two-month-old infants placed on the edge of the visual cliff tends to decrease (Campos *et al*., 1970) which implies that the infant is interested in the visual aspects of the apparatus. If the infant were afraid of the visual cliff (and hence perceived depth) then it would have shown an increase in its heart-rate. This study was replicated in Schwartz *et al*. (1973) who further showed that increases in heart-rate in response to the visual cliff occur at the time when the infant develops mobility. Thus before this point the infant merely perceives a difference which stimulates interest, but does not perceive depth.

Retinal image

Bower *et al*. (1970) presented infants with one object just out of reach and another object at twice the distance but twice the size. This results in the infant perceiving the two different objects with the same retinal image size. Infants were found to be significantly more likely to reach for the nearer object of the two, which suggests that there may be some innate aspects to depth perception. However, this method can only be tested on infants when they are able to reach out with their arms, and hence the possibility that depth perception may begin to develop about the time the infant is able to do this cannot be ruled out.

Defending against approaching objects

An interesting method of testing for infants' abilities in depth perception is to monitor their responses to approaching objects, especially those on a collision course. Two-week-old infants were found to move their arms and head as if to defend themselves against the object, suggesting that some depth perception is innate (Bower *et al*., 1970). Other studies have found that infants can even discriminate between approaching objects that will hit them and approaching objects that will miss them (Ball and Tronick, 1971). However, since small head and arm movements can be interpreted as either under-developed defending actions or as random movements, this evidence for innate perception of depth is inconclusive.

Developmental theories of perception

Piaget's enrichment theory

Piaget's (1952) enrichment theory is that perception develops with the infant interacting with the world by performing operations and noticing the results of their actions. The sophistication of these operations is said to develop over several stages.

The most critical period of perceptual development is the **sensorimotor stage**. In this first stage, infants under the age of two years learn to coordinate their sensory and motor skills. The infant relies on innate sensorimotor schemas, such as mouthing, grasping and touching objects. These innate schemas develop through experience by comparing new sensory information with the existing schema. Piaget emphasised the influence of the infant's action in its perceptual development; however, this influence may be over-estimated since in one study, infants who had the most crawling experience showed no more depth perception than other infants (Arterberry *et al*., 1989). In addition, five-month-old infants who have limited ability and experience with independent mobility do not tend to reach for objects that are out of reach.

Shaffer's three-stage theory

Shaffer (1990) argued that there is not one but three stages of perceptual development during the first year.

- The first stage, 0–2 months, is described as a **stimulus seeking stage** in which the infant develops the ability to make general visual discriminations between stimuli.

- In the second stage, 2–6 months, which is described as a **form constructing stage**, infants can perceive numerous forms and shapes.

- In the third stage, 6–12 months, which is described as a **form interpretation stage**, infants begin to make sense of what they perceive.

Findings from the visual cliff studies tend to lend support for the existence of these stages.

The nature–nurture debate

The key question is whether perception is innate or whether it is nurtured by the environment. According to the above studies, many aspects of perception appear to be innate, although the evidence can be difficult to interpret when using infants. Other methods for answering the question include distortion studies, readjustment studies, deprived environment studies and cross-cultural studies.

- **Distortion studies**. In the late nineteenth century, G. M. Stratton developed a method of dramatically altering his visual world by wearing a lens on one eye that turned the world upside down (with the other eye covered). Within five days he reported that he could walk around and write comfortably. In total, he wore them for eight days, after which the world he saw was immediately recognised. This shows that the visual system is highly flexible and adaptable. Hess (1956) placed a similar prism lens to chickens, with the result that they never completely learned to adapt, showing that the visual system of animals may be less adaptive than that of humans.

- **Readjustment studies**. SB gained sight at the age of 52, having been blind from birth. Within only a few days he began to understand his visual sensations. However, aspects such as depth perception and understanding of visual forms were only partially acquired, and his visual sensations were at times more of a hindrance than a help, and he often preferred to sit in darkness in the evenings (Gregory and Wallace, 1963). The implication is that visual abilities are either innate (and degenerate without use) or that they require experience to develop. Von Senden (1932) presented a summary of 66 such cases and concluded that some aspects of vision appear to be innate (identifying a figure from the background and visually tracking an object) while others are learned (depth perception and identification of more complex visual forms).

- **Deprived environments**. Riesen (1950) raised chimpanzees in total darkness until the age of 16 months and found that their perception of simple forms was severely impaired. Wiesel (1982) sewed one eye of a kitten shut and found that if it is done early enough the eye remains blind. Blakemoore and Cooper (1970) found that by restricting the animal's visual environment from birth, it found the perception of certain visual forms extremely difficult (see the Crucial Study on Blakemoore and Cooper's restricted visual environment study below).

- **Cross-cultural studies**. Segall et al. (1966) found that people from Zulu tribes were unable to perceive the Müller-Lyer illusion. This might imply that because their visual environment contains few rectangles, straight lines and regular corners, they were unaffected by top-down processing (and hence implying the importance of environmental influences in perception). Annis and Frost (1973) found that Canadian Cree Indians who lived in the countryside were very good at determining whether two lines were parallel regardless of whether they were presented as diagonally, vertically or horizontally, yet Cree Indians who lived in the city performed poorly when the lines were presented diagonally. The explanation offered is that exposure to the vertical and horizontal lines of the city makes perception of diagonal lines more difficult. Other studies such as Gregor and McPherson (1965) found no differences between rural and urban dwelling Aborigines on a number of visual illusions. A problem with cross-cultural studies is that they rely on self-report measures and their verbal responses may be difficult to interpret accurately. Another is the fact that they have been based mainly on two-dimensional visual illusions and may tell us little about visual perception in the natural visual world.

CRUCIAL STUDY – RESTRICTED VISUAL ENVIRONMENT STUDY

By restricting an animal's visual environment at birth, it may be possible to understand how the visual system develops. Blakemoore and Cooper (1970) restricted the visual environment of cats from birth and as soon as their eyes opened from birth kittens were placed in a drum that had only vertical or only horizontal lines. After five months the kittens were placed in a normal environment and behaved normally except that they were virtually blind for lines that were at right angles to those of their earlier restricted environment. For example, kittens kept in drums that contained only vertical lines tripped up over ropes stretched out in front of them. The cells in the visual cortex of kittens kept in vertically lined drums were later found to be unresponsive to horizontal lines (similarly for kittens kept in horizontally lined drums cells were unresponsive to vertical lines). The study suggests the importance of the environment in perceptual development, especially during the early critical phase of development.

Quick test

1. What is the 'externality' effect?
2. Briefly describe the visual cliff study of Gibson and Walk (1960).
3. Outline Piaget's enrichment theory of perception.
4. Outline Shaffer's three-stage theory.
5. Provide the details of two types of studies that have addressed the nature–nurture debate in perception.

Section 5

End of chapter assessment

Questions

1. How do we perceive colour?
2. Compare and contrast two theories of object recognition.
3. Examine the evidence for the view that the visual system receives enough information from the environment for perception to be accurate.
4. To what extent is visual perception dependent upon exposure to a visual environment?

Answers

1. You can begin your answer by stating that in order to evaluate theories of colour perception we first need to discuss how light enters the eye and is transformed into an image received at the cortex. You can discuss operations at the retina and the main pathway to the visual cortex. Introduce the Young-Helmholtz theory of colour perception and make the point that it has intuitive appeal. Say that it cannot account for colour blindness, however. Describe the opponent process theory as an alternative account and say what the advantages of this theory are. You can conclude by providing evidence that both theories have something to say about how we perceive colour.

2. This is a straightforward question. Take each theory in turn, beginning with the weakest. Outline the theory as clearly as you can and provide evidence for and against it. You could then go on to discuss the Bruce and Young model as an example of how feature detection theory can be applied to particular aspects of perception such as perceiving a face. The usefulness of discussing this theory is that you can indicate the broader importance of the topic.

3. In answering this question begin by making the point that the view outlined in the question is that of Gibson. You should then go on to describe Gibson's theory of direct perception, paying close attention to the concept of affordances. Outline a number of perceptual phenomena that seem to support this view. You can then introduce Gregory's theory as an alternative to this view. Outline Gregory's theory and say how it has been applied to the study of visual illusions. You can describe studies that have looked at the effects of expectation, motivation and emotion on perception, and you can use these as evidence of the influence of top-down information in perception.

4. While the question asks you directly about the influence of the environment on the development of perception, you can discuss the developmental process itself. For example, you can describe studies that show how perception emerges gradually and through stages, and here you can introduce Piaget's theory and Shaffer's theory. The study of the visual cliff is of crucial importance to this question so a clear outline of this study will help you get good marks. You can then move on to studies that show clearly the roles of the environment in the development of visual perception.

Section 6

Further reading

You would have to search hard to find a better text on perception than:

Coren, S., Ward, L. M. and Enns, J. T. (1994) *Sensation and Perception*. New York: Harcourt Brace.

Chapter 3
Attention

Chapter summary

Most of the time we seem to be 'bombarded' by numerous stimuli coming in through all of our senses at the same time. Despite this, we usually have no difficulty in focusing attention on one stimulus while ignoring others, and this suggests that we have an exceptional ability to filter out unwanted stimuli. Further, because this act seems effortless and because we are unaware of how we do it we have the illusion that it is a simple and straightforward process. In this chapter we discover how difficult the issue of selectivity in attention is to explain, and we review several theories and methodologies designed to understand attention.

Assessment targets

Target 1: Understanding what focused auditory attention is and how it is studied
Research into auditory attention has concentrated on how we are able to focus on sound and ignore surrounding noise, such as focusing on a conversation in a noisy environment. Several theories of how we do this are compared and contrasted. Question 1 will assess you on this.

Target 2: Understanding basic issues in studies of divided attention
Why can we do some tasks simultaneously with another task, while other tasks seem to require so much concentration that we cannot cope with any distraction? The study of divided attention considers this question and asks whether attentional capacity is fixed. Question 2 is designed to test you on this.

How will you be assessed on this?

Attention is a popular topic in cognitive psychology and is ideal for an in-class practical. The issue of capacity limitations in attention is a popular essay or exam question.

Section 1

Focused auditory attention

In this section you will be introduced to the issue of capacity limitations in attention, explored through the study of auditory attention. We illustrate the most important research methods used in this topic and present the main theories of selective attention.

The cocktail party effect

One of the first investigators of auditory attention was Colin Cherry in the 1950s. His interest, as an engineer, was whether one could build a machine that could selectively filter out unwanted sounds, in order to make sense of a particular signal (such as speech in a noisy environment). Humans can do this quite easily and without a great deal of effort, most of the time. However, the ease with which we can do this betrays the fact that it is a complicated process.

Cherry (1953) presents us with the 'cocktail party' effect, which is an example of the incredible achievement of auditory selective attention. Suppose you are having a conversation with someone at a cocktail party (as you do). Unless the surrounding noise is unusually loud, it is quite easy to hear and follow what they are saying (provided they are speaking a language you understand and are not mumbling, of course). You might not notice, for example, the particular piece of music being played in the background because you are focusing your attention on what the other person is saying. Also, around you lots of other conversations are going on and similarly you don't really hear what other people are saying because of your focus on the current one. However, supposing the couple chatting a few metres away from you were to mention your name. It is quite likely, since we are all concerned to some extent over what other people say about us, that you will hear your name being mentioned. The question which arises is, how were you able to detect a word (your name) in a conversation that you were ignoring? How can you ignore something and yet at the same time hear it?

CRUCIAL CONCEPT

In order to try to understand this phenomenon Cherry (1953) developed the **dichotic listening task** that involves being presented with two different messages, one to each ear via a set of headphones. The task is to attend to one of the messages closely and involves ignoring the second message to an extent in order to do this successfully. To be sure that the participant is attending to the desired message, he or she is required to repeat the message out loud as accurately as possible, a process known as **shadowing**.

Early findings indicated that the task outlined in the Crucial concept above was more difficult if the physical features of the attended and unattended message were similar. For example, if both messages were spoken by the same person then performance was worse than if the messages were delivered by different speakers or if one was a male voice and the other a female voice.

A key question concerns how much of the unattended message participants could detect. In terms of physical characteristics. Early studies suggested that only gross physical features were noticeable. For example, if the sex of the voice of the unattended message changed participants would notice this, but would not notice if the message changed from English to German. Cherry reported that his participants were unable to recall any specific word in the unattended message and Moray (1959) claimed that participants were unable to detect a word even when it was spoken 35 times within a trial in the unattended message. From these studies it was concluded that only basic physical features could be detected in the unattended message and that this was because attention was selecting out the unattended message in order to focus on the task of shadowing one message.

Theories of focused auditory attention

Bottleneck theories
You might think that from these sorts of studies it would be relatively straightforward to produce a theory of selective auditory attention and the above findings imply some sort of filtering process whereby the attended message is filtered in and the unattended message is filtered out. This is the basis of Broadbent's (1958) filter theory. Since the amount of information coming in from both channels (the attended and unattended messages) is more than can be coped with reasonably well then one message needs to be inhibited or ignored. The main features of the model are (see Figure 3.1) as follows:

- **Sensory store**. Incoming messages are held in a sensory store very briefly.
- **Sensory filter**. One message is filtered in and the remaining are filtered out (except for their basic physical features). Messages filtered in receive further processing, while filtered out messages are eventually lost.

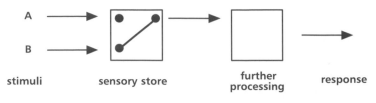

Figure 3.1 Broadbent's filter model

These elements of attention are said to process messages in the following way:

- The filter operates on the basic physical characteristics of the messages (e.g. sex of the speaker, type of sound).
- Filtering is a 'winner-takes-all' process, which means that only one message is selected for further processing, the rest are lost.
- Filtering is done consciously, in that people decide what they want to listen to. Furthermore, people can switch their attention from one message to another.
- The first stage of further processing is to identify the main components of the message (e.g. the words).

Evaluation

Broadbent's model accounts for the apparent finding that very little information, except gross physical features, of the unattended message get noticed. Filter theory also accounts for the fact that performance on the shadowing task is reduced when the similarity between the two messages is increased. An important aspect of Broadbent's approach is that he adopted an information processing perspective and presented one of the first 'box and arrow' diagrams of a mental process. Information processing theorists make the assumption that people's mental activity mainly involves processing information. They adopt the computer metaphor – that people process information in a similar fashion to the digital computer. We have input (sensory stimulation), we process the input (selectively filter them or abstract meaning), and we emit a response (talk back, laugh, and so on). One criticism of information processing theory is that it ignores meaning (see the discussion on Searle's Chinese Room example in Chapter 9), and that might be where Broadbent's theory begins to break down.

CRUCIAL STUDY: GRAY AND WEDDERBURN (1960)

If selective attention works on a winner-takes-all principle and is based on physical features rather than the meaning of the message, then if a participant was instructed to attend to the message in the left ear and ignore the right, this should not be difficult. However, suppose that the messages were presented like this:

Left ear   *Right ear*
Dear, 7, Jane   9, Aunt, 6

If the participant is asked to repeat all the items presented then Broadbent's theory predicts that recall would consist of either 'Dear, 7, Jane' or '9, Aunt, 6', since they would be attending to one channel only. However, not only can participants recall **all** of the items, they recall them as two units 'Dear Aunt Jane' and '976'. In other words, participants do not group the items based on the channel they were presented in but on their meaning. This finding is important because it suggests that more than just the physical characteristics are processed in the unattended message. Broadbent certainly did not consider that the meaning of the unattended message would receive processing.

As well as the Gray and Wedderburn (1960) study, other studies reveal that the meaning of the unattended message can be processed. For example, Treisman (1964) has shown that participants will switch between the two channels when the messages themselves are switched. If the unattended channel was not processed for meaning then participants would not know that the messages have been switched, they would just assume that the topic of the material has changed. Findings such as these led Treisman to develop her 'attenuation' model of attention.

CRUCIAL TIP

When thinking about the issues in this section, examine how you selectively attend to things in your environment. For example, when you are at home try writing an essay or reading a book with the radio on. Once you are deeply into your work make a note if anything, word or sound, on the radio catches your attention and distracts you from your work. Is it an unusual sound that distracts you or the voice of someone you like or strongly dislike, or is it a particularly favourite tune? Ask yourself how the theories discussed in this chapter fit in with your observation. Activities like this can often inform us about the plausibility of a theory.

Treisman's attenuation model

The key modification in Treisman's model is the assumption that, at the early stage at least, information is processed in parallel and selection is made at a later stage (see Figure 3.2).

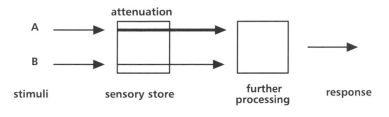

Figure 3.2 Treisman's attenuation model

The key features of the model are that early processing is not an 'all or none' or 'winner-takes-all' affair but rather that the main message gets through with other information being attenuated (made weaker). Thus the weakened message is still processed to some extent (hence it is also referred to as a 'leaky' filter model).

- Selection can be based on physical cues in the same way as Broadbent's model.

- If the attenuated information is consistent with the meaning of the message in the attended ear it can intrude and affect performance.

Evaluation

Treisman's model can account for the Gray and Wedderburn (1960) experiment, since the meaning of the message in the unattended ear is being attenuated (and still able to influence performance) rather than being completely ignored. Furthermore, unlike Broadbent's model, this model can better account for Cherry's cocktail party effect, since a significant message in the unattended channel (e.g. one's name) is being processed and not ignored, and hence attention can switch to that channel.

However, the attenuation model denies the possibility that stimuli may be selected at an even later stage of processing. There is some evidence that even more information can be processed in the unshadowed message than is suggested by Treisman's model.

CRUCIAL STUDY

Von Wright et al. (1975) used a classical conditioning procedure to pair neutral words with mild electric shocks. As expected when presented with the neutral words, participants showed a small increase in the galvanic skin response (normally taken to mean that they were responding like this because they were expecting the shock). However, when these words were presented in the unattended channel in a dichotic listening procedure, the galvanic skin response was still present despite the fact that participants were not attending to the words. This is made even more interesting by the fact that participants often showed the inflated GSR to the words even when they reported not hearing them. The implication is that unattended information can be processed for meaning, even nonconsciously. Corteen and Wood (1972) have reported similar findings.

Late selection models (Deutsch and Deutsch, 1963; Norman, 1968)

These results imply that all information is processed in parallel but that selection and filtering occurs much later on. Filtering is then based on whether the information is **pertinent** or not (i.e. the level of significance of the information to the individual).

CRUCIAL CONCEPT

Pertinence (the word **salience** is also used for the same concept) refers to the significance of a stimulus. Pertinent stimuli can either be those that are personally important to us, such as the sound of our own name or the sight of those we care about, or they are those that have a direct bearing on the current task (such as a set of traffic lights when we are driving). The concept is related to the 'goal-directed' nature of human behaviour and mental processes – we don't passively sit around waiting for stimuli to hit us but rather we are always engaged in an activity and trying to achieve something. This concept may help explain the cocktail party effect and is something that Broadbent clearly did not give enough consideration to.

The pertinence model appears to be more parsimonious (it can explain things more simply and elegantly) as an explanation of selective attention than Treisman's model. Consider, for example, the findings of MacKay (1973). In this study sentences that contained words with more than one meaning were presented, e.g. 'They were standing near the bank'. This could be taken to mean either 'They were standing near the **river bank**' or 'They were standing near the **money bank**'. Participants interpreted the sentence depending upon whether the word 'river' or 'bank' was presented in the unattended channel. The word provided a context in which to interpret the sentence (hence bank becomes pertinent to the word river or money). Clearly, the meaning of the information in the unattended channel is not filtered out at an early stage.

Quick test

1. Sketch diagrams of Broadbent's model and Treisman's model.

2. What are the main differences between the two models?

3. Describe one important experiment on focused auditory attention.

4. What is the significance of the finding?

Section 2

Divided attention

In this section we will be addressing the issue of limitations in attention but from a different angle. Rather than get participants to focus on one task and then see how much they were aware of other information around them, an alternative is to find out whether attention can be divided among several tasks. We describe a number of research methods used to study this topic and present the main theories of divided attention.

CRUCIAL CONCEPT

Divided attention concerns our ability to 'multitask', i.e. whether we can attend to more than one task at a time. While the dichotic listening task involves trying to attend to only one message, in studies of divided attention the task is to attend to more than one source of information. The questions concern how well we can do more than one task at a time, what kinds of dual tasks are achievable and which are not, and how can we explain this ability.

Early studies have shown two important factors that determine our ability to multitask:

- **The similarity of the tasks**. Allport *et al.* (1972) asked participants to learn a set of words while shadowing a spoken message. They found that the words could be learned when they were presented visually but not when they were presented as spoken words. However, if messages were sufficiently different then both could be attended to.

- **How well practised we are at the task**. Spelke *et al.* (1976) found that, with practice, students could learn to read a story while writing down a list of words read out to them.

Why do we have these limitations on performance?

Norman and Bobrow (1975) argued that the major factor that determines our ability to multitask is that our attentional resources are limited. Furthermore, this ability can also be affected by the quality of the information we receive (e.g. mumbled speech).

Kahneman (1973) also suggested that the amount of resources we give to a task is flexible. For example, we are more alert at times or more motivated to complete a task than at other times. There may also be an upper limit to the amount of resources that are available. Kahneman argued that this upper limit and the amount and type of information we **choose** to attend to is determined by an 'allocation policy', which is itself determined by several factors:

- **Our physiological state**. If we are feeling full of energy then we have more resources to allocate than when we feel tired.

- **Our enduring dispositions**. The amount of attention we give to tasks is dependent upon what type of people we are: our personality, our habits and our long-term goals.

- **Our momentary intentions**. Some stimuli may receive more attention than others because they are deemed more relevant to the task, the context we are in can affect what we attend to, and our current mood or personal concerns can affect what we attend to and what we choose to ignore.

This type of theory is known as a capacity theory since it is based on the notion that there is a general-purpose limited-capacity central processor:

- The central processor is a hypothetical mental structure that deals with ongoing tasks.

- It is said to be of limited capacity in that it has an upper limit in the amount of information it can deal with in any one moment.

- It is general-purpose in that it can deal with all kinds of information and tasks. For example, it is not restricted to dealing with information from a single modality.

Evaluation

The assumption of limited capacity has been challenged by several authors, since attention can be successfully divided under certain conditions and can be improved with practice. Furthermore, the assumption of a single general-purpose processor may be incorrect. It may be that several processors exist, each with a specific purpose. For example, consider the desktop PC. Although it has a main processor for doing such things as running programs, opening and saving files or making calculations in a spreadsheet, it also has a separate processor for playing CDs. In Kahneman's model the central processor divides its resources between the ongoing tasks, and while this is mostly true for the PC, the brain may have more specialised processors.

This idea has led to multiple-resource models of attention (e.g. Navon and Gopher, 1979). The idea is that it is not just the amount of resources a task requires that is important but the type of information required. Some tasks can interfere with each other not because they both require a large amount of resources but because they require the same type of

41

resources. For example, reading a book requires processing language and counting to 48 in fours requires processing numbers. With a little practice, these tasks can be done at the same time without interfering with each other and causing errors. However, shadowing spoken words and reading a book both require language processing, so may easily interfere with each other even with practice. Such interference is referred to as 'crosstalk' and a good example is the Stroop Effect (see Critical study below).

CRUCIAL STUDY – THE STROOP EFFECT (STROOP, 1935)

Imagine a list of words written in different ink colours. Suppose that you were asked to name the colour of the ink. The task is straightforward. However, if the word to be named was itself a colour word and it was printed in a different colour (e.g. the word BLACK printed in blue ink) then the task is not so easy. The Stroop effect is found when participants are slower to name the colour of printed words when the colour word and its printed colour mismatch than when they match. The effect has been replicated many times and is highly reliable. It has been used to explore the influence of anxiety and depression in selective visual attention (see Chapter 8).

Controlled and automatic processes

To some extent, the ability to perform more than one task depends on how accomplished we are at each task. Being able to drive and listen to a talk show on the radio (without crashing) depends on how experienced the driver is and their proficiency with the language and the topic of the discussion. For learner drivers, the radio discussion is a complete distraction and can interfere with driving (otherwise they take in little information from the discussion).

Schneider and Shiffrin (1977) have provided an extensive research programme to address the issue of how behaviour may become 'automated'. They argue that when learning a new skill, a lot of attention or controlled processing is required, but when we are skilled we can do the task without paying much attention to it at all. During skill acquisition, the behaviours required to carry out the task well become automated, which means that they are performed so well that they do not require many attentional resources and in that sense can be performed automatically.

CRUCIAL CONCEPT

Generally, **automatic processes** are said to be:

- rapid – a skilled driver can change gear quicker than a novice;
- effortless and make few demands on attention – the skilled driver can change gear while concentrating on a conversation and not thinking about driving;
- unavailable to consciousness – a novice driver will probably recall most of his or her attempts to change gear during a lesson whereas if you were to ask a skilled driver to demonstrate how they change gear they will probably perform the task less well than if they just did it in a normal driving situation;
- unavoidable – when we repeatedly do something it becomes a habit and we cannot avoid doing it, like looking in the rear-view mirror before overtaking (well, for most people).

CRUCIAL CONCEPT

Controlled processes, on the other hand, are said to be:

- slow – since controlled processing is applied to novel situations, we aren't aware of a reliable way to respond quickly;
- effortful and make heavy demands on attention – the learner's concentration on the task is intense;
- completely conscious – a lot of conscious effort is allocated to a new task.

The results of a series of experiments reported by Schneider and Shiffrin (1977) may be explained by the distinction between automatic and controlled processes. The experimental design is quite complicated but to give you an idea think about the following everyday example. Suppose that you are driving from Oxford to York and you are not familiar with the route. You know that you have to head towards Birmingham, so you are looking out for signposts to Birmingham. However, when you are near to Birmingham (you don't want to go to the city centre – as pleasant as it is!) you have to look out for signposts to Leicester. In doing so you will still see signposts to Birmingham but you will have to ignore them. This type of route we might call a **varied mapping** and this is so because the target city changes and as it does so we have to ignore targets that we were previously searching for (once we are on route for Leicester, we have to ignore signposts to Birmingham). Contrast this with going from Oxford to York needing only to follow signposts to York. We might call this type of route a **consistent mapping** because the target city is the same and we never have to ignore signposts to York at some later time. The Schneider and Shiffrin (1977) experiment involves a search task, looking out for a target letter. The two conditions are illustrated below:

	Varied mapping	Consistent mapping
Trial 1: Search for T among	V C H T G R Y	V C H T X R Y
Trial 2: Search for G among	P C H T G J Y	X D R Y G P B
Trial 3: Search for J among	V T G H Y J M	V F L J S M U

Note that for the varied mapping condition the search targets appear in other conditions, whereas in the consistent mapping condition the target only appears in the list of letters when it is a target and not in the other trials.

The number of distracters (the number of items appearing in the display during a trial) was varied, as was the presentation time of the list. Sometimes the target was present and sometimes it was not. The results showed that reaction time in the consistent mapping condition was the same regardless of the number of items in the display or the presentation time. Participants said that the target appeared to 'pop out' and it did not require much effort. However, for varied mapping reaction time was longer the more items there were in the set. In an earlier study, Kristofferson (1972) trained participants on either a varied mapping or a consistent mapping scheme for 30 days. The results indicate that performance at the task with a consistent mapping improved with practice but did not do so with the varied mapping condition. Schneider and Shiffrin (1977) interpret these findings by arguing that automaticity of a task requires a consistent mapping. In our example, it implies that learning the route from Oxford to York is much easier when we only have to look out for the signposts to York than when we have to look out for signposts to a city and only later have to ignore signposts to that city.

Evaluation
The notion of automaticity has been challenged. Hirst *et al.* (1980) report individuals who were able to learn to read while taking dictation. Since both tasks are not in the same form as a 'consistent mapping' there should not be, according to Schneider and Shiffrin's account, any opportunity for automaticity. Hirst *et al.* (1980) argued that automaticity had not taken place, but rather participants had learned to restructure the tasks so that they could do them simultaneously (for example by learning to share attentional resources between the two tasks).

Quick test

1. What limits our ability to perform more than one task?

2. According to Kahneman (1977), what three things determine the amount of attention we give to a task?

3. What are the characteristics of a 'general-purpose limited-capacity central processor'?

4. Describe the main features of an automatic process.

5. Describe the main features of a controlled process.

Section 3

End of chapter assessment

Questions

1. Which model of focused auditory attention can best explain the cocktail party effect?

2. What governs our ability or inability to perform two tasks at the same time?

Answers

1. Your answer should almost certainly begin with an explanation of the cocktail party effect. Then go on to describe the dichotic listening paradigm and discuss the early findings. You could then outline Broadbent's and Treisman's models and describe a couple of studies that help us to discriminate between the two theories. Finally, raise the issue of pertinence and conclude that late selection theories (such as those of Deutsch and Deutsch, 1963 and Norman, 1968) are better able to account for the cocktail party effect.

2. Begin your answer by saying that the question is pitched within divided attention research and say that these studies were aimed at identifying whether there are capacity limitations in dividing attention between two or more tasks. Outline the findings concerning task similarity and the amount of practice and then go on to identify theories that try to account for these limiting factors. Focus on Kahneman's theory and say what one's 'allocation policy' is said to be determined by. Discuss the view that there exists a general-purpose central processor with a limited capacity and how this contrasts with the alternative multiple-resource theories of attention. Finally, no essay of divided attention should leave out a discussion of automatic versus controlled processing, so describe these and say how these constructs can inform us about our ability to perform two tasks at the same time.

Section 4

Further reading

Coren, S., Ward, L. M. and Enns, J. T. (1994) *Sensation & Perception*. Harcourt Brace. Chapter 15.

Cowan, N. (1998) 'Evolving conceptions of memory storage, selective attention and their mutual constraints within the human information processing system', *Psychological Bulletin, 104*, 163–91.

Johnston, W. A. and Dark, V. J. (1982) In defence of intraperceptual theories of attention. *Journal of Experimental Psychology: Human Perception and Performance, 8*, 407–21.

Internet sites

http://psych.hanover.edu/classes/hfnotes3/index.html (someone's lecture notes!)

http://ling.ucsc.edu/~chalmers/mind.html#attention (consciousness and attention essays)

Chapter 4
Learning

Chapter summary

An important underlying assumption behind cognitive psychology is that learning and behaviour are governed by laws. As we discussed in Chapter 1, just how such laws might be discovered has been one of the main sources of controversy since the earliest scientific psychological investigations began. Despite the turbulent history of psychology, the methodology and the basic assumptions behind the study of animal learning appear to have been indifferent to these changes. Yet in practice, animal learning research has been at the helm of the controversy. The study of connectionism (Chapter 9) has also been influenced to some degree by animal learning theory, the common link being the doctrine of the associationists who argued that the unit of memory is the association of ideas, and learning theorists have provided some basic rules about how associations can be learned. For these reasons, it is important to consider the main elements of learning theory.

Assessment targets

Target 1: Understanding the foundations of classical conditioning

You will understand something about the philosophical roots of learning theory and the early findings of Pavlov. You will be able to explain the main phenomena of classical conditioning and you will be able to describe the roles of contiguity and contingency in learning. Question 1 will assess you on this.

Target 2: Understanding some of the principles of operant conditioning

You will be able to identify the differences between classical and operant conditioning, as well as the main principles of the latter. You will be able to explain the findings from several maze learning studies, as well as Skinner's schedules of reinforcement. Question 2 will assess you on this.

Target 3: Illustrating a number of applications of learning theory

You will be able to illustrate how the principles of learning theory can be applied in such settings as advertising, therapy, the classroom, prisons and in the home. Question 3 will assess you on this.

How will you be assessed on this?

Learning theory is one of the first topics some cognitive psychology courses present, and it is a way of providing some of the history that led to the cognitive revolution. Comparisons of classical and operant conditioning, and comparisons of contingency and contiguity are likely candidates for exam questions. You may also be asked to discuss applications of learning theory, either as a course essay or as an exam question.

Section 1

Classical conditioning

In this section you will read about the roots of learning theory and how the study of animals can bring insights into the study of human learning. You will study Pavlov's conditioning procedures and the main phenomena of classical conditioning.

Animal learning

One reason why animal learning theory has been so prominent in shaping the development of psychology is because it is relevant to human learning and human memory. On the relevance to humans Pearce (1987) notes that 'an accurate model of animal intelligence would provide a tremendous spur to its study in humans', and armed with such knowledge it is likely that 'considerable insights into the workings of the human brain will follow'. Animals are less complicated than humans: their behavioural repertoire is comparatively much simpler and their brains less developed. Despite the differences, the similarities are such that valid comparisons between human and animal learning and memory may be made.

Some of the neurophysiological similarities are quite astounding: the same types of neurons are found across species, including humans; all neurons communicate via synapses, and with similar substances. In fact neuronal 'signals are so similar in different animals that even a sophisticated investigator is unable to tell with certainty whether a photographic record of a nerve impulse is derived from the nerve fibre of a whale, mouse, monkey, worm, tarantula, or professor' (Kuffler, 1984). To some extent, much of the data on animal learning can be observed in humans. Some researchers have suggested that basic laws of conditioning appear to be universal across species (e.g. Turrkkan 1989).

Animal learning theorists seek to discover how animals learn about the relationships between events in their environment. Some events (such as the arrival of a predator) can be predicted from other events (such as the appearance of a shadow) and animals need to learn about such relationships to survive.

CRUCIAL CONCEPT

Animal learning theory began as an attempt to formalise ideas from the associationists (David Hume, John Locke, John Stuart Mill, F. C. Bartlett, and S. Lockery). The basic assumption of **associationism** was that mental phenomena consist of sensory impressions, and internal copies of these are linked together through ideas. They argued that the symbols used in any culture, especially religion, are examples of the formation of associations. For example, the cross is a Christian symbol and is associated with ideas such as sacrifice and devotion.

For the associationist school (e.g. Hume, Hartley, J. S. Mill, Locke), the existence of **mental associations** is intuitively obvious. For example, a picture of a joint of meat can elicit its smell, the sound of a voice can elicit a face, a particular song may elicit personal memories, and so on. However, the associationists argued that such links were not confined to associations between sensations, but also to other more complex forms, such as conceptual or linguistic relationships. For example, each line of the Lord's Prayer may be a cue for the next line, and each letter of the alphabet may cue the next letter.

The associationists attempted to derive 'laws' of association. The most fundamental of these were that memory of events, objects, people, ideas and so on are linked through (1) a **contiguity in space**, and (2) a **contiguity in time**. Hence events occurring in the same place or at the same time become associated with each other, such that the sensory impression of one may trigger the mental representation of the other. It is interesting to note that cause-and-effect was not considered logically justified. Indeed, Hume stated that as a philosopher of science he did not believe in cause and effect, yet as a human he did since the inference of cause-and-effect relationships is essentially human.

CRUCIAL CONCEPT

As learning theory has progressed, most of the controversy has surrounded the question of **contiguity** versus **contingency** when asking what the precise relationships that animals learn are. Contiguity is a view that we learn a relationship through mere contact in time (we learn that two things are associated because they occur together in time); for example, we 'learn' that two people are friends because they are always seen together. Contingency refers to learning that something predicts the occurrence of something else (for example, the ringing of a door bell predicts that someone is waiting at your front door for your attention).

Pavlov (1927) was the very first to systematically address this question. He suggested that if an animal could learn arbitrary associations, such as the ringing of a bell and the presentation of food, then the animal was merely learning contiguous relationships and not contingent ones. Pavlov further suggested that the association between a stimulus and a response was describable as a physical one, i.e. they are linked via 'nervous connections'. This type of learning has become known as **classical** or **Pavlovian conditioning**. Other forms of conditioning are known as **operant** or **instrumental** conditioning.

CRUCIAL STUDY

Classical conditioning is an important way of learning responses in new situations. Under normal circumstances, when a stimulus of biological significance such as food is presented to an animal, some behaviour or reflex will be immediately evoked, such as salivation. Pavlov (1927) first observed that by repeatedly ringing a bell immediately prior to feeding time, dogs would begin to salivate **before** the food became visible. He speculated that 'nervous connections' between the sensory registration of the ringing bell and the salivatory response were formed during this repeated experience, enabling an 'anticipatory' response to be learned. Such a finding provoked further investigation, not only by Pavlov, but also by many subsequent researchers. Such work has uncovered a wealth of related phenomena that were thought to be generalisable across species, including humans.

In classical conditioning, it is said that when an unconditioned stimulus (UCS) such as food is presented to an organism, an unconditioned response (UCR) such as salivation is evoked. The repeated pairings of a conditioned stimulus (CS), say the sound of a bell, and a UCS result in the formation of a conditioned response (CR) with the occurrence of the CS alone, that is to say, salivation at the sound of the bell.

Pavlov pioneered research into:

- the acquisition of CS–UCS associations;
- the unlearning of associations, known as extinction;
- the ability of the CS to form further associations with other previously neutral stimuli, known as second-order conditioning;
- the effects of altering the time interval between onset of the CS and onset of the UCS (the interstimulus interval, or ISI);
- the effects of conflicting associations (Pavlov was one of the first to develop a theory of neurosis based on conditioning principles).

Acquisition and extinction

Pavlov (1927) found that the acquisition rates of CS–UCS associations could be replicated using different animals, which suggests that such rates may follow a general law. The rate of acquisition follows an S-shaped, or 'sigmoid' curve where the vertical axis represents the magnitude of the response (a measurement of the frequency or intensity of the response, say the number of drops of saliva) and where the horizontal axis represents the stage of conditioning (usually the trial number). This curve indicates that learning is initially slow but is shortly followed by a period of rapid learning. This high rate is then tempered by a gradual rise to a peak.

When the learned CS is presented alone, i.e. it is presented in the absence of the UCS, the magnitude of the CR decreases until eventually it disappears. However, it is sometimes observed that during the latter phases of the extinction procedure the CR suddenly, but briefly, reappears. The cause of this reappearance, known as 'spontaneous recovery', is not well understood.

Generalisation and discrimination

Suppose some noise such as a tone was used as a CS in a conditioning experiment. Suppose further that this tone was pitched at 'middle C'. If the pitch was altered slightly while testing for a response, would the CR be observed? Results of such tests reveal that the closer the similarity of a novel stimulus to the CS, the more equivalent is the magnitude of the CR. For example, a CR trained to a CS consisting of a tone of 1,000 Hz generalises within the range 800 to 1,200 Hz.

CRUCIAL CONCEPT

Generalisation is important for all animals, including humans, since the variance of a single stimulus can be so great that without this ability every variation, however small, of a single stimulus would need to be learned. Clearly, this is a vital capacity as it is rare that the exact same stimulus will be encountered twice. Likewise, it is equally important to know where this generalisation boundary should end, that is discriminating between biologically significant and non-significant variations of a stimulus.

CRUCIAL CONCEPT

Temporal contact, or contiguity in time, refers to the fact that close contact in time between the CS and the UCS seems to be essential for learning to occur.

The temporal relationship between the CS and UCS is studied by varying the time between CS onset and UCS onset and observing the resulting conditioning rates. It is possible to identify four variants of temporal contact that produce reliable differences in the rate of learning:

- **Trace conditioning**. This is where the CS precedes the UCS but is terminated prior to or at UCS onset; acquisition rates are high (see Figure 4.1).
- **Delay conditioning**. This method produces the highest acquisition rates; this is where the CS precedes the UCS but stays on with the UCS.
- **Simultaneous conditioning**. Very weak conditioning occurs during simultaneous conditioning, where CS onset and UCS onset coincide.
- **Backward conditioning**. No conditioning is observed during backward conditioning, where the UCS precedes the CS.

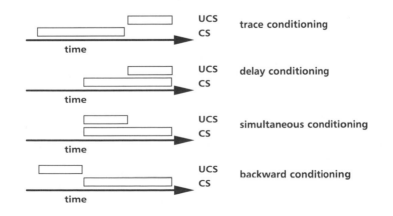

Figure 4.1 Four temporal arrangements of the CS and the UCS

If the duration of the CS and the duration of the UCS are held constant, then trace conditioning displays the longest ISI, delay conditioning will have a shorter ISI, while zero ISI implies simultaneous conditioning and negative ISI implies backward conditioning.

The findings of ISI studies were initially difficult to explain since it was thought that it was the simultaneous pairings of the CS and the UCS that resulted in learning. Hence optimal ISI was expected to be 0 ms or thereabouts. Explanations as to why these various temporal contact procedures should be ordered so, in terms of rate of CR acquisition, concern the predictive nature of what is learned in classical conditioning. Animals learn that the CS predicts the UCS, and hence this learning is more rapid when in classical conditioning experiments, the CS precedes the UCS.

Contingency and 'blocking'

It has been suggested that classical conditioning is the learning of a predictive relationship between the CS and the UCS (Kamin 1969, Rescorla and Wagner, 1972). In other words, the strength of the CS–UCS association increases with respect to the probability of their concurrence, and is contingent upon the CS being a reliable **predictor** of the UCS (Rescorla, 1968). Close temporal presentation of the CS and UCS, it is assumed, results in the increase in the associative strength between their neural representations (Hebb, 1949; Rescorla and Wagner, 1972).

CRUCIAL STUDY

The idea of contingency, i.e. that the CS is a predictor of the UCS, is highlighted by the 'blocking' effect first reported by Kamin (1969). A control group of animals is conditioned to evoke a CR to two simultaneous CSs (CS1 and CS2, which are followed by a UCS). On presentation of CS2 alone, the CR still occurs. However, the blocking group is initially trained to produce the CR to CS1 only, before being subjected to the control procedure (CS1 + CS2, followed by the UCS). Subsequently, when tested, the blocking group shows significantly fewer CRs to the presentation of CS2 when it is presented alone. Thus, after both procedures, the blocking group shows a smaller CR to CS2. A reasonable explanation is that for the blocking group the CS1 was sufficient to predict the onset of the UCS. Subsequently, when exposed to CS2, it is in effect ignored. This study shows that learning is based on contingency, that is whether or not a stimulus predicts another event. In the case of the blocking group, CS1 may predict the UCS more reliably than will CS2.

Secondary or higher order conditioning

Once a CS–UCS association has been learned then it is possible to form an association with the CS and a second CS even in the absence of the UCS. The first CS can act as a UCS for a new CS. Again, when the second CS reliably produces the CR, it too can be used to condition a third CS. Secondary conditioning is learning in the absence of a UCS, and where previously neutral stimuli may acquire both the power to form further associations with other neutral stimuli.

Hull (1932) was the first to suggest that higher order conditioning may be responsible for the learning of complex skills or 'habits'.

CRUCIAL TIP

Many students when writing about learning theory, merely provide answers to the question: what do you know about classical conditioning? Hence they write down everything they can remember about the topic. I have seen many such essays receive a fail grade. You must address the question. Typically, something very specific will be asked, such as the role of contingency or contiguity in learning.

Inhibitory conditioning

So far an established CS has been considered as being excitatory, that is the CS representation excites the UCS or CR representations. In such cases it may be said that the CS signals the imminent arrival of the UCS. However, a CS may also signal the omission of the UCS. A CS that does this is known as a **conditioned inhibitor**. For example, pigeons learned to move away from a light when food was only delivered while the light was off (Hearst and Franklin, 1977). Another demonstration of conditioned inhibition is described by Zimmer-Hart and Rescorla (1974) in which the CR was suppressed during the combined presentation of a CS1+CS2, but at its maximum during only CS1 presentations. This suggests that CS2 inhibited the CR. It is usual to suppose that conditioned inhibitors form a negative association with the CR (denoted CS−).

CRUCIAL CONCEPT

Inhibitory conditioning is a useful concept because not only can stimuli predict the occurrence of something, they can also predict the omission of something. Suppose you have a friend, person A, who is nearly always very pleasant to you. She laughs at all of your jokes and generally makes you feel good. However, when she is accompanied with another friend, person B, she is very cool towards you and shows you none of these positive attitudes. After some time, you will come to predict that person A plus person B equals the omission of pleasant exchanges. Yet you will predict that person A alone equals the presence of positive exchanges. Thus person B is an inhibiting stimulus and you would learn not to seek out their presence.

Pre-exposure effects

When a stimulus is repeatedly presented to an animal and this stimulus has no obvious consequences, i.e. it is not regularly followed by a UCS or an acquired CS, then later attempts to condition this stimulus are disrupted (Baker and Mackintosh, 1977). It is common to say that repeated exposure to a stimulus that does not signal any specific event results in the reduction of a response to that stimulus. This process is known as latent inhibition, since it inhibits future learning. **Sensory preconditioning**, on the other hand, is the exact opposite of latent inhibition. When two neutral stimuli repeatedly occur together, then the conditioning of one of the pair to a CS enhances the conditioning of another. For example, if neutral stimuli CS1 and CS2 occur together, then training CS1 with a UCS results in more rapid conditioning for CS2 when it is later paired with the UCS. Pre-exposure effects seem to indicate that no reinforcement (association with a UCS or established CS) is required for conditioning.

Quick test

1. Give one reason why psychologists study animal learning.

2. What did the associationists believe about memory?

3. Using the terms, UCS, UCR, CS and CR, state what is learned in classical conditioning.

4. What is meant by the term contiguity?

5. What is the difference between trace conditioning and simultaneous conditioning?

6. What is 'blocking'?

7. What is inhibitory conditioning?

Section 2

Operant conditioning

Whereas in classical conditioning responses are typically reflexive (salivation, hand withdrawal from heat and the eyeblink reflex, etc.), animals display other behaviours that are not necessarily elicited by specific stimuli. These spontaneous responses, or what Skinner referred to as **operants**, are species-typical behaviours (such as pecking, pawing, running, moving the head, and so on). Stated simply, operant conditioning is learning that an operant or action may have specific consequences. This is in contrast to learning when one event signals another as in classical conditioning. Viewed in this way, operant conditioning is, then, a more active process than classical conditioning.

Thorndike (1911) pioneered work in this paradigm, postulating the **Law of Effect**. This states that actions which are followed by some form of 'satisfying' stimulus are more likely to occur in the future, and that the greater the level of satisfaction the greater the strength of the bond between the response and its believed consequences. Thorndike defined satisfaction as a stimulus that does not invoke avoidance but rather one that invokes behaviour designed to attain it. The word 'reinforcer' has come to replace 'satisfying stimulus', and is used to denote objects or events that modify behaviour in some way.

A criticism of the concept of reinforcement is that a reinforcer is only defined by its effects and we cannot predict them accurately in advance. For example, suppose that psychologists believe that a slap in the face is a negative reinforcer. But if a barmaid slaps me in the face and then I frequent the pub more often then the slap has to be regarded as a positive reinforcer. In other words, only the effects of a stimulus can tell us whether it is a positive, negative or no reinforcer.

CRUCIAL CONCEPTS

Primary reinforcers may include desirable stimuli or outcomes (**positive reinforcers**) as well as aversive stimuli or outcomes (**negative reinforcers**). It is assumed that responses are continuously emitted, perhaps being randomly selected 'until the right one shows up' (Skinner, 1969, p. 134). That is, a range of behaviours is made until a desirable state in the immediate environment occurs. Such responses are said to be contingencies for reinforcement. For example, in the 'conditioning chamber' the experimenter rewards particular responses; in real situations some behaviours are more likely to lead to the discovery of desirable stimuli, such as food, than others are. In both situations the probability that these responses will recur is increased.

Most of the early work on operant learning was conducted on rats learning to find food in mazes. Indeed, it was Tolman's belief (a major contributor to this field) that everything important in psychology could be reduced to the processes involved in a rat at a decision point in a maze. While this may be rather overoptimistic, some very important issues have been raised by animal maze experiments. However, as well as a number of reliable concepts and sophisticated theories, a few controversies and theoretical problems have emerged from such work.

Place learning

Animals such as rats are especially good at learning the locations of reliable sources of food. This ability is fully exploited by psychologists interested in the process of place learning, especially the kinds of mental associations that might be formed. Are the responses of a rat finding a goal location in a maze a sequence of chained responses, so that one response automatically triggers the next one, or does it learn its environment as some mental or cognitive map?

Maze learning involves learning to coordinate serial behaviour towards the goal state. Many types of other skilled behaviours involve learning to do precisely this (see Chapter 7 on the state space approach to problem-solving). One of the first findings in the paradigm of operant conditioning was the discovery that the time lapse between the moment of reinforcement and the action responsible for it is crucial, but that such time intervals could be much longer than in classical conditioning. When this time lapse is minimal conditioning is most efficient. However, conditioning with delays of up to twenty minutes are still possible.

In an attempt to explain how conditioning with such large time delays was possible, especially in maze learning, Hull (1943) developed the **goal gradient hypothesis**. He supposed that finding the goal box of a maze was experienced as reinforcing for the rat. This reinforced the move into the goal box, thereby making this response at this point in the maze more likely to occur in the future. It also reinforced the association between the goal location and the food found there. This latter effect is crucial to the theory for it suggests that on future trials the location visited immediately prior to the goal box would also come to be associated with food (through secondary conditioning). This 'chaining' of the responses made at each location would eventually be extended backwards to the start location.

Evaluation

Despite this apparent success, **response chaining** has a number of problems, and from these the competing **cognitive map hypothesis** emerged. A major premise of Hull's theory is that action sequences are formed as a set of chained responses. However, a number of studies have questioned this assumption. For example, Tolman (1936) found that when a learnt maze (Figure 4.2(a)) was redesigned with straight alleys that went off in different directions (Figure 4.2(b)), rats tended to choose the alley, which was closest in direction to the goal location (route B in Figure 4(b)), rather than closest to the first choice point of the original design (route A in Figure 4.2(b)). If responses were chained, then the rat should have chosen that path from the start location nearest to the original path (route A). To account for this behaviour, Tolman suggested that animals utilise environmental cues or landmarks to develop a cognitive map of the environment – a mental representation of the relationship between different landmarks.

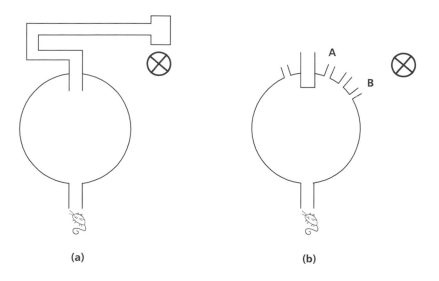

(a)   (b)

Figure 4.2 The maze used by Tolman (1936). When the learned route was blocked, rats chose the route that led directly towards the light (B) rather than the route closest to the learned route (A), indicating that the rats learned a spatial map of the environment rather than a chain of responses

The cognitive map hypothesis

More recent studies have demonstrated that rats do use external cues (external to the maze) such as filing cabinets or windows in learning about mazes. For example, rats were placed in a circular pool of milky water where a small, dry platform, not visible at the surface level, was placed in a fixed location (Morris *et al.*, 1982). Since rats dislike being placed in water, they swam around until they found the platform, whereupon they rested. After being repeatedly placed in the pool, they learnt to swim directly to the platform. When placed at new points in the pool the rats still swam almost directly towards the platform. Experiments in animal place learning such as this have shown that if all external cues are eliminated, then the probability of finding the goal is reduced to chance levels. Taken together, Morris *et al.* (1982) argued that this is evidence that rats use a cognitive map.

Evaluation

The cognitive map is not compatible with behaviourist assumptions. It is not about response chaining but having an **internal model** of the world, a term that the Behaviourists were keen to avoid. It is now generally accepted that the cognitive map theory is a better explanation of place learning than response chaining.

Schedules of reinforcement

A different approach to operant learning was adopted by Skinner. Rather than study animals learning their whereabouts in a maze, Skinner focused on the frequency and timing of reinforcement in order to examine the strongest and weakest forms of learning (acquisition) and unlearning (extinction).

Skinner's main findings are that the power of reinforcement depends upon whether it is given over a fixed or varied interval, or whether it is contingent upon a particular frequency of responding. There are two main types:

- **Continuous reinforcement**. The simplest (but most unrealistic) form of reinforcement is to provide it every time the desired response is made.
- **Partial reinforcement**. Reinforcement is not continuous but depends on the number of responses or the amount of elapsed time.

These are further subdivided into the following:

- **Fixed interval (FI)**. Reinforcement can only occur after a fixed interval of time and when after the interval the desired response is made. For example, an animal might only be reinforced on the first appropriate response after one minute. An example of fixed interval is a wage slip at the end of the week or month, provided at least once when response is made (i.e. turning up to work and doing the job). Skinner found that the animal initially responds at a very low rate but this rate soon picks up. Behaviour shows a cyclic pattern where responding is highest near the time of reinforcement (known as the FI scallop). Because of this scallop, it is not a good schedule for encouraging continuous responding. An effect of this you may be aware of is the scheduling of exams, e.g. at the end of term or semester. This predicts that the peak of responses will occur near the moment of 'reinforcement', that is students will cram in their revision a week or so before the exam.
- **Variable interval (VI)**. Reinforcement occurs after a specified interval of time and when the desired response is made. The interval can change from trial to trial, thus it can be 5 seconds on one trial and 2 minutes on the next. An example of this is reading your e-mail. You click on 'Read Mail' and your response is rewarded over variable intervals of time (sometimes you won't get an e-mail for a couple of hours, but at other times they might be seconds apart). Responding on this schedule appears consistent throughout the trials (i.e. a straight line on the graph). This is a better way

of scheduling exams (i.e. when the students aren't told which week they will be in!), since the students will work continuously.

- **Fixed ratio (FR)**. Reinforcement depends upon the number of responses made regardless of time. Animals show consistent responding on this schedule. However, if the ratio requirement is too high animals show **ratio strain**, which is characterised by long pauses in responding. The student equivalent of this might be if a course has a large number of assignments then the student might lose interest in studying, and show long periods of avoiding it. The reason is that a lot of work has to be done before the reward is given.
- **Variable ratio (VR)**. Reinforcement depends on a number of responses, and this number is varied on a trial-by-trial basis. Like VI schedules, VR results in responding that is consistent over time. An example of a VR schedule is the fruit machine. It pays out only after a certain number of coins have been inserted and this number is variable.

Schedules of reinforcement and extinction

The process of extinction is the attempt to eliminate the response by no longer giving reinforcement. For a continuous schedule, the extinction process works very quickly. This is not surprising: if the reinforcement is highly predictable then responses will cease when it is no longer reinforced.

Behaviour acquired through partial reinforcement is more difficult to extinguish (e.g. Lewis and Duncan, 1956). Since reinforcement was less predictable anyway, its omission is less surprising so responding will continue longer than when it is continuously reinforced. This can explain, for example, why fruit machines can be so addictive: if the machine never paid out then you would soon stop playing. However, since it pays out on a partial reinforcement schedule (VR in fact) then it is more difficult to stop. Avoidance behaviour is difficult to extinguish and this is because the behaviour is always reinforced (the potential threat is not experienced).

CRUCIAL CONCEPT

Methods of reinforcement provide ways of establishing a range of desired responses. However, in some cases the desired response might be too specific or the response made too infrequently to reinforce directly. The method known as **shaping** is used to reinforce related behaviours rather than the specific behaviour itself. For example, suppose a rat is to be trained to press a lever. Since lever pressing might not be part of the animal's usual behaviour, the experimenter reinforces the rat for moving in the direction of the lever. Once this behaviour is acquired, then the experimenter only reinforces the rat when it is within a few inches of the lever. Subsequently, when the rat has learned that being close to the lever is a good way of obtaining food, the experimenter only reinforces the rat when it touches the lever. In shaping, then, the reinforcement becomes more specific as behaviour approaches the desired response.

Research on these schedules enabled Skinner to achieve some remarkable behaviour in animals. For example, through selective reinforcement pigeons were able to play a sort of table tennis game, and the story goes that the US military explored the use of pigeon-guided missiles. The idea is that the pigeons are trained to peck certain keys in the presence of a particular target. This way, the pigeon, perched inside a missile and looking out through a small window, would be able to guide itself to the desired target.

Evaluation

Skinner generalised these findings to human behaviour. Indeed, it has been argued that he overgeneralised his findings in his claim that all behaviours are acquired through contingent reinforcement, from learning language to learning bad behaviour. Despite these criticisms, learning theory has been applied in a wide number of settings. In the next section we examine the legacy of learning theory by looking at how it has been applied to human behaviour.

Quick test

1. What are the main differences between classical and operant conditioning?

2. What is meant by the term 'reinforcement'?

3. Describe Hull's theory of response chaining.

4. Outline the cognitive map hypothesis.

5. Describe two of Skinner's schedules of reinforcement.

Section 3

Applications of learning theory

In this section we examine applications of learning theory to human learning, and in doing so we will evaluate the usefulness of the approach in understanding human behaviour and human problems.

Can humans be conditioned?

Before one can apply learning theory to humans, we first need to establish that humans can be classically conditioned and that human learning can be guided by contingent reinforcement.

Early demonstrations of human conditioning showed that:

- the eye-blink response can be conditioned to a tone (Spence, 1969);
- skin conductance can be conditioned to a tone (Öhman *et al.*, 1975);
- human judgement can be classically conditioned (Levey and Martin, 1975);
- blocking effects are also observable in humans (Trabasso and Bower, 1968);
- conditioning principles may be at work in advertising (Gorn, 1982; Smith and Engel, 1968);
- reinforcement principles may be used to modify behaviour in schools and prisons (Hall *et al.*, 1968; Phillips, 1968).

Some have claimed that classical conditioning might also occur on the psycho-sociological level. For example, Turkkan (1989) claims that personal attributes may be transferred by association. For example, person A (the CS) may take on attributes associated with person B (UCS) by being seen frequently together (paired). Recent studies show that such conditioned learning can be developed in the lab (Baeyens *et al.* 1990).

--- CRUCIAL STUDY ---

An interesting study by Smith and Engel (1968) also demonstrates that conditioning can also occur without conscious awareness that it is taking place. Photographs of cars with or without the presence of a very attractive woman standing next to the car were shown to a group of male subjects. Despite the denial in almost all participants that the attractive women had influenced their ratings of the desirability of each car, their evaluations were much higher for those cars accompanied by attractive women.

Another study of this effect is that by Levey and Martin (1975) on postcard evaluation. Fifty scenic postcards were presented to human subjects who were asked to rate them according to how much they liked or disliked each picture. For each subject the two most liked and two least liked were selected for the second part of the experiment. Each of these cards was paired with a neutral card (valued as neither liked nor disliked) and presented on a viewing screen. A neutral card represented the CS while a liked/disliked card represented the UCS. Each was paired according to a standard trace conditioning paradigm. In the third part of the study, subjects were asked to rate the neutral cards again. It was found that their ratings of the neutral cards had been affected by whether they had been paired with liked or disliked postcards. Neutral postcards paired with liked postcards themselves became more liked than neutral postcards paired with disliked postcards.

Operant conditioning theory of depression: learned helplessness

In an operant conditioning experiment first reported by Seligman and Maier (1967), animals were discovered to learn to cease producing responses that would otherwise have avoided a shock. The experiment involves two phases and three groups of animals. In the first phase, all animals were placed in hammocks. Group Escape were given electric shocks that could be avoided by pressing a panel with the nose, Group Yoked were given the same number of shocks as Group Escape but were unable to avoid the shocks, and Group Naive received no shocks. In the second phase, each animal was placed in a chamber in which an occasional shock was delivered. If the animal moved to the other end of the chamber, the shocks ceased. Within a few trials Group Escape and Group Naive learned to avoid the shocks. However, Group Yoked was unable to learn to avoid the shocks. Instead they had learned that they were 'helpless'. This study and many variants of it have formed one basis of theories of depression in humans, by supposing that depression is a reaction to a series of events in which the adverse consequences were believed to be outside the person's control. In order to explain why some people get depressed and others do not under the same circumstances, Seligman introduced the notion of **attribution**. For example failing an exam might be attributed to external factors ('The lectures did not prepare us for this exam') or internal ones ('I'm hopeless at exams'). According to the theory, individuals who attribute failure to internal sources are more likely to become depressed.

Classical conditioning theory of phobias

Intense fear of a particular object or situation may have been acquired through classical conditioning. A CS is paired with an extremely aversive and fearful event or stimulus (the UCS). Subsequently, the CS becomes feared and is avoided. An example might be a child who cuts itself on barbed wire (UCS) while stroking a rabbit (CS). The child then learns to fear rabbits.

One problem with the conditioning theory of phobias is that the things that people fear tend to have some basis in rationality. For example, fears of snakes and spiders might merely represent what our ancestors feared, and indeed some varieties of snakes and spiders are harmful. Phobias of inane objects, such as socks, sticky tape, grass and so on, are rarely reported. Nevertheless, there is evidence that intense fears can be acquired through classical conditioning (Davey, 1992).

Behaviour therapy

If some psychological disorders are acquired through conditioning, then it should be possible to eliminate them through conditioning-based procedures. Several of these have been designed, such as the following:

- **Systematic desensitisation**. The principle of counterconditioning can be used to associate the feared object with something pleasant. For example, Jones (1924) first used this method to eliminate fear of rabbits in a young boy, pairing the rabbit with eating. The rabbit was gradually introduced over a period of days each time the boy was eating. Wolpe (1958) coined the term systematic desensitisation and used it by getting the individual to imagine various feared objects and situations during periods of deep relaxation, thus associating the feared stimulus with a relaxed state.

- **Aversion therapy**. Rather than cure fears, aversion therapy is aimed at curing addictions or unwanted habits such as smoking. The technique of counterconditioning is used to associate behaviours involved in the habit with something extremely aversive, such as vomiting. Raymond (1964) used this procedure to help a 14-year-old boy quit smoking. The boy was given injections of apomorphine, which induces nausea, while he was smoking. Subsequently, the boy felt quite ill the next few times he tried to light up. This lasted for several years, apparently.

- **Classical conditioning for enuresis**. Mowrer (1938) developed a treatment for enuresis (bed-wetting) that is based on classical conditioning principles. Moisture detecting equipment is attached to the bed and when the bed becomes wet the equipment sets off a loud buzzer that wakes the child. The claim is that the sensation of a full bladder (CS) becomes associated with the buzzer (UCS) and hence the child wakes (CR) to the feelings of a full bladder. Studies have shown this to be a very successful technique (Doleys, 1977).

Unlike many other methods of therapy, behaviour therapy treats a disorder as merely unwanted behaviour. It is not assumed that the disorder is the result of some inner conflict (e.g., as in psychoanalysis) or the consequence of a dysfunctional family and so on. A more dominant approach in clinical psychology recently is cognitive-behaviour therapy, in which counterconditioning principles are used in tandem with other techniques based on cognitive principles.

The token economy

There are numerous reinforcers that are used socially. Perhaps the most common one is praise, and giving praise for certain behaviour usually results in an increase in that behaviour. For children, attention can be the strongest reinforcer and it seems that they will do anything (including behaving badly) in order to attain it. However, there are settings where praise and attention can act as poor reinforcers, such as with prisoners, disruptive children or individuals with severe learning difficulties. An alternative is the token economy, in which points or tokens are given for desirable behaviour and these can then be exchanged for sweets or other goodies.

At a residential centre called Achievement Place juvenile delinquents were given points for appropriate behaviour and these could be exchanged for snacks, money or special privileges. There were significant gains in good behaviour, including a major increase in the amount of homework completed (Phillips, 1968).

Token economies have also been used successfully in the workplace to reduce the frequency of accidents (Fox *et al*, 1987). The method has also been successful in prisons by increasing the amount of time prisoners spent improving themselves through study, and in one case significantly raising IQ (Kandel *et al*., 1976).

Problems with the token economy include the following:

- **Extinction**. When the token economy is terminated, behaviour may return to its 'pre-token' form (Wolf *et al*., 1987).
- **Tokens as bribes**. One objection to the token economy is that the reinforcer is nothing other than a bribe. However, as Lieberman (2000) argues, society is very welcoming of negative reinforcers, such as prison itself, being 'grounded', being slapped and so on, and all of these are unpleasant (as well as ineffective): '… reinforcement [such as the token economy] can be more effective than traditional forms of discipline in at least some circumstances, and avoid harmful side effects that sometimes come with punishment' (p. 262).
- **Extrinsic motivation**. The desired behaviour is motivated towards obtaining tokens or points rather than through an internal desire to behave in more socially acceptable ways. However, the benefits of changing behaviour can often outweigh the negatives.

Learning theory and child rearing

Many parents use punishment as a way of controlling their child's behaviour. But the evidence that punishment works is not impressive. The negative effects of punishment include the following:

- **Fear**. Since punishment involves the use of aversive stimuli, and aversive stimuli can induce fear, then the risk is that punishment over a long term can increase fear and anxiety. Increased anxiety can also, in turn, hamper the ability to pay attention (Cheyne *et al.*, 1969).
- **Avoidance**. If a child is punished for not achieving a certain standard on a specific task then rather than try harder the child might avoid the task altogether (Martin, 1977).
- **Increases in aggression**. The pain associated with punishment can under some circumstances promote aggression. Furthermore, a child brought up in an environment where physical punishment is the norm may learn to see aggression as a normal way of behaving.

Alternatives to punishment

According to the principles of conditioning there are several effective ways of encouraging desired behaviour and minimising unwanted behaviour without recourse to punishment:

- **Withdrawal of attention**. Children often seek the attention of others, especially parents and teachers. When a child is misbehaving, carers are naturally tempted to attend to the child. However, the attention may be rewarding and hence can reinforce the behaviour. An alternative is to ignore the child and hence not provide a reward for the behaviour. However, this is only likely to work for minor misbehaviours, and advocates such as Wierson and Forehand (1994) suggest including withdrawal of attention in conjunction with reinforcement for good behaviour.
- **Reprimands**. Carers often respond to a misbehaving child by 'telling them off' or reprimanding them. Often reprimands are used inconsistently, are shouted out and result in argument. O'Leary (1995) has studied the use of reprimands and claims that they work best when they are:
  - **consistent** – if a child is told off once for a particular behaviour then the child is always told off for doing it;
  - **immediate** – the time between the behaviour and the reprimand should be minimised;
  - **brief** – often carers get involved in arguing about a particular behaviour. The advice is to not engage in such arguments and to keep the reprimand brief;
  - **firm in tone** – the use of anger is claimed to be unnecessary and undesirable. A firm tone is better than a yell.
- **Time-out**. The misbehaving child is removed to place that is less reinforcing, such as sitting in the corner of a room watching other children play but not being allowed to join in (White and Bailey, 1990). Time-outs used in the home such as 'go to your room' may be ineffective since the child's room is a reinforcing environment. Research shows that time-outs work best when they are brief (one to two minutes) and when the child is gently constrained.

Quick test

1. Cite two studies that show that humans can be classically conditioned.

2. Describe one application of learning theory in the clinical domain.

3. What is a token economy?

4. What are believed to be some of the negative effects of punishment?

Section 4

End of chapter assessment

Questions

1. Outline how contingency **and** contiguity are important for learning in classical conditioning.

2. How do learning theorists explain how sophisticated behaviour (such as spatial knowledge, addiction, skills and so on) is acquired?

3. Outline and evaluate one application of learning theory.

Answers

1. Above all else, you should notice that this is not a 'write down everything you know about classical conditioning' question but asks something quite specific. The question really asks: if classical conditioning involves learning a new response (CR) to a stimulus (CS) then what is the relationship between the CS and the CR during and after learning? Is it a contiguous one in that mere contact in time is necessary and sufficient for learning or is a predictive relationship learned, such that the CS predicts the occurrence of the UCS?

   Of course, starting out your essay with a description of classical conditioning is essential. You should define the terms UCS, UCR, CS, CR and describe the procedure of a hypothetical classical conditioning study. Once the scene is set you can then go on to define contingency and contiguity. You could mention the views of the associationists here as they are relevant to the discussion.

   A discussion of the temporal features of classical conditioning (e.g. trace, delay and simultaneous procedures) can be used to discuss the critical feature of the temporal overlap as advancing the contiguity explanation.

   Other phenomena such as blocking, inhibitory conditioning, and pre-exposure effects can be used to outline the importance of contingency. Here the blocking effect is most important and a detailed discussion is required. You can conclude that congruity is important, but the studies generally demonstrate that contact in time in not sufficient by itself and that the animal learns a predictive relationship between the CS and the UCS.

2. This question asks you to identify one or two theories of operant conditioning and to apply them to some aspect of sophisticated animal or human behaviour.

   You could choose theories of place learning to answer the question since there are a number of different views on this. An outline of the chaining theory of Hull is a good theory to discuss since it lays out what the early conditioning theorists believed: that complex or skilled behaviour involves the acquisition of lengthy S–R chains. Provide the reader with details of the backchaining theory as a way the animal learns to navigate a maze. You could then introduce the view of Tolman, who suggested that animals learn something more than just behaviour chains.

   Another theory you could discuss is that of Skinner and his work of schedules of reinforcement. These outline different ways in which we acquire behaviour and how easily, or otherwise, it can be unlearned. The concept of shaping is particularly important for the behaviourist since it can explain how complex behaviour can be moulded by the type of reinforcement given.

3. This is the sort of question that students seem enjoy most! In answering it, choose any one area of research you think allows you to the best opportunity to discuss the advantages and disadvantages or strengths and weaknesses of the approach. This is because ultimately your mark depends on how and whether you demonstrate your skills of analysis and evaluation.

Behaviour therapy, the aetiology of anxiety, the token economy, and child-rearing and the effects of punishment are equally valid applications.

A word of advice on your choice is that you don't get more marks for discussing two applications when one is asked for. Despite the fact that this shows greater **breadth** of knowledge, when the question asks for one application, it generally means that the examiner is looking for *depth* in your answer.

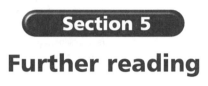

Further reading

I can only suggest one text for learning theory, and it is the superbly written:

Lieberman, D. A. (2000) *Learning, Behaviour and Cognition*, 3rd edn. Belmont, CA: Wadsworth Thomson Learning.

Chapter 5
Memory

Chapter summary

All human mental life and behaviour involves memory. Perceiving the world around you involves using your memory so that you can recognise and categorise what you see, hear, taste, touch and smell. Likewise, the study of memory underpins most of the other areas in cognitive psychology, and although a considerable amount of research has been devoted to memory, our understanding of memory is far from complete. In this section we will cover research into three main areas: immediate memory, episodic memory and semantic memory. In Chapter 10 recovered memory and false memory are covered through an example essay question.

Assessment targets

Target 1: Understanding how memory in the short term is studied
A key area of memory research is how information is retained over a short period. Trying to remember a telephone number or a shopping list without writing them down are everyday examples of the use of immediate memory. You will be able to describe some findings in this area and also a number of important theories that attempt to account for these findings. Question 1 will assess you on this.

Target 2: Understanding how episodic memory is studied
Research on long-term memory is vast. In Section 2 this discussion will be restricted to issues around one of the two main ways of dividing memory, that is into episodic and semantic memory. You will be able to outline the differences between these two and you will be able to describe a number of findings. You will also be able to outline and evaluate the theories that have been devised to account for the findings on episodic memory. Question 2 will assess you on this.

Target 3: Understanding theories of semantic memory
The area of research into semantic memory is heavily theoretical, so you will learn about three main theories: schema theory, semantic networks and connectionist networks. (To further understand the latter approach, please refer to Chapter 9.) Question 3 will assess you on this.

How will you be assessed on this?

I cannot imagine a course in psychology that does not feature the study of memory. Memory is an essential aspect of cognitive psychology. It also appears in most of the other areas of psychology. You should expect essay questions, exam papers and lab practicals on memory. Some aspect of memory may also feature in your final-year dissertation or independent study module (if your course has them).

Section 1

Memory in the short term

In this section you will learn about how short-term memory is studied, what the main findings are and what types of theories have been constructed. Several important techniques commonly used in short-term memory research will be outlined and a number of key theories will be explained.

Memory metaphors

An important question is how memories are stored. Philosophers and psychologists have used a variety of metaphors for thinking about memory and most of these are spatial, that is it is assumed that memories are stored in mental locations. Aristotle compared memory to a wax tablet, Plato compared it to an aviary and John Locke compared it to a cabinet.

Later metaphors began to draw on the technology of the time. For example, in the 1950s memory was being likened to a **telephone exchange system**, and then when the **computer** was developed psychologists found its most sophisticated metaphor yet. More recently, the **connectionist metaphor** has come to the fore and this has gone hand in hand with the development of neural network technology in engineering and computer science. Cognitive models of memory are therefore embedded within either the traditional computer metaphor or the connectionist metaphor (see Chapter 9). The earliest models of memory in the 1950s focused on the dual store theory that is based on the computer metaphor: since computers consisted of short-term and long-term information storage, so human memory was conceived of as consisting of dual storage systems.

CRUCIAL CONCEPT

Long before the computer was developed, the early psychologists had already speculated about **dual storage systems**. For example, William James (1890) divided all memory into primary memory and memory proper. Primary memory was considered to be that which we are immediately conscious of and memory proper was that which required 'recollection' to 'revive it' back into consciousness. This concept was then extended in the 1950s and 1960s and the terms **short-term store** (STS) and **long-term store** (LTS) were coined.

Broadbent's model

Broadbent likened cognition to an electronic communications system through which information flows. The **S-system** receives external information, which it stores very briefly and then passes selected portions of the information into the **P-system**. This system contains that which we are consciously aware of. The S-system and the P-system collectively represent primary memory. Since primary memory is of limited capacity, information can only be retained through the process of rehearsal. Secondary or long-term memory was a more permanent store, and information is held there after being rehearsed in short-term memory. Rehearsal was conceived of as a form of inner speech. For example, if given a telephone number to remember you might repeat it to yourself mentally.

Evaluation

In order to test the idea that rehearsal involves inner speech, Conrad (1964) tested recall for similar and dissimilar sounding items. Participants were presented with a list of letters that either sounded similar (such as T and V) or different (such as T and X). One group of participants read the letters aloud as they were presented and another group read them silently. It was found that the errors made by both groups were based on the sound of the letters (for example, they were more likely to confuse T with V than T with X during recall).

Similar findings are reported in Baddeley (1966). These results imply the use of subvocal rehearsal when participants were reading the letters silently.

CRUCIAL STUDY

Further evidence is provided by Murray (1967) who devised a procedure known as articulatory suppression. One group of participants were presented with a list of words and were required to say the word **the** repeatedly out loud (the articulatory suppression group). Another group were shown the words but not required to repeat the word **the**. Predictably, the errors made by the non-articulatory suppression group were based on phonemic similarity. However, the errors made by the articulatory suppression group were not based on phonemic similarity. This demonstrates that participants normally subvocalise the items as they are being learned, and when this is not possible, the information is not stored as an acoustic code.

A second question concerning Broadbent's model is the issue of **capacity limitation**. Miller (1956) found across numerous experiments that primary memory appears to be limited to '**The magic number seven, plus or minus two**', which was also the title of his paper. His work identified a limitation on the ability to process information in the short term. This limitation he measured using the memory span technique. The experimenter begins by presenting a list of items aurally, beginning with a manageable number and then increasing the number of items by one in each phase. The participant has to recall the items in the correct order. As the number of items is increased so too are errors and the point at which the participant makes errors at least 50 per cent of the time reflects the number of items they can recall as their memory span. About 90 per cent of the adult population can recall at least five items in order but not more than eight.

CRUCIAL CONCEPT

Clearly, if items are presented in a meaningful way (e.g. 1–9–7–8) then this will increase the memory span. Miller termed the grouping of information in this way as **chunking**. When chunked items are used, participants can still recall, on average, seven plus or minus two chunks. It was argued that seven items are maintained in primary memory through rehearsal.

Another method of preventing rehearsal is the **Brown-Peterson technique**. The experimenter reads out a consonant trigram (such as **DYB**) and then a three-digit number. The participant's task is to count backwards in 3s or 4s from the three-digit number for a specified time. After this the participant had to recall the three letters. The time spent counting backwards was varied from 3 to 18 seconds. They found that the number of items correctly recalled declined as the time was increased, and this is taken as evidence that rehearsal is used to keep items in primary memory, and that without rehearsal information decays rapidly.

Waugh and Norman's model

Waugh and Norman (1965) extended the Broadbent model in an attempt to understand the relationship between primary and secondary memory. They introduced the notion of **displacement** in primary memory, which is that as a new item enters so a previously held item must be lost or displaced. Rehearsal of items transfers the information into secondary memory, which has no capacity limitation. Rather than decay as an explanation of the Brown-Peterson effect they preferred the explanation that the few items that were recalled were due to rehearsal and that the main reason for information loss was displacement of the items by the items entering primary memory during the counting task.

Atkinson and Shiffrin's model

Atkinson and Shiffrin (1968) introduced the terms **short-term store** (STS) which closely resembles Broadbent's use of the term P-system or primary memory, and **long-term store** (LTS) which is equivalent to the S-system or secondary memory. STS is a temporary memory store and information in it is always lost eventually, but LTS is a permanent store although information may be modified through learning. Information enters LTS via the STS and an item retrieved from LTS has to pass through STS. They defined a number of control processes that manipulate information in STS and that are under the volition of the individual. **Rehearsal**, **coding** and **retrieval** are control processes of the individual. Of these retrieval was said to be most interesting, as although it seems like an effortless process, searching for information in a vast store of information predicts that it should take much longer than it does.

Although the Atkinson and Shiffrin model includes rehearsal as a way of storing information, it is assumed that information can be stored even in the absence of any intention to do so. As evidence that this occurs Hebb (1961) had previously shown that in a serial recall task, when a particular list is repeated intermittently in a long series of trials, the participants showed improved recall for that list over the other lists, even though participants were unaware of the repetitions. Atkinson and Shiffrin argue that this occurs because each time the list is presented some of the information is transferred into LTS. Thus their model is not an all-or-none affair and assumes that partial information can be stored and retrieved. For example, the tip-of-the-tongue phenomenon is explained by their model as being caused by the activity of partial rather than complete traces in memory.

Evaluation

One of the advantages of the Atkinson and Shiffrin model is that it was expressed as a mathematical model and hence yielded precise, testable predictions. Previously, theories of immediate memory were vague and described in brief terms. Much evidence used to support the model have come from research on the serial position curve.

CRUCIAL CONCEPT

The **serial position curve** is characterised as an inverted-U and is obtained through tests of free recall for items presented for a brief period. Its main features are the high accuracy of recall of the first few items, known as the primacy effect, and the high accuracy of recall of the last few items, known as the recency effect.

According to the Atkinson and Shiffrin model, in serial recall primacy occurs because of the better rehearsal of the first few items. It is better because initially there are fewer items to rehearse. Recency can be explained by the displacement effect in STS, as the earlier items are pushed out of STS by newer items. Middle items are then poorly recalled because (1) they receive fewer rehearsals, and (2) as they are more volatile than the earlier items that do receive rehearsal they are pushed out by the later items.

The model predicted that if recall was delayed then primacy will remain but recency will be lost. This is due to the fact that rehearsal of the earlier items pushed them into LTS but this is not so for the most recent items. This prediction was confirmed in Glanzer and Cunitz (1966) and Postman and Phillips (1965). A second prediction is that recency should remain regardless of the length of the list, since the most recent items remain in STS as they push out or displace earlier items in the list. Many studies have shown this to be the case, e.g. Murdock (1962).

However, there are many findings that the model cannot account for. For example, while Glanzer and Cunitz (1966) found a method whereby recency could be eliminated, they did this by using a distracter at the end of the list. However, when a distracter is used throughout the list, e.g. after each and every item, a strong recency effect appears (Bjork and Whitten, 1974). The model cannot explain this finding. Koppenaal and Glanzer (1990) suggest that with continuous distracters, participants learn to time-share, that is they begin to alternate their attention between rehearsing the items and performing the distracter task. The essential problem with the model is that there is too strong a separation between STS and LTS, and as Neath (1998) points out STS is dependent upon LTS: 'Information recalled from long-term memory has to pass through short-term memory on the way in and on the way out … Any response from any task should reflect both stores, and, because of this inherent contamination, it would seem impossible to separate the types of code' (p. 77). Indeed, many studies show that many of the results found with short-term memory can be replicated over much longer timescales (Neath, 1998).

Working memory

The distinction between short-term and long-term memory stores is no longer deemed plausible. How then can memory over the short term be characterised? The most influential theory is that of working memory (Baddeley and Hitch, 1974; Baddeley, 1986), and it is conceptualised as a location where many cognitive operations are carried out. Its main features are:

- **central executive** that coordinates activities in working memory;
- **visuo-spatial sketch pad** for processing visual information;
- **phonological loop** for processing auditory information.

The phonological loop is further divided into the phonological store, which stores speech-based information, and the articulatory control process, which translates visual information into speech-based information. Memory traces are assumed to decay rapidly over one or two seconds unless refreshed by the articulatory control process which controls subvocal rehearsal. The phonological loop was devised to account for the following:

- **The phonological similarity effect**. Items that have similar sounds are confused. For example, the list BCDEPT is more difficult to recall than the list QSXKGN (Baddeley, 1966). Furthermore, phonemic similarity results in a large number of transposition errors (for example, the sequence BFCUTJ being recalled as BFTUCJ with the phonemically similar C and T exchanging places in the sequence recalled). The effect occurs in the model due to covert rehearsal as the list is being presented.

- **Articulatory suppression**. According to the model, when rehearsal is prevented the phonological similarity effect should disappear. The evidence supports this prediction (e.g. Baddeley, Lewis and Vallar, 1984).

- **The irrelevant speech effect**. When irrelevant speech is played in the background serial recall is severely disrupted (Colle and Welsh, 1976). The model explains this finding as intrusions in the phonological store from the irrelevant speech. It further predicts that articulatory suppression should remove the effects of irrelevant speech and that irrelevant non-speech-based sounds in the background will not produce the same reduced performance as irrelevant speech. These predictions were supported by the findings of Salamé and Baddeley (1982).

- **The word-length effect**. In serial recall, short words are recalled better than long words (Watkins, 1972). Baddeley, Thomson and Buchanan (1975) found that if one set of words takes less time to pronounce than another set of words, then memory for the shorter items is better. The model accounts for these findings by supposing that memory span is determined by the time each item takes to be subvocally rehearsed, and predicts removal of the effect with articulatory suppression. Indeed, when subvocal rehearsal is prevented throughout a trial there is no word length effect (Baddeley, Lewis and Vallar, 1984).

Evaluation

There are several findings that contradict the working memory model. First, the irrelevant speech effect is not restricted to speech but can be produced with pure tones (Jones and Macken, 1993). Second, the word-length effect is more pronounced when the items are presented visually than aurally (Watkins and Watkins, 1973), and further, that the opposite effect can also occur (that shorter words can sometimes be recalled less well than longer words). A more general problem with the model is that it is expressed as a series of statements rather than as a mathematical or computational model (although there have been attempts to devise connectionist models of working memory, e.g. Burgess and Hitch, 1992).

Activation theories

Rather than conceiving of short-term memory as a special location in memory where information leaves and enters (as in the Atkinson and Shiffrin and working memory models), immediate memory may merely be those areas of memory that are currently active (Cowan, 1993). The idea is that immediate memory is that part of our knowledge that is currently in a heightened state of activation, and that only a small portion of knowledge may be in the state of activation at any one time. Activations decay through time unless rehearsed and a central executive directs attention and controls which information will be at the centre of attention.

Evaluation

Cowan's activation model disposes of the need for a specialist, discrete short-term storage system, and is one that is also consistent with the connectionist metaphor (see Chapter 9). There are a number of problems:

- Such a model is too general to make precise predictions (about the effects of serial recall, for example).

- Activation is not clearly defined. What does it mean to say that some bits of knowledge are in a heightened state of activation? One possibility is that activation may reflect increased activation of neurons that represent particular memories, but this is not clear.

- The notion of decay of information through time. As pointed out by Neath (1998) 'time is not a causal agent: iron rusts over time, but time should not be given a causal role; some other activity (usually defined as interference) that unfolds over time should be the causal agent.' Therefore, models of immediate memory should consider the role of inhibition or interference.

Activation models, such as the feature model (Nairne, 1990) take account of the many criticisms of previous models, but the feature model too is not without its problems.

Quick test

1. Outline Broadbent's model of immediate memory and provide at least one criticism of it.

2. Outline Atkinson and Shiffrin's model of immediate memory and provide at least one criticism of it.

3. Which effects was working memory designed to account for?

4. What are the problems with working memory?

5. Briefly describe the activation approach to immediate memory.

6. What are the criticisms of the activation approach?

Section 2

Episodic memory

In this section you will be examining the different ways in which memory is studied, such as the division of episodic and semantic memory systems, and the way that knowledge is acquired through either explicit or implicit learning.

Distinguishing between episodic and semantic memory

Tulving (1986) is usually credited with distinguishing between episodic memory (memory of when something happened) and semantic memory (memory for facts and knowledge). He raised five issues concerning the two types of memory:

- **Time**. Memory can either be time-based or independent of time. For example, recalling your first day at college is dependent upon time (i.e. you remember the events as occurring on the first day), but the information you learned in your first lecture that day (such as Baddeley's theory of working memory) is not dependent upon knowing when you learned it.

- **Types of associations**. Episodic memory is closely related to personal events and is autobiographical in nature. Semantic memory concerns the associations between concepts (e.g. that between restaurants and eating, for example) and is knowledge that is not necessarily of a personal nature.

- **Retrieval**. Retrieval of semantic memory seems not to be dependent upon the learning situation. However, for episodic memory, the learning context is important during retrieval, and retrieval can strengthen the information.

- **Interference**. Semantic memory appears to be less susceptible to interference than episodic memory.

- **Independence**. Although the two systems are sometimes dependent (you need semantic memory in order to recall a particular episode in your life, but you don't need semantic memory to recall the Kings and Queens of England), they can be thought of and treated as two independent memory structures.

Memory dissociations

How can we test whether two memory systems, such as semantic and episodic memory, are truly independent? The **dissociation technique** is to attempt to manipulate one memory type without affecting the other. So, if an experiment shows that episodic memory can be affected but not semantic memory then this could be taken as evidence of the distinction. For example, suppose the recall of time-related information of an experimental task was weak when tested one month later but the recall of the materials studied was intact then this might be evidence of the distinction. (This method is not without its critics, and one problem for the approach is that if the two measures used are different – and in many ways they **have** to be – then one type of information might merely be more difficult to recall than the other. This might be because the participant paid more attention to one aspect of the materials than other aspects.)

CRUCIAL CONCEPT

An important distinction in memory that has been extensively studied is that between explicit and implicit memory. **Explicit memory** refers to stored information that we can consciously recollect and talk about. **Implicit memory** refers to stored information that affects our behaviour but which is difficult to verbalise (such as being able to speak grammatically correctly, but not being able to state the rules of grammar).

Dissociation tasks have been used to draw a distinction between **explicit** and **implicit** memory. Tasks used are those that affect explicit memory but leave implicit memory intact. An example is the observation of Clarapede (reported in Baddeley, 1992) on individuals with amnesia. The doctor gives the patient a pinch while shaking hands when being introduced. The patient flinches and asks why he did that. Some days later, the doctor returns to the patient and attempts to shake hands. Since the patient is amnesic he or she has no recollection of ever meeting the doctor; however, the patient is reluctant to shake hands and cannot explain why. This demonstrates the possibility that explicit memory (in this case memory of the initial meeting) and implicit memory (feeling reluctant to shake hands the second time around) are separate.

Episodic memory

Two main areas of episodic memory which have been extensively studied are the effects of context on retrieval and memory for when something happened, which includes autobiographical memory.

Context effects

When we use our memory, we are said to be retrieving information. Various cues seem to affect the ability to retrieve information, and many of these are dependent upon the circumstances of when the information was acquired.

CRUCIAL CONCEPT

The **encoding specificity** hypothesis formulated by Tulving and Thomson (1973) is that the best conditions for retrieval are those that are most similar to those during encoding or learning.

An example of encoding specificity

Suppose that three groups of participants are required to learn the same list of words that were presented in different categories, such as a list of fruits, place names and so on. One group are required to free recall as many items as possible, the second group are given the category labels (e.g. fruit, place names) of the words presented earlier and asked to recall as many of each (congruent cued recall), while the third group are given cued recall but using categories of words that did not appear in the list (incongruent cued recall). The group given congruent cued recall do better than the group given free recall, and the group given incongruent cued recall perform the worst (Roediger and Payne, 1983). According to the encoding specificity principle recall in these cases is dependent upon the presence and quality of appropriate cues.

As well as particular cue words, environmental cues can improve recall. Godden and Baddeley (1975) gave divers lists of words in one of two conditions, underwater or at the surface. They were then tested either in the same or different setting. The divers who recalled the most words were those whose learning and test conditions were the same. Smith *et al.* (1978) found similar effects when the context was the same or a different room at learning and at recall.

CRUCIAL CONCEPT

A distinction is made between **context alpha**, which refers to aspects of the immediate environment, and **context beta** (or **interactive context**), which refers to things close to the ongoing activity (Wickens, 1987). For example, while reading the sentence 'The man robbed the bank' at home in your study, context alpha is the study environment, and context beta is the word 'robbed' that helps you distinguish the meaning of the word 'bank' as a place to keep money from its alternative meanings, such as 'river bank'. The above examples refer to context alpha.

CRUCIAL STUDY: CONTEXT EFFECTS AND RECOGNITION

Light and Carter-Sobell (1970) presented sentences to participants that included two capitalised and underlined words, as in 'The STRAWBERRY JAM tasted great'. Participants were forewarned to expect a recall test of the underlined and capitalised words. The recall test consisted of old sentences (ones presented in the list), new sentences (ones that did not appear in the list), and modified sentences that consisted of an old and a new item, as in 'The TRAFFIC JAM was terrible'. Participants were told to identify any of the underlined and capitalised words as old or new, irrespective of whether they appeared in a different sentence or with a different word next to it. The results show that when JAM was presented in the exact same context it was recognised 65 per cent of the time and when it was in a new context it was recognised about 25 per cent of the time. This study demonstrates the effects of context beta, as the sentence (i.e. the task) provides the cue for recognition.

Internal states as contexts

Just as environmental or task-related stimuli can elicit context-dependent memory effects, it appears that one's internal state can produce similar effects (**state-dependent memory effects**). For example, Bartlett and Santrock (1979) changed the states of participants so that they were in either a happy or sad mood, and found better recall when the moods matched between learning and recall than when they were different. In Chapter 8, we discuss similar results that have been reported by Bower (1981) and the implications they have for understanding emotional disorders.

Goodwin *et al.* (1969) reported the state-dependent memory effects of alcohol. They found some interesting and unexpected results. As you would predict, the best performance occurred for participants who were sober during learning and recall; however, the worst performance occurred when the participants were 'tipsy' during learning and sober during recall – even worse than when participants were tipsy during learning and during recall. Very similar findings have been reported with marijuana (Eich, *et al.*, 1975), and with nicotine (Peters and McGee, 1982).

Autobiographical and temporal aspects of memory

When we recall something from the past, we not only recall aspects of the event itself but also we have a sense of when it occurred and how long ago this was. A feature of my own memory that I find quite intriguing occurs when I leave my office and go to my car. I can park my car in several places but most of the time I instantly know where I parked it in the morning. Surprisingly, where I parked it yesterday and all of the days before that do not seem to interfere with my knowing where it is today. It is as though previous memories are automatically overridden.

Memory for when something occurred is one of those areas of research aimed at understanding an aspect of mental life that we seem to achieve effortlessly. However, research shows that (1) this is a difficult area to theorise in, and (2) people are not very good at locating an event in time accurately.

Some findings on memory for when something occurred are as follows:

- We know (from the previous section) that recall is better for the beginning and ends of a sequence (the primacy and recency effects), but this is also true for autobiographical memory (Baddeley, Lewis and Nimmo-Smith, 1978).

- When people estimate when something happened they tend to make the error that it happened more recently than it did (Thompson *et al.* 1988). This is known as forward telescoping.

- If there is a long interval between two events then estimates of when they occurred are better than if the interval is short (Underwood, 1977).

- Memory for the time, day of the week, time of the month, the month, the year of a single event can be independent of each other (Friedman and Wilkins, 1985). That is, you may be able to recall the time of your first visit to the union bar at university, but may not recall the day of the week or time of the month very accurately.

- For rare events, and these tend to be particularly special events for us such as our wedding day or the birth of a child, temporal memory can be very accurate from the actual time of the day to the day of the week and so on (Friedman, 1993).

Models of temporal memory

Many explanations have been offered for the way in which we are able (or unable) to recall the time of a particular event. The main types of theories are as follows:

- **Strength theory**. People make judgments about when an event occurred by assessing the strength of its memory trace. One problem for this theory is that it cannot account for primacy effects where events that happened earlier can sometimes be recalled better.

- **Organisation theories**. Estimating the time of an event is based on its distinctiveness, and distinctiveness automatically occurs because information is stored spatially in memory (rather like a tape recorder stores information sequentially). Three problems with this approach arise in explaining primacy effects, telescoping and the independence in the ability to recall the time, day, month, year and so on.

- **Time tagging**. The time is automatically recorded in memory when something happens and is tagged in with the memory of the event (Hasher and Zacks, 1979). An obvious problem with this theory is that it cannot predict when time estimates will be accurate and when they will be inaccurate, such as in telescoping.

- **Perturbation theory**. Item and order information about an event are stored separately, but associations are formed between items and their order in a sequence (Estes, 1972). The model is expressed as a relatively simple equation and can account for many observations in memory for sequential information. However, although it describes the findings well it is weak in offering psychological explanations of the findings.

- **Inference model**. People use multiple sources of information about the time of an event and then make an inference. In other words, if you were to recall the time of your first lecture at university, you might infer that it was a Monday (since this seems quite likely), it was either 9 a.m. or 2 p.m. (since these are typical lecture starting times), and it was late September or early October (since this is when the first term of university usually starts). So, multiple sources of information can give rise to quite an accurate estimation of time. The theory can explain recency effects (more cues are available for recently occurring events than events long ago) and also primacy effects (by relating them to landmarks in our personal history). The theory can also explain the finding that events more separated in time are easier to put a date to than events close in time, through the general cognitive principle that information that is more separated in time can be easier to discriminate. The strengths of the theory are that it can account for the findings and it can offer a plausible psychological explanation.

Memory for specific events: flashbulb memory

For some events we can recall the exact time and date it occurred because we deliberately make a note of it. For example, we remember the date of the terrorist attacks in the US as 11 September because that is one way in which it is recorded and labelled. For events like these we seem to be able to recall other more minor details. Can you remember where you were when you heard the news that a plane had hit the north tower of the World Trade Center in New York? Can you recall how you heard the news, what you were wearing, whom you were with and what activity you were engaged in? Do you remember this moment like a photograph?

According to Brown and Kulik (1977), when a major event occurs people record many important and not so important details of it in memory rather like the way a photograph preserves information indiscriminately. They coined the term **flashbulb memory** to refer to the photograph metaphor for when the details of an extremely surprising or shocking event are printed accurately in memory. Their studies were based on events such as the assassination of President John F. Kennedy in Dallas, Texas, and it seems that people are able to recall clearly not only the event itself but also other minor details of the moment they heard the news. They postulated that the emotional impact such an event has promotes rapid and durable imprints of the situation.

Evaluation

Studies of flashbulb memory have focused on major events such as the explosion of the Space Shuttle *Challenger*, the resignation of the British Prime Minister Mrs Thatcher, the

71

death of Diana, Princess of Wales, and the assassination of the Swedish prime minister Olof Palme. Many studies claim to have found evidence for a special flashbulb memory mechanism. However, other studies suggest that memory for such events can be explained by normal memory mechanisms. For example, when such events occur people tend to talk about them and tell people how they heard the news (rehearsal). Secondly, people are continually reminded of the event through the news media, and this may remind them of the time they heard the news. Finally, many studies show that memory for the details of how such news was heard can be very inaccurate (see Crucial Study below). Weaver (1993) argues that when the experience of such an event occurs people are compelled to remember the event, but their memory is no better than that of more innocuous events.

CRUCIAL STUDY: FLASHBULB MEMORY (NEISSER AND HARSCH, 1992)

The day after the Space Shuttle disaster, 106 people filled out a questionnaire which asked about how they heard the news, where they were, who they were with and so on. About three years later, 44 of these participants were contacted and filled out the questionnaire a second time. The mean score after three years was 2.95 correct out of 7, and 25 per cent of the participants were wrong on every question. This was despite the fact that participants rated their confidence in the memory very highly, 4.17 out of 5. Hence, although they claimed to still have highly vivid images of the event and a good deal of confidence in their memory, their memories were not as accurate as the flashbulb memory theory would predict.

Eye-witness testimony

An important and well studied aspect of episodic memory is the memory of the eyewitness. Since a person can be convicted on the basis of the testimony of a single eyewitness, the reliability of this kind of memory has major implications. One example is that of Jennifer Thompson who identified Ronald Cotton as the man who had raped her at knifepoint. Cotton was convicted and given a life sentence. Some years later new DNA evidence revealed that it could not have been him and identified another man as the rapist. Her testimony had been convincing enough for a jury but her memory was erroneous (O'Neill, 2000).

CRUCIAL STUDY – EYEWITNESS TESTIMONY (LOFTUS, 1979)

Participants watched a traffic accident and were then asked one of the following:

How fast were the cars going when they **contacted** each other?
How fast were the cars going when they **hit** each other?
How fast were the cars going when they **smashed into** each other?

Eyewitness responses were influenced by the verb used in the question. **Smashed** produced the highest estimates of speed and a week later participants who had heard the word **smashed** recalled the accident as being more violent than participants who had heard the words **contacted** or **hit**. The study demonstrates not only that memory for an event is not necessarily a true record of an event, but that different methods of questioning can yield different responses for the same memory.

The study by Loftus (1979) shows that the wording of a question can influence the recall of a memory, but other studies have also shown that an object mentioned after an event can often be mistakenly recalled as having been there (Dodson and Reisberg, 1991). It appears that when a new object is mentioned it is integrated into the old memory and subsequently indistinguishable from what was originally seen.

Eyewitnesses may provide detailed accounts of events and the amount of detail has been found to correlate with the likelihood of a conviction (Bell and Loftus, 1989), even when the detail can be irrelevant. In addition jurors tend to be impressed by the confidence of an eyewitness. However, we have seen in previous sections that confidence and memory accuracy do not always correlate well. There are now strict guidelines on how evidence should be abstracted from eyewitnesses in the US.

Quick test

1. Describe one study of context effects in memory.
2. List two or three findings on memory for when something occurred.
3. Outline two theories of remembering when something happened.
4. What is flashbulb memory?
5. What are the main criticisms of flashbulb memory research?
6. Describe one way in which eyewitness accounts may be erroneous.

Section 3

Semantic memory

Semantic memory is our knowledge of the world, from general to more specific and specialised knowledge. In this section you will be studying three influential views of semantic memory: schemas, semantic networks and connectionist networks. The discussion of the last is brief since it is covered more fully in Chapter 9.

Schemas

'Would you like to try the wine, madam?' It is most likely that you know what this sentence refers to. It is the moment at a restaurant when someone at the table is asked to try the wine to check that it is not a bad bottle. Your knowledge of the sequence of events that takes place when you visit a restaurant is probably very detailed. Knowledge may be organised as schemas, thus we may have schemas for eating out at restaurants, schemas for football, schemas for college life, and so on. A feature of schematic memory is that given partial information, we are able to recall the entire schema, as in the restaurant example. Memory organised in this way may serve a **cognitive economy**: that we do not need to be told about every detail, we can infer much of the information. Indeed, people often say things like 'You know when . . . ' as in 'You know when your phone goes off at the cinema . . . ' When we talk in this way we are announcing the schema we are about to refer to and it saves having to explicitly state a large amount of information.

CRUCIAL CONCEPT

A **schema** is 'an organised knowledge structure that reflects an individual's knowledge, experience, and expectations about some aspect of the world' (Neath, 1998, p. 328). When we hear someone telling us something or when we begin reading text, we often automatically infer the schema that is being referred to. Several candidate schemas may become active in semantic memory until further information is received, whereupon only one schema remains active.

CRUCIAL STUDY – ACTIVE SCHEMAS
(BRANSFORD AND JOHNSON, 1972)

Participants were presented with a piece of text and were asked to rate the text on how easy or difficult it was to understand. An abstract of this text is:

The procedure is actually quite simple. First you arrange items into different groups. Of course, one pile may be sufficient depending on how much there is to do. If you have to go somewhere else due to lack of facilities that is the next step, otherwise you are pretty well set. It is important not to overdo things ... It is difficult to foresee any end to the necessity for this task in the immediate future, but then one never can tell. After the procedure is completed one arranges the materials into different groups again. Then they can be put into their appropriate places...' (p. 722)

One group of participants rated the passage as very difficult to understand and another group rated it easy to understand. The only difference was that the second group were told beforehand that the text they were about to read was about doing the laundry. The experiment shows that by informing participants about the subject of the text, they can then activate their schema for doing the laundry and hence better comprehend the passage.

Evaluation

The most obvious criticism about schema theory is that it is quite vaguely specified and cannot yield many precise predictions. The concept is not new and Plato had a version of memory that is consistent with the notion of the schema. However, this does not mean that the concept cannot form the basis of a more detailed theory of semantic memory, and semantic and connectionist networks attempt to do this.

Semantic networks

One way in which schematic knowledge may be organised is through hierarchical arrangements of concepts. In other words, units of knowledge may be associated with each other through meaningful links.

A semantic network consists of a collection of nodes (Collins and Loftus, 1975). Each node represents a concept, such as animals and categories of livings things. Nodes are connected according to their relationship. For example, the node **Animal** is connected to both **Living thing** and **Bird** nodes. They are connected by the semantic association **is a**, since an animal is a living thing and a bird is an animal. Furthermore, the nodes can be arranged hierarchically according to categorical information, and in this example, **Living thing** is the top node, **Animal** is at the next level and **Bird** is at the lowest level. However, **Bird** can have nodes at even lower levels, as in **Penguin** since it is a type of bird, and also **Wings** since a bird has wings (the connection in this case is **has**).

According to the theory, when information is retrieved one node becomes active and activity then spreads throughout the network. An example of spreading activation is that if you heard the word **Bird** then nodes such as **Animal** and **Wings** will become active. Furthermore, if you were asked, true or false, whether a penguin is a bird, the relevant nodes in your semantic network would become active and enable you to answer the question.

Some information can be recalled 'directly' and other information has to be inferred. For example, 'Is a robin a bird?' can be answered directly because it is most likely that this has been learned directly. However, 'Is a penguin a mammal?' might require an inference since we may have never directly learned that a penguin is not a mammal. In these cases, response times to the former questions will be shorter than those to the latter types of questions. Collins and Loftus (1975) predict that the time taken to respond to these types of questions will directly relate to their distance in a semantic network. This prediction has been confirmed.

Evaluation

One of the main problems with semantic network theory is the concept of spreading activation itself. How does the system know when to stop spreading its activation? Suppose a word, like **Bird**, was associated with 10 other words. Then those 10 words become activated when the word **Bird** is presented. Those 10 words may each be associated with a further 10 words, and those further 10 words with another 10 words, and so on. After only a brief moment, activation of the word **Bird** would activate tens of thousands of other words in semantic memory.

Connectionist networks

In a connectionist network there is a collection of units or nodes where each node represents a concept. Connections between nodes represent learned associations. Activation of a node will activate other nodes associated with it. Connections between nodes are not programmed into the network. Rather, the network learns the association by 'exposure' to the concepts.

This model of semantic memory has a number of psychologically plausible concepts, such as the following:

- **Generalisation**. Given partial information the network can retrieve a whole memory. For example, if we overhear someone talking about a key political figure in the UK named Tony (partial information), we can infer that the person being referred to is Tony Blair the British prime minister. Likewise, given a few details of a complete memory, the network can retrieve the memory in its entirety.

- **Fault tolerance**. In humans neuron loss is mostly constant, but this does not seem to have a dramatic effect (unless the amount is great or the damage is located in a particular area of the brain). Indeed, as neuron loss increases behaviour shows a **graceful degradation** – performance on a task gradually declines rather than disappears all together. The advantage of the connectionist network is that the loss of a handful of units will not result in the complete inability to recall the memory whole.

Chapter 9 discusses this approach in more detail. Connectionist networks are an increasing influence in theoretical cognitive psychology, so it is a useful topic to study.

Quick test

1. What is a memory schema?
2. Describe the basic features of a semantic network.
3. Describe one important psychological property of a connectionist network.

Section 4

End of chapter assessment

Questions

1. Describe and evaluate the Atkinson and Shiffrin model of short-term memory.

2. Outline ways in which episodic memory differs from semantic memory. What cognitive mechanisms have been suggested that help people recall the time of an event?

3. Outline and evaluate one theory of semantic memory.

Answers

1. There are four key things you should address when answering this question:

   (a) You should begin by defining short-term memory, and remember that these authors defined the term 'short-term store' and others refer to it as immediate memory or primary memory. You could mention here how short-term memory is said to differ from long-term memory.

(b) Next, describe the model in as much detail as you can saying what observations it was designed to capture.

(c) The next part of your answer should be to evaluate the model in respect of what predictions the model makes and how well new data fits in with the model.

(d) You then need to evaluate the model conceptually: are there any obvious flaws in the model? This would then nicely lead into a brief description of an alternative model, such as working memory or activation theory or both, and (without going into too much detail) you could say how better an explanation of immediate memory the alternative model(s) is/are.

You must also end your essay with a conclusion. Students often forget to do this and it is a place where good marks can be attained because it allows you to offer some final evaluative thoughts on the issue (and in this case the Atkinson and Shiffrin model).

2. First, note there are two parts to this question and typically your lecturer will expect both to be answered in order to achieve a pass mark. In this example, the allocated marks to each part are not given, and as a general rule you can assume that more marks are attached to the part that requires more evaluation. In this case it is the second part since it asks you to write about suggested cognitive mechanisms, in other words theories of memory for when something happened.

The first part of the question asks you to identify differences between the two types of memory, and the distinctions raised by Tulving (1983) are relevant here. You could also mention the method of dissociation to determine whether the two types of memory are indeed independent.

The second part of the question clearly asks you to describe two or more theories about episodic memory. It is a good idea sometimes to delay discussing any theory until after you have described some observations. Remember that theories are developed to account for the findings, so letting your reader know what the findings are can help them understand the theories you will go on to describe. You should mention some of the theories that are clearly problematic, saying that they cannot account for some of the main findings. You should include inference theory here, as it is a superior explanation to many others. As a demonstration of inference theory you could mention the research on flashbulb memory and conclude that inference theory can better account for the data than some hypothetical special flashbulb mechanism.

A point worth making here is that in my recommended answer I have introduced a discussion on flashbulb memory but it is not directly mentioned in the question. You will probably be advised **not** to introduce work that is not really implied by the question. However, when students lose marks for this, it is typically when there appears to be no link (or rather when the student does not make the link explicit). If you can identify a strong link between the main issue implied by the question and a slightly different line of research, then it is fair to include that material. You must, however, make it clear how it is related.

3. When you are asked to evaluate or describe one theory, you might be tempted to choose a theory that you understand better than any other theory. This is perfectly understandable. However, sometimes you can get more marks by writing about a theory that you do not understand so well, and this is because the theory is easier to evaluate (there are many more criticisms of the theory and such criticisms lead nicely into a discussion of the theory that replaced it).

Schema theory is easy to write about but difficult to evaluate clearly. It is therefore better to discuss semantic networks than schema theory since you can list the many problems with this approach. Furthermore, once you have described the concepts of nodes and associations your description of connectionist networks is that much easier, and you should discuss connectionist networks as an alternative and more psychologically plausible model of semantic memory.

Other students might be tempted to describe and evaluate the best theory of semantic memory to date, which is connectionism. This is fine if you are confident writing about connectionism, but if you are not then it is better to evaluate a weaker theory and use your knowledge of the better theory in your evaluation.

Section 5

Further reading

Neath, I. (2002) *Human Memory: An Introduction to Research, Data, and Theory*. Belmont, CA: Brooks/Cole Publishing.
Baddeley, A. D. (1990) *Human Memory: Theory and Practice*. Hillsdale, NJ: Erlbaum & Associates.
Andrade, J. (2002) *Working Memory in Perspective*. Hove: Psychology Press.

Chapter 6
Language

Chapter summary

Language is perhaps the most sophisticated of all human abilities. For this reason language is also possibly one of the most difficult areas to understand, despite the fact that there are numerous methods available to research language. In this chapter we consider some of the main elements of language, including reading and text comprehension. We then go on to examine a number of theories of the use of language and its relation to other cognitive processes, such as thought. How children acquire language is also discussed and several proposed theories are evaluated.

Assessment targets

Target 1: Explaining the main elements of language
In this section you will learn about the main elements of language such as, phonology, syntax, semantics, morphology and pragmatics. Question 1 will asses you on this.

Target 2: Describing and evaluating research on reading
This section will help you understand the research on reading and text comprehension. You will also read about the various forms of dyslexia and how researching these can inform our understanding of the cognitive processes in reading. Question 2 will assess you on this.

Target 3: Evaluating theories of the relationship between language and thought
You will be able to explain and evaluate theories that address questions about how language and thought are related to each other and whether one is constrained by the other. Question 3 will assess you on this.

Target 4: Understanding and explaining how the acquisition of language is studied
Linguistic competence seems to be acquired in a particular sequence. You will be able to explain the order in which certain aspects of language are learned. Aspects of language may be innate but most aspects seem to require appropriate environmental influences. You will be able to understand and explain the different theories of language development. You will also be able to answer the question about whether animals, such as chimps, can acquire the ability to converse with humans. Question 4 will assess you on this.

How will you be assessed on this?

The relationship between thought and language and the acquisition of language are both popular topics for essay and exam questions. Some of the issues discussed in this chapter may also feature in your lab practical classes.

Section 1

Elements of language

Spoken language can be broken down into a number of elements, such as phonology, syntax, semantics, morphology and pragmatics. These are important aspects of language that you need to study before being able to fully appreciate the issues discussed in Sections 2 and 3.

Language is a means of using words to communicate. However, it is also used to gather information from our environment. Anyone who has spent time in a country that speaks a foreign language is keenly aware of how difficult it is to communicate and obtain information about local affairs. Often when we are deprived of something, we fully appreciate its function and value.

In order to study language one needs to understand the types of physical and linguistic information involved, such as speech and the written word. We begin this section with an analysis of phonology, syntax, semantics and pragmatics before considering more general theories of language.

Phonology

The study of linguistic sounds is known as phonology. It concerns the production of sounds made by the mouth, tongue, vocal chords and so on, whose combined movements produce speech. The physics of the raw sounds produced in speech is known as acoustics. The basic unit of speech is the phoneme. One way in which languages differ from each other is in terms of the sorts of phonemes that are used. Phonemes can consist of consonants, such as /d/, /b/, or vowels, such as /i/, /a/. Phonemes can also be voiced (/b/, /k/, /g/, etc.) or voiceless (/s/, /t/, etc.), and are characterised as such based on the location at which the initial sound burst is made, whether it is in the vocal chords (voiced) or within the mouth (voiceless).

Syntax

A sentence consists of a number of words. The way words are put together to form sentences is known as syntax and it concerns the rules of language use, e.g. its grammar. The order of words within a sentence most often determines its meaning. For example, if we transpose two words in the sentence **the dog bit the man** to form **the man bit the dog**, we create an entirely different meaning. As we will recall from our English lessons, words are categorised as nouns, verbs, adjectives, adverbs, and so forth. In English, the first noun is the subject of the sentence and the second noun is usually the object. Between them is usually a verb. Thus the previous exemplar sentences are of the form **the (Subject) (Verb) the (Object)**, and this is known as an S-V-O word order. It has been estimated that 75 per cent of all languages use the S-V-O form (Ratner and Gleason, 1993). One exception is Japanese which uses an S-O-V form (**the dog the man bit**), and another is Welsh, which uses a V-S-O (**bit the dog the man**) word order (Ratner and Gleason, 1993).

Semantics

Syntax alone in insufficient to abstract meaning from a sentence. The obvious example of this is that it is possible to create sentences that are syntactically correct in terms of the S-V-O word order but have no meaning, as in the sentence **the jumper milked the sideboard**. The study of semantics is concerned with how we process the meaning of linguistic information.

There are five aspects of language important for the study of semantics (Bierwisch, 1975):

- **Ambiguity**. Words can have more than one meaning and this can make a sentence ambiguous, as in **go to the right table** – does this instruction refer to the **correct** table or the table on the **right-hand side**?

- **Anomaly**. This is a sentence with correct syntax but one that has no meaning, as in **tables fly long hairs in the air**.

- **Entailment**. In our use of language we often say something that conveys more information than that contained in the sentence, as in **Helen is my best friend**, which also reveals, by inference, that my best friend is female.

- **Conflicting meanings**. A sentence may contain items that appear to contradict each other, as in **my cat is not my pet**. Ordinarily, **my cat** and **my pet** would be synonymous, except that here the word **not** creates a conflict and it may mean that the cat is something more than just a pet.

- **Implication**. While words can have more than one meaning, so too can sentences, as in **Students hate annoying lecturers**. This could have two different interpretations: that students dislike those lecturers who can be annoying or that students dislike annoying their lecturers.

Morphology

While phonemes are the basic **physical** unit of speech, morphemes are the basic units of word meanings. Morphemes include prefixes (pre-, un-, mis-, dis-, and so on) and suffixes (such as -s, -ness, -d, and so on) as well as individual words. So, for example, the word **skirts** has two morphemes, **skirt** (article of clothing) and **s** (a suffix to denote more than one of these items). Morphemes such as most prefixes and suffixes are not words by themselves and hence are said to be **bound**. Morphemes that are words by themselves are said to be **free**.

In contrast to theories that stress the importance of syntax in the meaning of a sentence, the case grammar approach emphasises the importance of our knowledge of words and their relationship with other words in attaching meaning to a sentence. So while the syntactic approach informs us of how a sentence is constructed in the terms of the order of different word forms, it tells us nothing of the subject of the sentence.

> CRUCIAL STUDY: MCGURK AND MACDONALD (1976)
>
> McGurk showed participants a videotape of a person uttering simple consonant-vowel combinations, such as /ga/. However, the soundtrack was replaced with a voice uttering a different sound, such as /ba/. The soundtrack was synchronised with the lip movements on the videotape. Participants report not hearing /ba/, nor did they report hearing /ga/. Instead they reported hearing /da/, a sound that lies between the two. This phenomenon is know as the McGurk effect. The effect demonstrates that what we hear as speech is not just a simple combination of phonemes and lip movements of the speaker. One implication of the effect for film-makers is that comprehension of movies can be hampered when the voice-over is dubbed (as with films made in one language but dubbed with another language).

Pragmatics

Language is used differently in different contexts. Pragmatics concerns the social rules that determine how language is used in certain contexts. For example, you might describe your college differently to a future employer than you would to a close friend. In the former, you might emphasise the academic aspects of being a student at the college, but in the latter you might emphasise the social aspects of college life.

According to Grice (1975) conversations in different contexts vary according to four maxims. Thus a discourse can be:

- highly informative versus weakly informative;
- completely truthful or untruthful;
- most relevant or irrelevant;
- perfectly clear or completely unclear.

People vary each aspect depending upon with whom they are conversing. So, for example, someone who is lying to their boss about why they didn't turn up to work might use a discourse that is weakly informative, untruthful, irrelevant and unclear. On the other hand, the same person talking to a friend might use a discourse that is informative, truthful, relevant and clear.

Other rules of conversation have been identified that concern the type of utterance that might be used (Searle, 1979):

- An assertive is a statement of opinion or belief, as in **I am studying quite hard**.
- A commissive is a statement that commits the speaker to some action, as in **I am going to study for three hours this evening**.
- A declaration is a factual statement, as in **I spent two hours watching TV yesterday evening**.
- A directive is an instruction directed at the listener, as in **Carry these books for me**.
- An expressive is a description of the speaker's internal state, as in **I'm so pleased I got an A+ for my cognitive psychology essay**.

In each case it is the listener's job to respond appropriately and some statements require more of a response than do others.

Quick test

In the study of language:

1. What is phonology?
2. What is syntax?
3. What are semantics?
4. What is morphology?
5. What are pragmatics?

Section 2

Reading and text comprehension

In this section you will be reading about the cognitive processes involved in reading and text comprehension, and also when these processes break down, as in developmental and acquired dyslexia.

Reading

Reading involves many cognitive processes. First, you need to be able to identify the printed characters as letters and the letters as words. Secondly, you will need to hold individual words in memory so that you can understand a complete sentence and relate it to previous sentences. You will also need to be able to comprehend the text and integrate new information conveyed in the sentence you are currently reading with information acquired from previous portions of the text. Hence reading involves object recognition, immediate memory, long-term memory, semantic memory and many other processes.

Despite the involvement of so many complex cognitive operations, reading seems effortless and is usually very accurate.

Reading differs from spoken language in several ways. First, **reading is visual and spatial** whereas spoken language is auditory and time-dependent, and while **readers can speed up, slow down or pause**, listeners cannot do this as listening is dependent on the speaker (although it is possible in some cases to ask someone to repeat themselves). Also, **reading involves understanding word units that are separated by white spaces**, but speech is continuous and many words are co-articulated. The meaning of the words can be augmented in speech through the use of stresses and accents, but this is not possible with printed words (except with the use of italics to emphasise certain words). **Reading involves concerted attention and controlled eye movements** and it is usually difficult to do something else while reading. Speech, on the other hand, can be processed relatively easily while the listener is engaging in some other task (such as driving).

Eye movements and reading

Reading involves visual orienting to words across a page. We move our eyes most of the time and the most obvious reason is that there are a number of limitations in the visual system. For instance, we do not have a 360-degree visual field and most visual detail lies in a small region known as the **fovea**. Visual acuity gradually decays as we move from foveal to peripheral vision.

CRUCIAL CONCEPT

Movements of the eyes are known as **saccades**. There appear to be two types: Voluntary saccades are slower eye movements under direct conscious control, while express saccades occur automatically and are involved in correcting errors when we try to locate a visual target.

In an early study, Saslow (1967) reported that the saccade normally takes between 220 and 250 ms to perform, and that this can depend upon the properties of the stimulus being viewed (such as its brightness). This latency period of between 220 and 250 ms was found in similar studies and was reported in texts as **the** saccadic latency. However, Fischer and Boch (1983) found that under certain conditions monkeys frequently made very short saccades (80–100 ms). Soon after this Fischer and Ramsperger (1984) reported observing a similar rapid or express saccade but this time in humans, although it was slightly longer (110 to 130 ms). Therefore, we now distinguish between the **voluntary**, slower **saccade** and the **express saccade**, which is a very small involuntary movement of the eyes.

While saccades can be rapid they can also be quite inaccurate. It has been observed that a small secondary saccade normally follows a voluntary saccade to correct for fixation error. It is understood that saccadic errors of about 10 per cent are normal (Kowler and Blaser, 1995).

CRUCIAL CONCEPT

The region of vision between saccades is known as the **perceptual span** (Rayner, 1998).

During reading the perceptual span has a bias for letters to the right of the current letter being looked at. It has been shown that the span ranges from 4 letters to the left and 15 letters to the right of the current letter. This **right-sided bias** occurs because reading involves looking ahead to determine important features of the sentence, such as the length of the word and punctuation marks. Words that are highly predictable, such as the word **the**, are skipped during reading, but unusual words or misspelled words are scanned for longer periods and involve small saccades (Rayner, 1988). In addition, letters and words outside foveal vision are recognised during reading (Norton and Stark, 1971) and it is likely that this occurs because readers use their knowledge of words and their understanding of the text. This is especially so with skilled readers and implies that they do not fixate on each and every letter and word of the text during reading.

Saccades made during reading are also dependent upon reading ability. Good readers make larger jumps across the sentence, but poor readers make smaller saccades and often jump backwards towards earlier words in the sentence.

Reading and working memory

Since working memory is of limited capacity, individuals with a larger memory span tend to make better readers. This is because they have a greater capacity to utilise important cognitive resources during reading. For example, a large memory span aids processing ambiguous sentences (Miyake *et al.*, 1994), the ability to infer the meaning of unusual words (Daneman and Green, 1986) and the ability to understand complex sentences (e.g., Carpenter *et al.* 1994).

Routes involved in word recognition

An important research question is how readers interpret the meaning of words and what the processes involved are.

CRUCIAL CONCEPTS

The **direct-access hypothesis** is that readers directly translate the written word into meaning, i.e. perception of a particular pattern of letters directly activates a region in semantic memory (Baluch and Besner, 1991). The **phonologically mediated hypothesis** is that readers translate words into their speech form (internally, of course) before understanding their meaning (e.g. Wydell *et al.*, 1993).

Recall from the discussion of immediate memory, especially the discussion of working memory in Chapter 5, that there is good evidence that working memory operates primarily in an acoustic code. Errors made in working memory with similar sounding words also occur when the material is presented visually (Baddeley, 1966). This suggests that the phonemic quality of words might be important in reading. A third view is a combination of the first two, namely the dual-route hypothesis (Coltheart and Rastle, 1994).

Evaluation

Evidence that printed words are translated into speech sounds during reading comes from the finding that children who are more knowledgeable about phonemes are better readers (Seidenberg, 1995) and that children trained on phonemic skills become better readers than children trained on semantic skills (Byrne and Fielding-Barnsley, 1991). Evidence that reading might not involve internal phonemic expression comes from Bradshaw and Nettleton (1974) who presented words that were similar in the way they were spelt but were pronounced differently (such as **horse** and **worse**). When participants read the word pairs aloud, it took them less time to read the first word than it did to read the second word. The conflict between the visual similarity and the phonemic dissimilarity of the word pairs may have caused interference, and hence is likely to have slowed the reader. However, this was not so when readers were asked to read silently. As there was no interference, this suggests that words were not translated into speech sounds. Yet, McCuthcheon *et al.* (1991) have shown that adults read **tongue twisters** (e.g. **She sells seashells on the sea shore**) very slowly even when reading silently, and this indicates that printed words are translated into sounds.

CRUCIAL STUDY – LUO *ET AL.* (1998)

Participants were presented with word pairs and were asked to state, as quickly as possible, whether the words were related or unrelated in meaning. The key manipulation was whether the second word sounded the same as (was phonemically similar to) a word that was semantically related. For example under one condition, the second word, e.g. **BARE**, which sounds the same as another word, **BEAR**, that was semantically related to the first word, **LION**, produced more reading errors than pairs that were neither semantically nor phonemically related, such as **LION–BEAN**. Since participants did not read the words aloud, this pattern of errors suggests that they were producing the words phonemically but silently.

The direct-access hypothesis suggests that children should be taught to read through a whole-word approach (Crowder and Wagner, 1992), which is that children should not be encouraged to produce the sounds or focus on the sounds of words. There may be some value in this approach since in English, at least, there is not 100 per cent correspondence between the spelling of a word and its correct pronunciation. Conversely, the dual-route approach suggests a phonic approach to teaching children to read. This involves encouraging children to learn to read new words by attempting to produce the sounds of the individual letters (or sounds produced by combinations of letters, such as **sh**). Research shows that the phonics approach can produce better spellers than can no such training (Pressley *et al.*, 1996).

Text comprehension

As an illustration of the complexity of reading and comprehending text, Medin *et al.*, (2001) tell the story of how, during the 1960s, US computer scientists attempted to devise a computer program to translate Russian into English. To test their program, they translated English sentences into Russian and then back into English. The major problems involved in translating text become apparent by the following effort of this program: 'The spirit is willing but the flesh is weak' was returned back into English as (after first being 'translated' into Russian) 'The vodka is good but the meat is rotten'. (I have just logged onto an online translation service (http://translation2.paralink.com/), and I typed in the same sentence, translating the text first into German and then from German back into English, with equally disastrous results: 'The spirit is ready, but the meat is weak'). Such literal translations miss one of the beauties of language, which is the metaphor. The point is that the meaning of a sentence is more than just a particular combination of words.

CRUCIAL CONCEPT

Comprehending text is an **inferential process**: it involves making many inferences and forming coherent representations. For example, consider the sentences **The python caught the mouse** and **Jane caught the ball**. The first sentence yields the inference that the python caught the mouse in its mouth, and the second that Jane caught the ball with her hands. So rich are the inferences that when people are asked to recall these sentences some time later, many report the first sentence as **The python ate the mouse** (Brewer, 1977).

Carpenter *et al.* (1995) reveals that readers also create rich internal models of characters when reading a story. Kintsch (1994) developed a **processing cycles theory** of text comprehension, which is based on the idea that understanding a sentence involves integrating it into the context developed in the previous sentences. Each new sentence brings with it a new representation of the text, and this representation is constantly updated.

There is much research to suggest that, when reading, we make inferences that may not have been intended by the writer. In other words, we draw on information that is not present in the text (van den Broek, 1994). One factor that encourages this is the possibility that semantic memory is schematically organised. We saw in Chapter 5 that when given partial information about something we can recall its whole. So, for example, if you read the text 'Waiter!' your schematic memory of eating at a restaurant would become active instantly. Similarly, when reading a novel, the reader spontaneously makes inferences about the causes of events, such as the motivations of the characters and the likely outcome of a passage. This represents the constructivist view of reading: that readers actively construct meaning that goes beyond anything stated literally in the text (O'Brien and Myers, 1999).

In contrast, the minimalist view is that readers only make inferences when it is necessary to understand adjacent sentences (McKoon and Ratcliff, 1992). One method they developed is to present a paragraph for comprehension and then give a word recognition test. Words that actually appeared in the text should be recognised quicker than words not presented in the text but are likely to have been inferred. For example, given '**The director and the**

cameraman were ready to shoot close-ups when suddenly the actress fell from the fourteenth storey', a likely inference is **death**. McKoon and Ratcliff (1986) found that responses to inferred words were slow but only on an immediate test. Furthermore, they suggested that minimal encoding had taken place, such that participants infer something bad has happened. Minimal encoding may be useful for avoiding inappropriate inferences since further details emerging from the text might contradict an inference made from the earlier text. A considerable amount of research has been carried out in an attempt to resolve this debate, but it has yet to be resolved.

CRUCIAL STUDY – HUITEMA *ET AL.* (1993)
INFERENCES MADE DURING READING

Text similar to the following was presented to participants:

1. Dick had a week's vacation due
2. and he wanted to go to a place
3. where he could swim and sunbathe.
4. He bought a book on travel.
5. Then he looked at the ads
6. in the travel section of the Sunday newspaper.
7. He went to his local travel agent
8. and booked a ticket to Alaska.

Sentences 1 to 3 imply that Dick wants to go to a sunny beach. However, this inference is contradicted in line 8. Notice that the points where these inferences are made are separated by several lines. Huitema *et al.* presented four different types of stories: a far/inconsistent story (as above), a near/inconsistent story (where the contradiction occurs on the next line), a far/consistent story (where two non-contradictory inferences are separated by several lines), and a near/consistent story (where the two inferences occur in adjacent sentences). Participants tended to read the inconsistent stories slower than the consistent stories (which should be expected when inferences contradict each other), but the distance at which the two inferences appear in the story (whether near or far) did not influence reading speed. These results provide difficulty for the minimalist view, which predicts that reading speed should be influenced by the distance of two inferences. Instead they support the constructivist view.

Findings from Huitema *et al.* (1993) and Klin *et al.* (1999) have shown that readers build up inferences from a text, even when the inferences are at some distance apart, and this further suggests the use of long-term memory in reading. It also indicates that readers look to make inferences that are consistent with those already made from earlier passages of a text.

Reading disorders

CRUCIAL CONCEPT

Dyslexia is a disorder that affects reading ability but other cognitive processes are normal. There are two main subgroups of dyslexia: **developmental dyslexia** and **acquired dyslexia**. The former develops during childhood, but its origin is not well understood, while acquired dyslexia results from brain damage.

Developmental dyslexia

It is not clear whether the disorder has a neurological origin or a psychosocial origin. However, it is known that in dyslexia there is poor development of the magnocellular pathway (Eden *et al.*, 1996), a structure involved in the visual detection of movement, direction and depth. Furthermore, although in the normal brain language functions are specialised in the left hemisphere, in individuals with dyslexia, there is an unusual symmetry of function between both hemispheres (Bishop, 1990). Pollatsek and Rayner (1990) examined the eye movements of individuals with dyslexia and found that they make a larger number of smaller eye fixations, with much jumping back to earlier words in the sentence (which are known as **regressions**), and reading is generally slower than in normal readers. Dyslexia is also characterised by poor awareness of the phonological features of speech. For example, transposing the first sounds of two words (reading **mustard-salad** as **sustard-malad**) is difficult. There also appears to be a deficit of the perceptual span for words but not for other types of stimuli.

Acquired dyslexia

Many insights can be gained by trying to understand cognitive disorders, most of which result from brain damage. The **connectionist approach** (discussed in greater detail in Chapter 9) is an extremely useful method for testing cognitive theories since brain damage can be simulated in a connectionist network (by removing a number of processing units or by reducing the values of connection weights). If the 'lesioned' network behaves in a similar way to individuals with a specific disorder then the network may provide a plausible model of both the underlying process (reading) and the deficit. Acquired dyslexias have received a great a deal of attention from language researchers and connectionist modellers. The two main types of acquired dyslexias are peripheral dyslexia and central dyslexia. There are some similarities between developmental dyslexia and acquired dyslexia in terms of the deficits in reading.

Peripheral dyslexia

Alexia is one form of peripheral dyslexia and is characterised by a weak ability to visualise words as single units, such that reading is achieved by attending to words letter by letter. A simple test of alexia should reveal abnormally long word-naming times for long words (Warrington and Shallice, 1980). The disorder may be due to an inability to process letters in parallel (Patterson and Kay, 1982) or the loss of stored visual memory for printed whole words (Warrington and Shallice, 1980).

Neglect dyslexia is another form of peripheral dyslexia in which words located on one side of the visual field receive minimal processing (they tend to be ignored). Reading errors are characterised by the omission of words on one side of the page. The disorder may be due to an attentional deficit (Riddoch *et al.*, 1990) or to damage to brain areas responsible for representing information on the neglected side of the visual field.

Central dyslexia

In phonological dyslexia the ability to name words is unaffected, but naming nonwords is severely impaired. In surface dyslexia, reading of words and nonwords is normal but the reading of exception words (words that have an irregular correspondence between the way the word it pronounced and its spelling, e.g. **subtle**) is impaired (Patterson et al., 1985).

The dual-route model of reading can account for central dyslexia. Phonological dyslexia may be the result of an impaired phonological encoding route, while surface dyslexia may be the result of an impaired direct reading route. The existence of these two distinct disorders implies that they result from two independent processes in reading.

In deep dyslexia, a variety of reading errors are made, such as those based on the meaning of words (**sword** read as **dagger**), those based on visual and semantic similarity (**shirt** read as **skirt**), and the poor ability to read nonwords. A possible cause of deep dyslexia is that there may be damage to both routes of the dual-route model. An alternative account is that individuals with deep dyslexia attempt to read with their right hemisphere rather than the left hemisphere which is specialised for reading (Saffran *et al.*, 1980).

Connectionist models of reading and dyslexia

In Chapter 9 we present a description of the connectionist approach to modelling cognition. Several connectionist models have been designed to simulate language functions, especially reading. Furthermore, these models can be tested by making 'lesions' to the network. The subsequent errors made by the network may (or may not) adequately simulate brain damage (for example, reading errors in acquired dyslexia).

Quick test

1. In what ways does reading differ from understanding speech?
2. What is meant by the term perceptual span?
3. Describe the direct-access hypothesis of reading.
4. Describe the phonologically-mediated hypothesis of reading.
5. What is the evidence for the dual-route hypothesis of reading?
6. Describe two studies on the use of inferences during reading.
7. Describe one type of developmental dyslexia.
8. Describe one type of acquired dyslexia.

Section 3

Language and thought

In this section you will be reading about theories of whether language is determined by the way we think or vice versa.

Surprisingly, some behaviourists had views on the relationship between language and thought. For example, one theory was that thought could be regarded as inner speech. One researcher allowed himself to be given a curare derivative that caused paralysis and hence prevented any subvocal speech. If thinking was merely a form of inner speech and if speech were prevented, then thinking should stop. Despite almost total paralysis, he reported still being able to think.

A number of other studies have revealed that thinking can occur independently of language. For example, participants shown a repeating sequence of cards gradually learned to correctly identify the next card, and they did so long before being able to articulate how they arrived at their decision (Humphrey, 1951).

─── CRUCIAL TIP ───

There are many everyday examples we could think of that demonstrate decision-making in the absence of any linguistic activity, internal or otherwise. For example, think of a physical skill that you have (playing tennis, sprinting, playing cricket, juggling, and so on) and try to articulate exactly how you make decisions while you are carrying out that skill. It is quite difficult in most cases. Therefore, it is clear that cognitive processes can occur independently of language.

The Whorfian hypothesis

Whorf (1956) developed a theory known as the **linguistic relativity hypothesis**. He argued that the linguistic system is 'not merely a reproducing instrument for viewing ideas but rather is itself the shaper of ideas, the program and guide for the individual's mental activity ... We dissect nature along lines laid down by our native language' (pp. 212–13). In other words, language shapes the way people make sense of and understand their world.

The theory has been modified in several ways, and there are strong and weak forms of the theory (Miller and McNeill, 1969). Each version varies as to the extent of the relationship between language and other cognitive processes:

- **The strong hypothesis: language determines thinking**. According to this view, a concept cannot be available to the speakers of a language if no word exists for the concept. On the other hand if a culture places great importance on a particular concept then it will have more words to reference the concept than other languages whose culture placed less importance on it. Supporting evidence most often cited for this is that one Eskimo language has 27 different words to describe snow (Boas, 1911). Snow words can refer to whether the snow is falling or has settled, whether it is lightly falling or is heavy, where the snow has fallen, and so on. Clearly, it would seem that the large number of concepts Eskimos have about snow has had an influence on their language. However, it could just as easily be argued that since snow is an important aspect of their environment, it is the environment that has influenced both their language and their thinking. However, Martin (1986) has since suggested that Eskimos have no more words to describe snow than any other language of people who live in warmer climates.

- **The weak hypothesis: language affects perception**. Farb (1974) showed one way in which language is able to influence thinking. Japanese women living in America were interviewed in both English and Japanese. When asked to complete the sentence (asked in Japanese): 'When my wishes conflict with my family's …', they responded with '… it is a time of great unhappiness', but when asked the same question in English they replied with '… I do what I want'. Hence different attitudes were revealed depending upon which language was used. According to Farb, this is evidence that language expresses cultural ideas and attitudes.

Evaluation

The main problem with these studies is that it can be misleading to infer cognitive processes from language (Greene, 1975). As an example of this, while Hopi Indians use the same word for 'insect', 'air-pilot' and 'aeroplane', this does not mean that they categorise these as being the same kind of object. English speakers do not categorise a pause, a decent snooker score and a fracture as part of the same concept when using the word **break**.

CRUCIAL STUDY – UNLEARNING TO DISCRIMINATE BETWEEN PHONEMES

Perhaps one of the strongest sources of evidence that language can influence perception comes from Miyawaki *et al.* (1975), who studied infants' perception of phonemes. In order to determine how well infants can discriminate between sounds, Miyawaki *et al.* used the sucking technique. When an infant is presented with something novel its rate of sucking on a dummy increases. If the stimulus continues then after a while the sucking rate drops back to baseline. The sucking rate can be directly measured and recorded. Japanese infants were presented with the phoneme /l/, which caused an instant increase in the sucking rate. The phoneme was sounded continuously until the sucking rate returned to baseline. Then the sound was changed to a repeating /r/ and the sucking rate increased, which indicated that the babies were able to detect the change and hence were able to discriminate between the /l/ sound and the /r/ sound. Remarkably, however, Japanese adults are unable to make the same discrimination. Thus, although at birth Japanese people can discriminate between these two sounds, they gradually lose this ability as adults. The reason why this ability is unlearned, of course, is because the Japanese language itself does not discriminate between them. Both sounds can be used in the production of the same word.

The verbal deprivation hypothesis

According to Bernstein (1961), most sophisticated forms of thinking are dependent upon language. Bernstein distinguished between universalistic meanings and particularistic meanings.

- Universalistic meanings refer to knowledge that exists independently of any specific context. Universalistic meanings require an elaborated linguistic code.

- Particularistic meanings refer to immediate, specific ideas or examples, which are often tightly dependent on the context in which they occur. Particularistic meanings require only a restricted linguistic code.

Bernstein argued that socialisation and the class system expose individuals to either code: restricted code for the working class and elaborated code for the middle class. Because of the differential exposure to linguistic use, middle-class children begin school with a distinct advantage over working-class children who are verbally deprived.

Evaluation

The main critic of this approach is Labov (1970) who argued that working-class children are exposed to a linguistically rich environment, albeit in a distinct dialect rather than a standard form. Labov argued that differences between elaborated and restricted codes is less significant than Bernstein thought. Labov (1972) studied black children's use of English and concluded that the black linguistic code used was of comparable complexity and sophistication to standard English.

The developmental view

Piaget's view was that knowledge is the precursor to language and that language is only one of several ways in which knowledge can be represented. As the child experiences the world, he or she uses language to represent this experience both in terms of knowledge and in terms of social interaction. For Piaget then, thought can influence language development much more than language development can influence thought.

Vygotsky's view: language and thought are separate

Vygotsky argued that language and thought are entirely separate and have different origins. Thought, he argued, is a cognitive activity that occurs as the child experiences its environment. The child needs to store memories about the world in order to understand it and to adapt to it. Language on the other hand is a social activity that arises from hearing it from others and from communicating with others. Much of everyday language is affiliative (involved in acting socially and developing social relations) – it commonly exists as 'small talk'. Language is not always cognitive in the sense that is not always about transmitting knowledge in an elaborate way. The cognitive functions of language, he argued, are served by inner speech, which acts as a way of monitoring and structuring mental activity. Young children often produce egocentric speech, in which the child's speech reflects what is in its own mind without reference to any listener. This is because the child is unable to separate the two main functions of language, which are cognitive and social.

Accents and dialects

Lyons (1981) distinguished between three variations of a language:

- an accent, which is a regional or social variation in the pronunciation of words;
- a dialect, which is a variation of a language that has its own grammatical rules and vocabulary;
- an idiolect, which is a personal style of language use that includes speech patterns and speech habits. Most individuals have more than one idiolect which they use depending on the social context.

Haugen (1966) argued that there is little qualitative difference between a dialect and a language and it depends on the number of people who speak it. For example, Flemish, which is used by Belgians who have a Dutch origin, is now considered as a language in its own right, but French-speaking Belgians once considered it a dialect of Dutch.

Giles (1973) found that the social status of an accent could influence the perceived credibility of an argument. Participants were exposed to arguments for and against capital punishment in different accents: standard pronunciation, a Welsh accent, a Somerset accent and a Birmingham accent. They were then asked to rate the quality of the argument presented to them. Arguments in standard pronunciation were rated the highest, even though the type of argument was counterbalanced between participants. Research shows that this effect is more pervasive than one might imagine.

CRUCIAL STUDY – TEACHERS' PERCEPTION OF ACCENTS

Edwards (1979) conducted a study that examined student teachers' perceptions of the reading abilities of children with either working-class or middle-class accents. They listened to tape recordings of children reading the same passage, and were then asked to rate the reading on a number of scales, such as 'intelligence', 'enthusiasm', 'happiness', and so on. The student teachers rated the middle-class children more positively than the working-class children, despite the fact that the only difference between the two samples of children was their accent. This implies that people infer intellectual and other personal attributes on hearing a particular accent. What is of great concern is that teachers should draw such incorrect inferences. Other research shows that teachers' expectations of pupils can have an effect on children's learning: expectations can become self-fulfilling prophecies. If a teacher has an incorrect belief about a child's intellectual capacity then it can adversely influence how that child is treated, which will in turn influence the child's educational performance.

Quick test

1. What is the **strong** version of the Whorfian hypothesis?
2. What is the **weak** version of the Whorfian hypothesis?
3. What was the view of Vygotsky on the relationship between language and thought?
4. Outline one study or theory on the issue of accents and dialects.

Section 4

Language acquisition

In this section you will be studying theories and research about how children acquire language, the stages they go through, and whether language acquisition is innate or requires appropriate input from the environment. You will also be studying research on the level at which animals can communicate with humans.

In Section 1, we discussed four features of language, such as the basic unit of sounds and the uses of language in different contexts. Shaffer (1993) claimed that these four aspects of language were acquired by children in the same order:

- phonology: the sounds produced in a language;
- semantics: the meanings of words and utterances;
- syntax: the rules that govern how words may be combined to make sentences (grammar);
- pragmatics: the ways in which language use is modified according to the context (e.g. talking to a child versus talking to a college tutor).

What is the evidence for this claim?

Evidence of early vocalisations

At three weeks the infant makes 'fake cries'. These occur in the absence of any distress and most likely reflect the infant's enjoyment at making sounds. Between three and five weeks the infant begins to coo, and by four to six weeks babbling begins to occur. Babbling sounds like random combinations of vowel and consonant sounds. After a while the infant shows echolalia, which is a repetitive sound, such as **mamama**. Up to eight months, babbling sounds are universal in the sense that they sound the same regardless of the language of the infant's environment (recall that in the previous section we saw that Japanese infants but not Japanese adults can discriminate between consonants). After eight months, babbling begins to be shaped by the language they hear in their environment.

By 18 months, the child has entered the one-word stage, and begins to utter single meaningful words, such as **mine**. From 18 months onwards the infant is in the telegraphic period, where words begin to be combined in way that is reminiscent of the way telegrams were once written (a sort of verbal shorthand), such as **Daddy chair**. Brown (1973) identified early rules that the infant uses in this stage, such as the basic word order rule: a sentence consists of subject-verb-object (e.g. **Daddy eats dinner**). Two-word utterances tend to be of the form subject-verb (e.g. **Daddy walk**) rather than **verb-subject** (**walk Daddy**), and reflects the same use of word order by adult English speakers.

Grammatical morphemes

As language develops, the child acquires the use of grammatical morphemes, such as prepositions, prefixes and suffixes (**in**, **on**, the use of **s** to denote the plural, **the**, and so on). All children appear to learn grammatical morphemes in the same order (de Villiers and de Villiers, 1973), starting with simple forms followed by more complex forms (e.g. **they are**).

CRUCIAL CONCEPT

Children's acquisition of linguistic rules can be evidenced by the mistakes they make, and one of these much studied is **over-regularisation**. The child notices that the past tense of a verb can be created by adding the suffix **ed**, which is the case for regular verbs (**pass/passed**, **like/liked**, **pick/picked**, and so on), but over-uses the rule for irregular verbs (e.g. **The dog runned away**). Irregular verbs do not conform to this rule (e.g., **go/went**, **come/came**, **see/saw**, and so on). Children's over-regularisation appears to follow several stages.

Pragmatics

Children also begin to alter their use of language according to the context. For example, Shatz and Gelman (1973) observed that four-year-old children used complex sentences when talking to adults about a toy but simplified their speech when talking to younger children.

Theories of language development

Nativist theories of child language

Chomsky (1965) presented a theory of language acquisition based on the idea that it is innate and hard-wired into the system. He argued for a language acquisition device (LAD) that enables children to acquire language.

CRUCIAL CONCEPT – NATURE VERSUS NURTURE

The issue of whether some abilities or characteristics (such as intelligence, language, personality, mental disorders, and so on) are inherited at birth (the naturist view) or acquired as a result of being shaped by the environment we live in (the nurturist view) arises in many areas of psychology. In terms of language acquisition, the naturist view is that we are born with specific brain structures that enable us to acquire language quite easily. The nurturist view is that to acquire language and to reach a high level of competence in its use requires exposure to a rich linguistic environment, especially in the early years.

Chomsky distinguished between surface structure, which are the actual phrases used in a sentence, and deep structure, which are the meanings of sentences. Transformational grammar allows us to transform the deep structure of a sentence into the surface structure of the sentence. According to Chomsky transformational grammar is innate. He further argued that there are linguistic universals, which are features found in every language. Thus we are all born with a universal grammar, and this determines the surface structure of sentences. For example, Hocket (1966) has identified 13 general properties that are common to all human languages. Five of these are listed below:

- **Arbitrariness**. Intrinsic connections between the symbols used in all languages and their meaning are not necessary. For example, the symbol or utterance **grape** has no obvious connection to the object **grape**. In other words, the symbols in language are abstract.
- **Cultural transmission**. Languages are learned by direct contact with their cultural origin.
- **Discreteness**. Languages each have a discrete set of phonemes.
- **Duality of structure**. All languages have a finite set of phonemes than can be arranged to form meaningful units in a virtually limitless number of ways.
- **Productivity**. In all languages it is possible to create a completely new sentence, which is unlikely ever to have been used before. An example I'm just inventing right now is 'Eamon, the person writing this book on cognitive psychology, is the most intelligent, good-looking, easy-going, and most generous man you could ever meet.' Now, I can be pretty sure that this sentence has never been written or spoken before by anyone!

Critical period hypothesis

Lenneberg (1967) argued that although language is innate, it does depend on a biological maturation process. As evidence of this Lenneberg (1967) reported that children who become aphasic before puberty, especially before the age of five, recover most or all of their lost language functions, whereas such recovery after puberty is slow and partial. Findings like these suggest that early opportunities to acquire language are critical for the development of competency in the language.

Evaluation

Studies of second language learning, such as that of Newport (1994) on Asian immigrants to the US, show that the younger the individual when entering the country the better they learned the language, which supports the critical period hypothesis. Other evidence has been taken from studies of deprived children, such as the case of the 'Wild Boy of Aveyron' and the case of 'Genie'. These studies show that if a child is not exposed to language, up to a certain age, then they never subsequently acquire it. However, other evidence is less clear. For example, Harley (1995) found that recovery rates from aphasia were not predicted by age. In terms of acquiring a second language, more recent studies suggest that when the same learning criteria are used for adults and children, adults are better on language learning tasks than children are. As McLaughlin (1984) points out, these findings pose problems for the critical period hypothesis.

--- CRUCIAL STUDY ---

Pinker (1994) refers to a study of Nicaraguan children of various ages who attended a new school for deaf children created by the government in 1979. Although they were not taught sign language directly, they developed their own system quite spontaneously. The sign language they created later became widely used (known as the Lenguaje de Signos Nicaragüense or LSN). Interestingly, younger children who were then taught LSN developed it further and in their own way. The sign language developed by these younger children (which became known as the Idioma de Signos Nicaragüense) included grammar. It has been argued that the inclusion of grammar occurred because these children were younger than those who created LSN. These spontaneous developments in the use of sign language support the critical period hypothesis.

Environmental theories

Skinner (1957) argued that language was acquired through operant conditioning. Parents reinforce the required utterances and so these become more likely to be repeated. As the linguistic abilities of the child become progressively more sophisticated so reinforcement become more selective. This process of reinforcement is known as shaping. He contended that children also learn through imitation: the child often tries to repeat what the parent says (called the echoic response).

Evaluation

Although children often learn language through imitation, the evidence for learning by reinforcement is generally not supportive. Brown *et al.* (1969) found that parents tend to reward children's speech on the basis of its truth rather than on the basis of the grammar used. The way parents influence their child's language development is through the way they speak to the children and through expansion, rather than through direct praise. Many parents, for example, use 'motherese' when talking to very young children. Motherese consists of sentences that are very short and simple, which gradually become longer and more complex as the child's own use of language develops (Shatz and Gelman, 1973). In addition, parents tend to expand the sentences uttered by their children. So, for example, the child might say **biscuit please** and the parent might respond with **Would you like a biscuit?** This expansion instructs the child on how grammatical sentences are constructed.

The interactionist approach

Social interactionists suggest that language acquisition depends on social stimulation. For example, Sachs et al. (1981) studied a young boy whose parents were both deaf and did not speak. By the time he was four his speech was below age level. Although subsequent speech therapy led to quick improvements, his impoverished speech earlier was due to exposure to an impoverished linguistic environment. Bruner (1983) proposed that instead of an LAD, children have an LASS (language acquisition support system), whose maturation depends on social and verbal interaction, especially with adults.

Animal language

While animals are able to communicate with each other through various signals, animals are not generally considered to use language. This may be because language is an innate ability that animals do not have. However, if an animal could be taught to use a form of language and communicate in moderately sophisticated ways this might provide evidence that would sit uncomfortably with the nativist position.

The problem with communicating with animals is that they are unable to vocalise the phonemes used in human languages because they do not have the necessary vocal systems. However, and for that reason, psychologists have attempted to teach animals, and especially apes, forms of sign language.

Gardner and Gardner (1969) taught an ape Washoe 132 signs of the American Sign Language (ASL) over a four-year period. She could use signs that referred to objects and the state of objects (such as **open**). In addition, despite the fact that the researchers did not use ASL in the presence of a second ape, Loulis, the latter ape learned to use 50 signs by being in the presence of Washoe, her teacher.

CRUCIAL STUDY: KANZI

Another remarkable study is that of Savage-Rumbaugh. (1986). Kanzi, a bonobo chimp, learned to communicate with humans through a keyboard containing numerous symbols. However, Kanzi acquired the ability by watching his mother, Matala, being trained to use the symbols. Kanzi could use the keyboard to request particular foods, and so on. For example, Kanzi could press the symbol for strawberry before going to the spot whether the strawberries were grown. In addition, Kanzi would go to the strawberry patch when the word strawberry was mentioned. He could also produce lexical combinations such as **more drink** and **apple me eat**. Savage-Raumbaugh *et al.* (1993) claimed that Kanzi's linguistic ability was equivalent to an 18 to 24 month-old human. This claim was based on comparing Kanzi and a daughter of one of the researchers, Alia (who took part in similar games and activities as Kanzi), on carefully controlled tests.

Some critics have argued that these animals were merely conditioned to use signs by being given rewards and that the animals did not acquire an understanding of the meaning of the symbols in the same ways that humans understand them. However, in many of these examples, the animals used combinations of symbols that they were not directly taught. For example, one ape referred to a zebra as a **white tiger**, which suggests more understanding than the critics have argued.

Quick test

1. What is the **nativist** view on language acquisition and who argued for it?
2. What is the **nurturist** view on language acquisition and who argued for it?
3. What is the **interactionist** view on language acquisition and who argued for it?
4. Describe one study on animals' acquisition of sign language.

Section 5

End of chapter assessment

Questions

1. What are the main elements of spoken language?
2. What evidence is there that readers make use of the pronunciation of words during reading?
3. 'Thought is itself shaped by our use of language.' Discuss this view with respect to the relationship between language and thought.
4. How has the study of animal language helped resolve the nature–nurture debate in language acquisition?

Answers

1. Some questions in your first year of study may simply test your knowledge rather than your skills of analysis and evaluation. For this question you should demonstrate your knowledge of the main elements of language by defining phonology, syntax, semantics, morphology and pragmatics. You should also give examples of each and you should describe one or two studies where possible. In this type of question, the more knowledge you demonstrate the more marks you gain.

2. Unlike question 1, this question asks you to evaluate and analyse different views on an issue. In particular it identifies the phonologically-mediated hypothesis in reading, i.e. that readers translate words into their speech form internally before understanding their meaning. However, we should be aware that this is only one view on the issue. Therefore, not only should you focus your answer on the phonologically-mediated hypothesis, but you should also mention it with respect to the direct-access route and the dual-route hypotheses. Following your description of these should follow an evaluation and you can draw on the studies described in Section 2, such as Luo *et al.* (1998). You should also discuss some of the evidence from central dyslexia that supports the dual-route hypothesis.

3. Begin your answer by making it clear that the view outlined in the question is that of Whorf (1956) and is known as the linguistic relativity hypothesis. You should then go on

to outline this hypothesis and variants of it (the strong and the weak versions). Provide some supportive evidence for the view (e.g. Miyawaki *et al.*, 1975) and evidence that is problematic (e.g. Greene, 1975). You could then discuss related theories such as Bernstein's verbal deprivation hypothesis and Piaget's developmental view. You can then advance a completely alternative view, such as Vygotsky's view that language and thought are independent. Finally, through a discussion of accents and dialects you can make the point that we often (incorrectly) infer much about a person's thought through the way they use language.

4. This is a difficult question for first-year psychology students, but it may be included to get you to think about difficult issues. A question such as this will certainly be used to test your skills of analysis and evaluation. You can begin your answer by defining the nature–nurture debate with respect to language acquisition (don't be tempted to drift into discussions of whether intelligence or aspects of perception are innate). Note that you don't have to begin with a discussion of animal language, you can outline the theories first. Therefore, mention the nativist theory and the environmentalist theory in general terms, then outline more details of both approaches. Having set the scene you can then discuss the many studies on animal language, citing many cases where animals have learned sign language. State that taken at face value these studies provide difficulties for the Nativist position. Finally, you can provide some evidence from studies with infants, and although the question focuses on animal language, you can justify your discussion of infants by saying that such evidence of the importance of the environment is more convincing.

Section 6

Further reading

Harley, T. (2001) *The Psychology of Language: From Data to Theory*. Hove: Psychology Press.

Clark, H. H. (1996) *Using Language*. Cambridge: Cambridge University Press.

Ellis, R. and Humphreys, G. (1999) *Connectionist Psychology: A Text with Readings*. Hove: Psychology Press.

Chapter 7
Problem-solving and creativity

Chapter summary

You have a problem when you want to achieve something but do not know **how** to achieve it. Of course, there may be occasions when you know **how** to reach the goal, but cannot face doing those things necessary to reach it (such as studying hard to get your degree). In this case the problem would be how to get yourself motivated (and for that you can read the Introduction to this book!). Generally, psychologists are interested in understanding how people reach a goal or achieve a task by thinking about the problem. In this chapter we discuss good and bad problem-solving strategies, the state space analogy for representing problems and their solutions, how experts acquire their expertise and the issue of creativity.

Assessment targets

Target 1: Describing the psychological approach to problem-solving
You will be able to describe studies of problem-solving, the sorts of common mistakes that are made during problem-solving, and the much used state space analogy. Question 1 will test you on this.

Target 2: Explaining how expertise is acquired
You will understand ways in which the expert differs from the novice and the stages the expert has gone through in developing their knowledge. Question 2 will test you on this.

Target 3: Defining and evaluating the concept of creativity
You will describe a number of definitions of creativity and explain the various ways it is studied. You will evaluate the notion of creativity and will look at the evidence as to whether the concept really exists. Question 3 will test you on this.

How will you be assessed on this?

Problem-solving is a central topic in cognitive psychology, so expect essay and exam questions, especially concerning how people solve problems and how problems can be represented.

Section 1

Problem-solving

In this first section you will be studying the various approaches psychologists take in researching this area. You will learn about the state space metaphor that is used to represent a problem and how it might be solved, as well as other ways of representing a problem. You will also learn about the strengths and limitations of this approach.

What is a problem?

We solve problems every day of our lives. For example, on a given day you could be faced with a number of problems: a flat tyre on your bicycle, an essay you haven't written needs to be handed in by 6 p.m., your daughter refuses to get dressed for school, your PC fails to recognise that it has a hard disk, or all of these (including the headache!). The solution to each problem may not be obvious, although they are certainly solvable.

Problems have three main features:

- **An initial state**. This is the position or state you are in when you begin working towards a goal or begin a task.
- **The goal state**. This is the position you will be in when the goal is reached or when you have completed the task.
- **The obstacles**. These are the things that prevent you, and get in the way of, reaching your goal.

For example, for the PC problem, the initial state might be turning the PC on, the goal state would be to sit in front of the PC with a word processing package open, and the obstacle might be a blank screen with a flashing cursor that remains this way for several minutes. Of course, another obstacle in this example is the user's lack of knowledge of operating systems and why PCs often 'hang up' in this way.

--- CRUCIAL CONCEPT ---

In order to solve problems people employ **plans** or **strategies**. A plan consists of breaking down the problem into a number of logically arranged sub-goals and solving each in turn. A strategy is a particular method for solving the problem and each problem may be solved by the use of different strategies. For example, to solve the PC problem, one strategy would be to seek help from a technician, and another would be to consult the manual (despite the overwhelming urge to hurl the thing out of the window).

How problems are solved

In order to solve a problem successfully, one first needs to understand the problem correctly. When faced with a problem we develop an **internal representation** of it. This means that we have a certain understanding of the problem, and this understanding will vary in accuracy and complexity. Greeno (1991) suggested that a good internal representation has three features:

- **Coherence**. The problem is understood within a specific context and we are aware of the constraints on the problem.
- **A close correspondence with the true nature of the problem**. Sometimes our understanding of the problem is incomplete.
- **It is built on relevant knowledge**. Sometimes people fail to use their background knowledge in understanding a problem.

Types of internal representations

Very often problems are solved by the use of an analogy or a representation of the problem that makes it easier to understand. Types of analogies are:

- **Symbols**. Some problems can be represented mathematically. For example, suppose you and a friend purchased some items for a day of studying at home. You purchased 3 bars of chocolate and 1 tin of biscuits and spent £4.60, while your friend spent £4.20 on 2 bars of chocolate and 1 tin of biscuits. A third friend sees the biscuits and wants to buy one too so asks you how much they cost. You solve this by representing the problem mathematically (and solving using simultaneous equations). The major difficulty with using symbols is in their translation. For example, some students are uneasy with using simultaneous equations. In one study, Schoenfeld (1985) found that about 30 per cent of students made translation errors when solving similar kinds of algebra problems.

- **Matrices**. A matrix is a table or chart useful for solving problems that are categorical in nature. An example is the table one uses to solve the popular logic problems found in puzzle books. Schwartz (1971) found that students encouraged to use a matrix to solve a logic problem were more likely to solve it correctly than students who used alternative strategies that employed different types of representation.

- **Diagrams**. One of the most common ways of solving a problem is to draw it as a diagram. This way, a simple form can represent a large amount of information. However, diagrams can suffer from the problem of 'functional fixedness' (see later section).

- **Visual imagery**. Like diagrams, visual images can contain a large amount of information, but they have the advantage over diagrams in that they can be 'irrational' as Koestler (1964) pointed out. Thus, they encourage problem-solving by breaking out of the boundaries of diagrammatic representations. According to Adeyemo (1994), visual imagery is commonly used when the task is to construct a figure – it is visualised before and during construction.

Problem-solving using the state space analogy

A problem can be likened to a maze in which there is a **start state**, a number of **paths**, several **dead ends** or **cul-de-sacs** and a **goal** (Newell and Simon, 1972). An **action** (such as turn left, turn right or go back) takes the problem into a different state (e.g. one step closer to the exit), and all of the locations or states of the maze collectively define the state space of the problem. To solve the problem one might use several strategies to determine which move to make and at which point.

Games such as noughts and crosses and chess can also be represented by the state space analogy. The starting state of noughts and crosses is an empty grid, and the first move (say X in the top left-hand corner) takes the game into a new state (or location in the maze analogy). A move by O into the centre square, say, takes the game into another distinct state. Every conceivable (and legal) configuration of X and O on the grid represents the game's state space (and in noughts and crosses there are, believe it or not, several hundred possible states). Similarly, in chess, the start state is the board configuration before a move has been made, and the first stage might be 'pawn to king 4'. This new state could lead to numerous other states next, depending upon how black makes her first move. In the maze analogy, the state or location created by white's first move has several 'paths' leading from it based on all of black's options, which I've just counted as being 20 (eight pawns, each with two options, and two knights, each with two options). As the game progresses the number of options increases dramatically (which is one reason why the game is so difficult to master) and it has been estimated that there are more possible game states in chess than there are known atoms in the universe!

CRUCIAL CONCEPT

In finding solutions to problems that can be represented in this way one uses a 'search' technique or **algorithm**. The idea is to search the state space of the problem for routes that lead to one of the goal states. In noughts and crosses, for example, you consider placing your X or O in one of a number of empty squares on the grid and then consider what your opponent would do next (see Figure 7.1).

CRUCIAL TIP

Try drawing the state space of the first few moves of noughts and crosses. This will help you appreciate the method as well as understand how such an apparently simple game can have a huge state space.

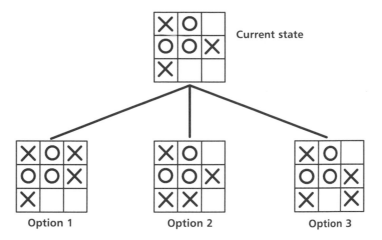

Current state

Option 1   Option 2   Option 3

Figure 7.1 An example of the problem space of a game of noughts and crosses.
By expanding the diagram to include O's possible replies to each move, and X's final move,
the diagram can be used to obtain the best result possible for X. Here X has three options,
and only option 2 can guarantee avoiding defeat.

--- CRUCIAL CONCEPT ---

A simple, though extremely long-winded, algorithm is to do an **exhaustive search**. This means considering every option and every possible consequence of each option.

In a game like noughts and crosses an exhaustive search is quite manageable and would help make sure that you did not lose the game. However, in more complex problems, where the state space could be huge, this method is unrealistic. For example, solving the anagram LSSTNEUIAMYOUL using only an exhaustive search would take a very long time since there are more than 87 billion possible arrangements of the 14 letters of the word SIMULTANEOUSLY (Matlin, 2002). Fortunately, problems can be solved using other methods, known as **heuristics**. A heuristic is a strategy for searching state space in a more meaningful way. For example, to solve the anagram you could try to arrange some of the letters that commonly go together, such as NE and OU and many words end with Y. In addition, we know that the first two letters could be LE, LA, SE, SI, or ME, and so on. We also know that the first two letters cannot be SS, LS, ML, and so on. By using our knowledge of language we can develop useful heuristics for solving this kind of problem.

A useful type of heuristic is the **hill-climbing** method. To use the maze analogy, we assume that the goal location is at the top of the hill and all we have to do is make sure the next step takes us further up the hill. In order to know how far up the hill we are, we use an evaluation function – some measure of how good each of the possible paths ahead are. For this we need some way of measuring how good a possible state is. In chess, for example, a state can be assigned a value according to a number of criteria, such as whether the next move gets the opponent into check, or whether it removes a player's piece (and how important that piece is), whether it increases control of the centre of the board, and so on.

One problem with the hill-climbing heuristic is that its success depends on the way the evaluation is formulated, and some will be clearly better than others. A second problem often cited against the hill-climbing heuristic is that it could not produce solutions that involve doing something that is temporarily bad but very good in the long-term. It is often the case that you have to take a step back in order to go forward. For example, in chess players often 'sacrifice' a piece in order to gain advantage over the opponent. In the **Tower of Hanoi problem** (see Figure 7.2), the solution involves taking a step that appears to be a move **away** from the goal. The hill-climbing heuristic would not yield such a move since it encourages the selection of moves that produce better board states. It could be argued, though, that this is not necessarily the case since it depends the **breadth** and **depth** of the search.

99

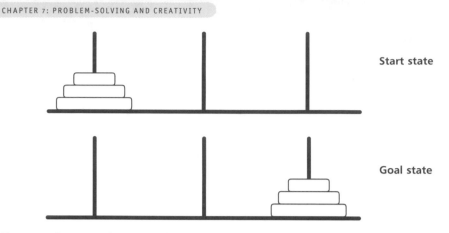

Figure 7.2 The tower of Hanoi problem. The aim is to move the rings of the tower from the first peg to the last peg by moving only one ring at a time and never placing a larger ring on a smaller ring.

Heuristics may employ a broad search, which involves considering a large number of immediate options (such as considering the next move of each of your pieces in chess). Heuristics may also employ a deep search, which involves considering the many implications of a single option (for example, imagining a long sequence of moves in chess – 'if I move here, and she moves there, then I could move here'). The success of the hill-climbing heuristic can depend on the depth of the search, and if this is large then it could conceivably uncover a sequence of steps where one of the steps results in a 'bad' state in the short term but a useful solution in the long term.

───── CRUCIAL CONCEPT ─────

A well-known heuristic is **means-ends analysis**. It involves breaking a problem down into a number of smaller sub-problems. If a number of ends (sub-problems) can be identified then all one has to do is to identify the means of solving each sub-problem. It seems that we use this heuristic for most everyday problems we encounter.

Greeno (1974) has found that people do tend to use the means-ends analysis when solving problems, and Ward and Allport (1997) have observed that working memory is very active when people try to organise sub-problems.

Ill-defined problems

Virtually all of the problem-solving strategies noted above involve what are called **well-defined** problems in which the goal is clear and there are well-understood paths or routes one can take. However, many problems do not have these characteristics and are **ill-defined** (Reitman, 1965). Types of ill-defined problems include how to get a university degree with minimum effort, how to stop the neighbour's dog from barking, how to get more money from those sponsoring our studies (usually our parents), how to get a date, and so on. While many of the methods described above may be suitable for well-defined problems such as the game of chess, the Tower of Hanoi problem or anagrams, it is not clear how they could be used to solve ill-defined problems such as those just listed. Of course, there are those who would argue against this, saying that the aim would be to convert an ill-defined problem into a series of smaller well-defined problems (Simon and Chase, 1973). However, since most of the research in this area has been on what could be called 'toy problems', it is not clear how these methods would 'scale up' to everyday, real-life problems.

Quick test

1. What is a problem?

2. What are the three main features of a problem?

3. Outline two types of problem representations.
4. Briefly describe the state space approach to problem-solving.
5. What is an algorithm?
6. What is means-ends analysis?
7. What is the difference between a well-defined and an ill-defined problem?

Expertise

In this section you will study the concept of the 'expert', how their problem-solving strategies might differ from those of the novice, and how experts acquire their expertise.

A common view of experts is that they either have superior memory or that they have superior reasoning skills. However, the view that they have some super general ability is not necessarily the case. Rather, experts have a significant amount of **domain-specific knowledge and ability**. This conclusion is brought about by the extensive research on expertise, and in particular research that compares the expert with the novice.

Much of this research has focused on masters versus beginners at chess. We know from the previous section that chess is a difficult game to learn because of the huge number of possible game states. One might assume that chess experts search deeper and broader when analysing their move, and that they can hold a large amount of information in their superior short-term memories. However, Chase and Simon (1973) have refuted this idea and show that the main difference between the expert and novice chess player is that the expert is able to **chunk information** in a more efficient way than the novice.

CRUCIAL STUDY – EXPERT CHESS PLAYERS (CHASE AND SIMON, 1973)

Three types of chess player were shown mid-games from chess that contained around 24 to 26 pieces for five seconds. The players were then asked to recall the position of each piece by reconstructing it using another chess set. The master chess player recreated 16 pieces successfully, the intermediate player recalled eight successfully, while the novice recreated only four successfully. However, when the same types of player were shown random board configurations (24 to 26 pieces arranged in random positions on the board) there were no differences in the number of successful reconstructions between them (each recalled about two or three). The reason why the expert's recall of random board configurations was so poor was that such a configuration is unlikely to be a typical board state and hence its meaning for the chess expert was no greater than for that of the novice. This study shows that experts do not have superior memories but rather chunk information in meaningful ways.

Similar studies have been carried out in other domains with similar results. For example, expert hockey players could remember more player positions that could non-experts when briefly shown a photograph from a game. In addition, expert volleyball players, but not non-experts, are especially good at identifying the location of the ball when shown a photograph from a game (see Allard and Starkes, 1991).

CRUCIAL CONCEPT

Experts appear to have developed more advanced **problem schemas**, which are knowledge structures for understanding problems within a specific domain.

Chi *et al.* (1981) studied expert versus novice physicists on a series of physics problems. They found that while the novice physicists grouped information about the problem in terms of their structural characteristics, expert physicists categorised information on the basis of the laws of physics (such as Newton's Third Law). Through extensive experience, experts have gained knowledge of specific configurations of information that they can apply to problems.

Lesgold *et al*. (1988) examined expert versus novice radiologists in their ability to detect disorders in X-ray films. Interestingly, experts were not only able to spot an abnormality more quickly but could also entertain several plausible diagnoses than could the novices. Novices tended to work backwards from a possible hypothesis.

Acquiring expertise

If we want to know how experts acquired their expertise then the simple answer is that they practised a lot. Simon (1980) estimates that it takes about ten years (or 10,000 hours) to acquire expertise in one domain. He argues that practice leads to 'automatic' actions in response to a problem.

Problem-solving can promote learning. However, the use of some heuristics, such as means-ends analysis, can hinder learning rather than help it (Sweller and Chandler, 1994). This is because experts themselves use schema-driven problem-solving methods and not means-ends analysis. Undirected problem-solving strategies can help the learner. In one example, Owen and Sweller (1985) gave a series of trigonometry problems and compared students who were instructed to calculate particular angles and sides (directed instructions) and others who were told to calculate as many angles and as sides as they could (undirected instructions). Greater learning occurred with the undirected instructions than with directed instructions.

A theory of skill acquisition: Anderson (1987)

Anderson has presented a theory of how skills are acquired and has implemented the theory as a computer program. In the theory skill acquisition occurs through a series of stages:

- **Stage 1**. The learner uses declarative knowledge. When we first learn something we adhere rigidly to the instructions we are given and we solve new problems by going over our knowledge we have acquired so far. That knowledge is declarative in the sense that it is of the 'facts and figures' variety. In learning to play a new piece on the piano, the learner first acquires knowledge of the notes to be played and by which fingers, and continually rehearses this knowledge through practice.

- **Stage 2**. The learner develops procedural knowledge. Based on procedural knowledge the learner can build up 'procedures' or knowledge of how and when to do some action. Anderson describes procedural knowledge as a collection of productions, which are rules in the IF … THEN form. Programmers will be familiar with IF … THEN lines in programming code. The general case is IF (some condition is met) THEN (take some specific action), e.g. IF (it is raining) THEN (take an umbrella). For our pianist, this stage might refer to the development knowledge of how to play a bar or a segment of the piece as one 'chunk'. So, when the learner wishes to play that part of the piece they play it automatically rather than by consulting the manuscript (and it is almost as though the fingers have a mind of their own).

- **Stage 3**. The learner refines and enlarges procedural knowledge. Through extensive practice and experience the learner can conceptualise knowledge in larger chunks. It is the stage where our piano player has learned the entire piece as a small number of units.

The theory has made predictions about the speed of learning that have been supported empirically (Anderson, 1993; Singley and Anderson 1989). It has also formed the basis of a computer-based tutoring system (Anderson *et al*., 1995).

Although means-ends analysis can sometimes hinder learning, there may be other heuristics that can be taught in helping people acquire expertise. Schoenfeld (1985) has shown that teaching heuristics does not improve learning and argues that although heuristics may describe some aspects of what experts do, they are not informative enough in letting the learner know exactly what to do. Parents often make similar mistakes with their children. For example, they may ask them to take care when playing on a climbing frame. However, the child may not have a good understanding of what the dangers are and the sorts of behaviours that can put them in danger. Rather, the learner needs to know how to implement heuristics (in the language of Anderson's theory, they need to be taught procedural knowledge).

Quick test

1. What did Chase and Simon (1973) discover about differences between the novice chess player and the grand master?
2. Outline Anderson's (1987) three stages to skill acquisition.
3. Does problem-solving promote or hinder learning?

Creativity

Most of the time, the major factor that determines whether someone will solve a problem or not is the extent of their knowledge. However, some problems are difficult to solve because prior knowledge 'gets in the way' of a solution. In this section you will be studying creativity and creative solutions. We will be asking whether there are special cognitive processes involved in creativity or whether more routine cognitive processes can be used to explain it.

--- CRUCIAL CONCEPT ---

One of the main obstacles to problem-solving is known as **functional fixedness**. It refers to the way we tend to think of an object only in terms of its common everyday function, rather than how it may be used differently in new contexts.

Consider the following problem devised by Duncker (1945). The task is to fix a candle to a wall. The only objects available are: a handful of drawing pins and a box of matches (and a candle, of course). The pins are too small to go right through the candle. Very few people solve this problem without any hints. Try this yourself before reading on.

The solution becomes obvious when you are told to think of the match box as a candle holder. All you then do is fix the match box to the wall with the pins, melt some wax into the base of the match box, and place the candle in the match box on top of the melted wax. (Alternatively, you could also push a pin through the base of the box into the underside of the candle.) The difficulty with this problem lies in seeing the match box as a useful object for solving the problem.

A related idea is that we tend to see familiar patterns when we look at something and our problem-solving is over-influenced by prior knowledge and prior conceptions.

--- CRUCIAL CONCEPT ---

Lateral thinking is the term used when we try to break out of seeing something in a conventional way.

Consider the nine-dot problem in Figure 7.3. You are to connect the nine dots using only four straight lines and the pen must not leave the paper. Have a go at this problem before you read on.

Figure 7.3 The nine-dot problem

The solution involves 'thinking outside the square' (see Figure 7.4). Most people attempt the problem by drawing lines within the square itself and this may be because the dots themselves form imaginary lines. Hence, prior knowledge of visual patterns can constrain our thinking.

Generally, it could be said that functional fixedness and 'thinking outside the square' involve some aspect of creative thought, and psychologists are becoming increasingly more interested in the study of creativity.

Measuring and defining creativity

Creative thinking is often characterised by the difference between convergent and divergent thinking (Guilford, 1959).

CRUCIAL CONCEPT

Convergent thinking typically occurs when there is one solution and the problem-solver gathers information and develops a single overall plan to home in on the solution.

CRUCIAL CONCEPT

In **divergent thinking**, the problem-solver gathers a variety of information and develops numerous strategies to find one of many possible solutions. Divergent thinking expands on the number of opportunities to find a solution.

Torrance and Witt (1966) developed a series of tasks to measure creativity which included such tasks as thinking of as many different uses of an everyday object as possible, such as a house brick. Another example, is to draw as many objects as you can that have a circular feature. Creativity is measured by:

- **fluency** – the number of objects drawn;
- **flexibility** – the number of distinct objects drawn (for example, if participants drew two types of door then this would score 2 for fluency but only 1 for flexibility);
- **originality** – the infrequency of the object in terms of how different it is from what other people draw.

Creativity measured in this way focuses on the product of the creative process, and the products must be both original and relevant in order to be considered creative. However, psychologists are more interested in the process of creativity (i.e. creative thought) rather than just the product.

CRUCIAL CONCEPTS

Studying creativity is hampered by the problem of defining it and knowing when it has occurred. One of the earliest definitions was provided by Wallas (1926), who proposed four stages of the creative process:

- **Preparation**. Before creativity occurs, the individual is carrying out some task or trying to achieve some goal and encounters a difficult problem.
- **Incubation**. After some time the problem-solver leaves the problem and does something else.
- **Illumination**. The solution suddenly occurs to the problem-solver in a flash of insight.
- **Verification**. As not all insights turn out to be useful, the possible solution is checked out and verified.

There are many examples from great thinkers who seem to have arrived at a creative solution to a problem through something like Wallas' four stages. However, Weisberg (1986) has studied these well-known cases and has tried to debunk the idea of these four stages. First, most solutions are identified during the problem-solving process itself and not during a period of rest from the problem. Second, Wallas' ideas may describe the phenomenology of the creative process and what it feels like but do not describe the process. For example, it is not clear what is meant by illumination and, more importantly, how the process of illumination occurs.

Studies on incubation and illumination

Incubation and illumination are dependent upon the notion of **unconscious problem-solving** and occur when we are consciously engaged in a different task away from the problem. However, despite numerous attempts to find empirical support for unconscious problem-solving, very little has been obtained. Smith and Blankenship (1991) argue that in such cases the problem-solver becomes **fixated** on an inappropriate strategy and when the problem-solver returns to the problem after a break from it, alternative strategies can be considered. Fixating on a single strategy can block off relevant knowledge that could be useful for solving the problem. Smith and Blankenship (1991) provided support for this idea by giving some participants misleading information in an attempt to simulate fixation on an inappropriate strategy. The findings were more consistent with blocking of relevant information than unconscious problem-solving.

It may be that creativity, rather than occurring as a sudden insight, occurs through a series of small incremental steps, during which previous methods and ideas become modified and elaborated (Weisberg, 1986). Weber and Dixon (1989) examined the historical development of a number of inventions. In many cases, inventions are merely modifications and refinements of already existing ideas and do not just suddenly appear.

Problem finding

Simon (1995) argues that ideas that are considered as creative seem to be brought about not just by finding an original or new solution but by reformulating the problem. Understanding how the problem emerged can lead to a potential solution. For example, suppose you want to stop some children from behaving badly in a classroom. Your belief about what causes their unruly behaviour will determine what solution you choose to employ. If you think it is because of a lack of discipline you might want the teachers to be stricter. If you think it is because the children are seeking attention from the teacher and from other children you might want them taught separately. Your solution is dependent upon how you view the problem. Dunbar (2000) examined the reasoning of molecular biologists over a one-year period. He claims that problem reformulation took place regularly within the research teams, often promoted by tough questioning in lab meetings.

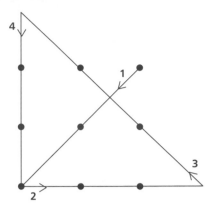

Figure 7.4 The solution to the nine-dot problem

Is creative thought that much different from noncreative thought?

According to Ward *et al.* (1999) the mental processes in what many people would regard as creative thought are no different to those of non-creative thought. They argue that creativity is simply the result of the combined activity of a number of mental processes.

CRUCIAL STUDY

Ward (1994) asked children to imagine that they had visited another planet that had alien life forms. They were then asked to draw the creatures. One could argue that the drawings that resulted were extremely creative and unusual. However, an analysis of the features that the children used in their drawings casts doubt on this assertion. For example, 89 per cent of the aliens were symmetric and 92 per cent had obvious sensory organs. Hence, the features of the aliens were much like creatures found on earth. Ward (1994) argues that their thinking was based on existing knowledge and non-creative thought processes.

Quick test

1. What is functional fixedness?
2. Define lateral thinking.
3. How might creativity be measured?
4. What is meant by problem incubation?
5. What did Simon (1989) mean by the term problem finding?
6. Describe the Ward (1994) study on drawings of aliens and say what the study demonstrates.

Section 4

End of chapter assessment

Questions

1. How do people solve problems?
2. How do people acquire expertise?
3. Is creativity a useful concept for explaining how people solve problems?

Answers

1. While students find broad questions such as this very attractive, it is fraught with difficulties, the main one being limited time (or words) in which to answer the question. It requires an overview of the area and an identification of the most important aspects. Weaker answers tend to focus on one aspect at the expense of others. However, in providing an overview details of one or two approaches can be useful.

   One way to approach a broad question is to begin by defining the key terms. Say what a problem is and what its main features are. Briefly discuss the issue of problem representations and how these can help or hinder problem-solving. Outline the state space approach and since this is much studied you can go into some detail here. In doing so, you must mention and define terms such as algorithm, heuristics and exhaustive search. Give a short appraisal of the state space approach and introduce the notion of well-defined versus ill-defined problems.

2. In contrast to the previous question, your answer to this one will be quite precise. Begin by saying what the common view of expertise is (that the cognitive processes of experts are more efficient than those of the novice). You can then go on to discuss how this view is debunked by research such as Chase and Simon (1973) who found that experts acquire the ability to chunk more effectively. You could also mention the study by Chi *et al.* (1981) on the use of problem schemas. Describe one theory of skill acquisition, such as that of Anderson (1987). Outline each stage of the process and give a brief evaluation of the theory. Finally, you could discuss how problem-solving strategies can be taught and in what ways this process helps or hinders learning.

3. For many issues in psychology, the prevailing view has often moved away from an intuitively appealing explanation to one that is completely different. The issue of creativity is one example. For this kind of topic, a neat way of writing about it is to outline the earlier view or views and then to discuss the ways in which the view has been overwritten. For example, you can begin by providing the earlier view of creativity, such as Wallas (1926) and especially his emphasis on incubation and illumination. Outline the evidence (or lack thereof) for these concepts. You can then introduce Simon's notion of problem finding and Ward's view that the cognitive processes in 'creative thought' are no different from non-creative thought.

Section 5

Further reading

Hayes, J. R. (1989) *The Complete Problem Solver*. Hillsdale, NJ: Erlbaum & Associates.

Robertson, S. I. (2001) *Problem Solving*. Hove: Psychology Press.

Chapter 8
Cognition and emotion

Chapter summary

In this chapter we will cover the study of emotion from the cognitive perspective. It could be argued that what the previous chapters miss is how cognitive processing can be coloured by emotion. This is a relatively new area of research, and in this chapter we address issues such as the relationship between cognition and emotion, their mutual influence over each other, and applications of cognitive theory in the therapeutic domain.

Assessment targets

Target 1: Understanding different viewpoints on the issue of the relationship between cognition and emotion

When we react with a strong emotion, such as fear, is it a rapid and fairly automatic response to something threatening or do we think about the threat before we react? Studying this chapter will help you understand the various viewpoints on this issue and how it is researched. Question 1 will test your knowledge of this.

Target 2: Understanding the extent to which cognitive processes can influence emotional states

If cognitive processes, such as memory, perception and thought, can influence our mood or emotional state, to what extent can they promote an emotional disorder, such as anxiety and depression? There has been a considerable amount of research devoted to this topic, and this chapter will help you understand this research and how the influence of cognition on emotional disorders can be studied. Question 2 will assess you on this.

Target 3: Understanding the extent to which emotional states can influence cognitive processes

Many psychologists argue that emotional states can affect cognitive processes. Most of this research concerns the influence of mood on memory and this chapter will familiarise you with research in this area. Question 3 is designed to test your understanding of this research area.

How will you be assessed on this?

Issues around the relationship between cognition and emotion are more likely to appear in your second or third years of study. However, you may be given a choice of essay topic, and if so then this area is a popular one among students. This is mainly because they find it less 'dry' than pure cognitive psychology. Topics from this chapter, such as the relationship between mood and memory, also form the basis of lab practical classes.

Section 1

Cognition and emotion: separate or interdependent?

There is a debate in the literature on the relationship between emotion and cognition. In this section, we review the main ideas on the issue.

Emotion does not require cognition

Zajonc (1984, p. 117) affirmed that 'affect and cognition are separate and partially independent processes … and although they ordinarily function cojointly, affect could be generated without a prior cognitive process'. One example of this is to imagine that you turn a corner and come face to face with a lion. What Zajonc is arguing is that your physiological reaction will occur **before** you have processed the sensory image of the lion cognitively. Zajonc (incidentally, most students pronounce this name as 'za-jonk' but the correct pronunciation is 'zai-yonce') discusses the 'mere exposure' effect as evidence of this distinction. When pictures are presented subliminally (too briefly to be consciously detected) participants later tend to rate as more liked those pictures they have been 'shown' than new pictures. This demonstrates that an affective response can occur without cognition.

CRUCIAL CONCEPT

The **mere exposure** effect is the observation that people will tend to like something simply because they have seen it before and have some familiarity with it (all else being equal). It may be a basic psychological process for both animals and humans, and has an obvious function: better to deal with something we have seen before than something novel or new which might be less predictable. The effects seem to contradict the adage 'familiarity breeds contempt', but I will leave you to ponder why they might both be true.

Emotion requires cognition

Lazarus (1982) has criticised the conclusion drawn from mere exposure experiments. If subjects prefer items they have 'seen' subliminally then they may still have processed the items 'cognitively', since we do not need to equate awareness with cognition. Lazarus argues 'Cognitive appraisal (of meaning or significance) underlies and is an integral feature of all emotional states.' In other words, Lazarus seems to be saying that the cognitive process of detecting or determining affect comes before any elicitation of emotion. Affective processing may involve detecting the goodness or badness as well as the significance or potency of a stimulus.

This theory of pre-emotional appraisal has three forms:

- a **primary appraisal** (identification of the event as being aversive, positive, etc.);
- a **secondary appraisal** (a check of the resources one has to cope with the event);
- and a **reappraisal** (monitoring and modifying both the primary and secondary appraisal processes).

CRUCIAL STUDY – COGNITIVE APPRAISAL: SPEISMAN *ET AL* (1964).

Subjects were shown a particularly gruesome and anxiety-evoking film (these included scenes in which people receive cuts, which are sometimes fatal). Participants were divided into three groups:

- one third of the subjects were informed, via the soundtrack, that the individuals who appeared in the film were actors (**denial group**);

- a second third of the subjects watched the film with an 'anthropologist' describing the events (**intellectualisation group** – the voice-over on the soundtrack sounds objective and factual, as though viewing strange customs);

- the other subjects watched the film without the soundtrack (control group).

In recording physiological measures of emotional arousal, it was found that both the denial group and the intellectualisation group showed significantly lower levels of arousal than the control group. Therefore, cognitive appraisals of events can significantly affect emotional reactions, and in this case reduce their intensity.

Evaluation

In general, Lazarus takes the view that cognitive appraisals (which need not be conscious) always precede emotional reactions. Zajonc's reply is that we have little evidence that these appraisals exist, they are nothing more than an article of faith. More recently, neuropsychologists have entered the debate providing new perspectives on the issue.

A cognitive neuroscience perspective

LeDoux (1989) argues that 'Emotion and cognition are mediated by separate but interacting systems of the brain.' The emotional system evaluates the biological significance of stimuli from the external world or the internal one (thoughts, images and memories). Further, this evaluation takes place prior to conscious awareness, and only the results of the evaluation are made conscious. Thus, LeDoux's appraisal theory has much in common with that of Lazarus, although LeDoux (1989) provides more details on how such mechanisms might operate. He distinguishes between cognitive and emotion processes according to their consequences:

> For example, the computations that determine that a snake is a vertebrate, that it is biologically closer to an alligator than to a cow, and that its skin can be used to make belts and shoes, have very different consequences than the computations that determine that a snake is likely to be dangerous (p. 272).

CRUCIAL CONCEPT

For LeDoux, **cognitive computations** in the brain provide information about a stimulus and its relationship to other stimuli (broadly, this is knowledge about the world), while **affective computations** (those that lead to emotions) provide information about the relation of the stimulus to the individual (in short, what the significance of the stimulus is for the individual). Cognitive computations may also lead to further cognitions (e.g. 'elaboration' – reasoning or thinking deeply about something). Affective computations lead to behavioural responses (e.g. avoidance), autonomic responses (increased heart rate, sweating, and so on), and humoral reactions (changes in brain chemistry, such as an increase in adrenaline).

LeDoux argues for a distinction between cognition and emotion on functional grounds – what is most efficient for adaptation: 'In the presence of danger it is more important to emit appropriate escape or defence responses than to ruminate over cognitive attributes of the stimulus' (p. 272).

CRUCIAL TIP

Before reading on, ask yourself what you understand by the term 'cognition'. How would you define a cognitive process? Then read on.

CRUCIAL TIP

Avoid using labelling terms such as 'phobics', 'depressives' and so on. Instead, use terms such as 'people with a phobia' or 'people who have been diagnosed with depression'.

But what is cognition anyway?

From this analysis what becomes clear is that the problem lies in what is meant by (and what is not meant by) the term 'cognitive process'. It may be a term that is too vague and imprecise, and means different things to different psychologists. It is interesting how the debate has moved from 'what is an emotion?' to 'what is cognition?' So, is cognition to be equated with conscious thought or with non-emotional information, or is it broader than that? Do the collective firings of nerve cells within a structure, such as the amygdala, represent a cognitive process?

This position is adopted by Parrot and Schulkin (1993), who argue that 'emotion and sensation cannot be independent from cognition' since 'for emotions to function adaptively, they must incorporate interpretation, anticipation, and problem-solving...'. They argue that emotion must be inherently cognitive since it requires appraisal and preparedness for action. If cognition is defined as that which is involved in interpretation, memory, anticipation and problem-solving (the list could be continued), then every emotion has a cognitive element, since emotion involves these processes. However, they argue that there are some cognitive processes that do not involve emotion.

Evaluation
We appear to have arrived at the position that while all emotional processes have a cognitive component, the possibility that all cognition can have an emotional component is doubted. Historically, the answer to the question has been determined by how cognition is defined.

Quick test

1. Briefly state the view of Zajonc on the relationship between cognition and emotion.
2. How does the view of Lazarus differ from that of Zajonc?
3. According to LeDoux, to what extent is emotion a cognitive process?
4. What is the concept of centrifugal organisation, and how do Parrot and Schulkin use it to address the question of the relationship between cognition and emotion?

Section 2

The influence of cognition on emotion: attention and anxiety

In this section we examine how cognitive processes, such as attention, can have under certain circumstances a negative impact on our emotional state. Several theories suggest that paying too much attention to things we find threatening can increase our levels of anxiety, and in the extreme case, promote an anxiety disorder. We examine the evidence for this assertion.

Anxiety, phobia, and attention

Imagine (or remind yourself!) that you are afraid of spiders. You are in the attic looking for grandpa's old photographs. You notice a sudden movement of something small, through the corner of your eye. What is it? Do you assume that it is nothing of importance and ignore it, or do you think it might be a spider? If the latter, then you slide down the ladder as quickly as you can, in a desperate attempt not to be eaten alive!

CRUCIAL TIP

Think of other fears that you or other people might have. Do you tend to notice those things associated with the fear very quickly? The next time you are a little afraid or nervous, monitor your own attention and note whether you are vigilant for the thing you are in fear of.

The spider-in-the-attic example demonstrates what has been found in people who are prone to anxiety – they tend to notice potential dangers and threats much more easily and sooner than people who are less prone to anxiety. Clearly, there is a pay-off for the anxious person who notices a threat sooner rather than later: they can take evasive action before being harmed. However, anxious people too often make the error of assuming that something is dangerous or threatening when it really is harmless and quite innocuous. This rapid switching of attention towards threat has been observed in the laboratory in anxious students as well as people diagnosed with an anxiety disorder.

CRUCIAL CONCEPT

Highly anxious individuals demonstrate an **attentional bias** for threat. It is has been suggested that attentional orientation towards threat over prolonged periods of time (e.g. years) can change a mildly anxious person into someone with severe anxiety. The evidence for this is not conclusive, however. At least it seems intuitively obvious that attentional bias might at least serve to **maintain** anxiety.

In many experiments, highly anxious individuals have been found to direct their attention towards items related to personal threat (e.g. words related to health, or photographs of mutilation, and so on) when these items appear alongside more neutral items (see review by Mathews and MacLeod, 1994). For example, when a smiling face and an angry face are presented at the same time on a computer screen, the anxious individual looks at the angry face first.

CRUCIAL STUDY – HOW ATTENTIONAL BIAS IS MEASURED (MACLEOD AND MATHEWS, 1988)

MacLeod and Mathews (1988) devised the dot-probe method. The idea is that a probe, such as an asterix (*), is presented on a computer monitor and the participant is required to press a button as soon as he or she sees the probe appear. Two words are presented on the screen, one on the left side and the other on the right side, and one word is a threatening word (e.g. **dagger**) and the other word is a non-threatening word (e.g. **number**). Suppose **dagger** is presented to the left and **number** to the right. An anxious person might orient towards the word **dagger**, while a low anxious person might look at either. The probe is then presented on the screen replacing the word **dagger**. If the participant is looking at **dagger** then they will be able to respond sooner than if they were looking at the word **number**. In this way it is possible to infer the direction of attention by analysing reaction times.

Specificity of attentional bias

Research has shown that what an anxious person fears most grabs most attention (MacLeod *et al.*, 1986; MacLeod and Mathews, 1988; Broadbent and Broadbent, 1988). As examples:

- people with a spider phobia attend to words such as **hairy** or **creepy**;
- people with a social phobia attend to words related to socialising (e.g. **party**);
- people with an eating disorder attend to words related to food (e.g. **chocolate**);
- anxious students tested just before their exams have been shown to attend to words related to success and failure (e.g. **error**).

The tendency for anxious individuals to attend to threat does not seem to depend upon conscious awareness or deliberate intent, as attentional bias has been found to exist even for stimuli that cannot be reported, such as when the words are presented subliminally (e.g. Mogg *et al.*, 1993). It may therefore be a behaviour that is difficult to control or suppress (and this then obviously has implications for therapy).

CRUCIAL STUDY – THE EMOTIONAL STROOP TASK (MACLEOD, 1996)

The selective allocation of attention to emotional stimuli has also been assessed using the **emotional Stroop task**. Participants are required to name the ink colour of emotional words as quickly as possible, while attempting to ignore their semantic content. Consistent with the notion of the presence of an attentional bias towards the content of threatening words, individuals with high levels of anxiety trait have been found to consistently display a disproportionate slowing to name the colour of the ink of threat-related stimuli.

Evaluation

As indicated above, it has been suggested that cognitive bias for threat is a contributory cause of clinical anxiety, because it leads to more information about potential dangers being perceived. However, while there is ample evidence for the existence of an attentional bias in anxiety, the evidence for a causal connection is very limited, and more evidence is required.

Quick test

1. What is meant by the term attentional bias?
2. Describe the dot-probe method of assessing attention.
3. Describe the emotional Stroop task.

Section 3

The influence of emotion on cognition

Ways in which emotion can affect cognition are examined in this section, through research on how mood can influence memory.

Mood and memory

One of the most studied areas on the effects of emotion on cognition is that of mood and memory.

CRUCIAL CONCEPT

State dependent memory (SDM) is the term given to the theoretical view that the recall of information is dependent upon the state of the brain during learning and during recall. The principle is that if the state of the brain during learning is very close to the state of the brain during retrieval, then recall will be easier than if these two brain states differ. As examples, taking eyewitnesses to the scene of the crime may enhance recall, and having an exam in the same lecture room rather than in a different room should improve recall of the material.

SDM is offered as an explanation for childhood amnesia. Few people can recall their early childhood experiences, especially before the age of five. This is consistent with the finding that there are distinct EEG differences between the brains of adults and young children (although this finding is predicted without recourse to a theory of SDM, such as the fact that the brains of young children are less developed).

SDM is also offered as an account of why drugs that influence some psychopathologies such as depression alleviate the disorder: the drugs change the state of the brain and hence make certain memories (in this case very sad personal memories) more difficult to retrieve.

SDM cues may be features of the environment or features of the internal state (arousal level, hormonal state, mood state). The 'functional state' of the brain may permit access to certain parts of long-term memory but restrict access to other parts.

CRUCIAL STUDY – MOOD AND MEMORY (BOWER, 1981)

The Bower *et al.* paper begins with an example from a Charlie Chaplin film. Basically, he is a tramp and meets a drunken wealthy gent in a bar. They get on well together, and the wealthy man looks after him – that is, until the wealthy man sobers up and can remember nothing of Charlie and why he is in his home, and so kicks him out. However, when the man gets drunk again he sees Charlie and treats him like a long lost friend. The message is that drugs such as alcohol can induce SDM-type effects (as well as others!). Bower set out to explore whether SDM effects can be reproduced in the lab using mood induction

---

In the first experiment of Bower *et al.* (1981) there were four phases:

1. Participants were induced into happy or sad state.
2. Participants learned a list of words.
3. Participants were induced into a mood state (either the same or different).
4. Participants were tested for recall on the list of words.

The results indicated that superior recall occurred when the mood state at recall was the same as the mood state during learning. Thus participants induced into a sad state during learning and then into a sad state again during the memory test recalled more words than participants induced into a sad state during learning and a happy state during the memory test.

In the second experiment, participants kept a diary and recorded any event that had an emotional impact on them. They were to record the time, the place and the gist of the event, and to rate its importance (on a −10 to +10 scale). Recordings were made over the period of one week. Participants were then induced into a happy or sad mood, and were asked to recall as much information as possible about the events that they had recorded. The results were that those induced into a sad mood recalled more information about their unpleasant events than their pleasant events and those induced into a happy mood recalled more information about their pleasant events than their unpleasant events.

Implications for our understanding of depression

The conclusion from Bower *et al.*'s (1981) study is that the current mood state is predictive of the type of material that is easier to recall. Thus, if a sad mood promotes the recall of unpleasant personal experiences then it is possible that a negative cycle of mood and memory is produced. As unpleasant memories are elicited during a state of sadness, so that recall deepens the state, and it is easy to see that if such a cycle were allowed to continue uninterrupted, then even over a short period a state of depression could result. In one sense people are already aware of this phenomenon, as it is present in our language, as in the phrases 'the rose-coloured glasses of the optimist' and the 'sombre grey outlook of the pessimist'. However, the implication of the study is that pessimism breeds even more pessimism.

Other studies have shown that the speed of recall of emotional material is affected by the emotional state of the individual. Mood-congruent material, such as lists of words related to sadness and disappointment learned by people in a state of sadness, is recalled **more quickly** than mood-incongruent material, such as lists of words related to being happy learned by people in a state of sadness (Teasdale and Fogarty, 1979).

In another study Lloyd and Lishman (1975) compared people with a clinical diagnosis of depression with non-depressed people, and found that the more severe the depression, the longer it took to retrieve a pleasant memory and the quicker it took to retrieve an unpleasant one.

Evaluation

SDM theory predicts that mood-congruent recall should not be restricted to states of depression but to other states as well, such as anxiety. However, it is interesting to note that a memory bias for unpleasant information has not been found in individuals with **clinical anxiety** (Mathews, 1994). Furthermore, Bower's version of SDM theory predicts **attentional bias** for unpleasant information in **depression**, and despite much effort to look for this effect, it has not been found.

Unfortunately, the findings from the Bower *et al.* (1981) study have been difficult to replicate (e.g. Bower, 1987). It may be that the effect is only present in extreme emotional states, such as clinical depression, but not in emotional states that correspond to everyday mood swings.

Quick test

1. What does SDM stand for?
2. Why might it be difficult to recall our dreams?
3. Briefly describe the method and results of Bower *et al.*'s diary study.
4. In terms of SDM effects, how does depression differ from anxiety?

Section 4

End of chapter assessment

Questions

1. 'There can be no emotion without cognition.' Discuss.
2. What is the evidence for an attentional bias in anxiety?
3. In what ways can mood influence cognitive processing?

Answers

1. Note that your first task in reading the question is to identify exactly what the issues are that inspired the question. This question is not asking about **how** emotion can influence and be influenced by cognition (which is covered in sections 2 and 3), but rather concerns whether emotion and cognition are separate processes or are mutually interdependent (Section 1).

   Ordinarily, you would be encouraged to begin your essay by defining the key terms mentioned in the question. However, in this instance your response is determined by how the terms emotion and cognition are to be defined in the first place. Therefore, you could begin by making this point and leaving your definitions towards the end of your answer. For example, you could begin with 'As this essay will show, whether there can or cannot be emotion without cognition depends largely on how cognition is to be defined.'

   Approach the question first, by identifying that it was Lazarus (1982) who first made this point and then second, by stating that despite this claim being contended by some researchers over the last few decades, it is consistent with current thinking. You can then introduce the arguments of Zajonc (1984) and of LeDoux (1989). Provide an extensive evaluation of these arguments and then go on to state that in order to draw any firm conclusions on the issue, we need to be clear what we mean by the term 'cognition'. Go through what could be meant by the term and then outline the views of Parrot and Schulkin (1993) and then Damasio (1994) (see Further reading at the end of the chapter), which represent the current mode of thinking on the subject.

Support your descriptions of the arguments with one or two key studies. You could, if you felt confident describe, **one** of the studies from Section 3 or Section 4 as an illustration of the relationship between the two.

2. Knowing the area that this question is referring to is easy. However, one problem with this kind of question is that it prevents you from discussing research in other areas (which you may have also revised). The danger then is to rewrite the question (in your head) to something like 'What is the evidence for attentional bias and a memory bias in anxiety and depression?' This is a common mistake that students make. Even though your knowledge is broader than what is required for the question, every minute spent answering the question directly is worth 30 minutes of time spent writing material that is not directly relevant to the question.

The material you should cover is from Section 2. You can devote some of your essay to describing how anxiety is induced in participants and you can describe the details of the two main methods used, such as the dot-probe method and the emotional Stroop task.

3. This question poses a similar problem to question 1. You need to be self-disciplined by adhering to the area of mood and memory and not be tempted to answer a different question (e.g. discussing attentional bias and anxiety). Your answer should focus on Bower's studies and you should mention the failure to replicate his earlier findings.

Section 5

Further reading

Three papers that set the debate about whether emotion can occur without cognition are:

Zajonc, R. B. (1980) 'Feeling and thinking: preferences need no inferences', *American Psychologist, 35*, 151–75.
Zajonc, R. B. (1984) 'On the primacy of affect', *American Psychologist, 39*, 117–23.
Lazarus, R. S. (1982) 'Thoughts on the relation between cognition and emotion', *American Psychologist, 37*, 1019–24.

More recent works on the issue are:

Damasio, A. R. (1994) *Descartes' Error: Emotion, Reason and the Human Brain*. New York: Grosset/Putnam.
LeDoux, J. E. (1989) 'Cognitive-emotional interactions in the brain', *Cognition and Emotion, 3*, 267–89.

A good overview of attentional bias and anxiety is presented in:

MacLeod, C. and Mathews, A. (1988) 'Anxiety and the allocation of attention to threat'. *Quarterly Journal of Experimental Psychology: Human Experimental Psychology, 38*, 659-70.

If your library subscribes to the journals *Cognition and Emotion*, *Cognitive Psychotherapy*, *Behaviour Research and Therapy* or *Cognitive Therapy and Research* then take a look at the latest issues for any good overviews/reviews and new developments.

Chapter 9
Computer models of cognition and connectionism

Chapter summary

There is a long history of the use of the computer metaphor in cognitive psychology. Indeed, developments in computer science were said to inspire, in part, the cognitive revolution. In this chapter we explore the computer metaphor by comparing aspects of the operation of the modern computer and human mental processes. The most recent development in this area is the connectionist approach and we outline the principles involved and evaluate the approach. The debate about whether or not computers could in principle be considered to think is discussed and we examine the implication of this debate for cognitive psychology.

Assessment targets

Target 1: Understanding and explaining what the computer metaphor is
Cognitive psychologists liken the mind to a computer. Both are said to have short-term and long-term memory and both are said to process information. Here you will gain knowledge of how the computer metaphor is put to use in cognitive psychology. Question 1 will test you on this.

Target 2: Understanding the principles of connectionist models
The connectionist metaphor has, to a large extent, taken the place of the computer metaphor. Here you will learn about why this is so and the principles which the approach is founded on. Question 2 will test you on this.

Target 3: Evaluating the debate about whether machines can think
In the early days of cognitive psychology a debate began about whether machines can, or could at some point in the future, think. This debate became useful for evaluating the computer metaphor in terms of how useful it is as a description of how humans think. Here you will read about this debate and gain an interesting insight into how thought might be defined and whether computers are able to capture thinking processes. Question 3 will test you on this.

How will you be assessed on this?

Topics in this chapter are often set in the first year for a number reasons. First, it is a good introduction to the computer metaphor, so prevalent in many of the topics on which the previous chapters are based. Second, many tutors may wish to expose you to the connectionist metaphor quite early on so that you can understand its influence throughout cognitive psychology. Third, many students find the issues covered here extremely interesting, especially the question about whether machines can think. It is most likely you would have the opportunity to write a course essay, rather than be set an exam question on these topics.

Section 1

The computer metaphor

The use of the computer metaphor is pervasive in cognitive psychology. Here you will be studying exactly how the computer metaphor is applied and the sorts of models that have been developed that simulate some aspect of cognitive psychology.

Computers carry out their tasks according to a specially written program. A program is a language that the programmer uses to get the computer to carry out particular tasks. Most of the tasks involve either numerical operations or operations on words (non-numeric text is known as a string by programmers).

An **algorithm** is a set of routines in the program that describes the series of steps that need to be taken in order to achieve some task. People may use algorithms every day of their lives. For example, consider the algorithm for making a cup of coffee:

1. Fill the kettle with water
2. Turn on the kettle
3. Put some coffee in a cup
4. When the kettle has boiled, pour some water into the cup
5. Pour some milk into the cup

We also use algorithms when we try to teach someone a skill. However, because computers cannot think by themselves the instructions need to be very precise indeed. So, while most people would be able to follow the algorithm described above, how would an alien fair at the task? For example, what do we mean by **fill** in step 1? Do we really fill the kettle or is this a figure of speech? Also, in steps 3, 4 and 5, how much is **some** exactly? It follows that the instructions we give a computer must be completely unambiguous. In other words, computers are very **stupid** and will interpret every command **literally**.

And the point is?

The aim of this discussion is to illustrate the similarities that might exist between algorithms and the way people think. If human thought can be described as a collection of algorithms then three things might be possible:

- First, we may have identified a specific way of **describing mental processes**. Once a psychologist is familiar with what an algorithm is, he or she can understand the details of theories that are described as algorithms.
- Second, it may be possible to **simulate human thought** on the computer.
- Third, it may be possible to **design machines** that can do things that humans do. The first two describe the information processing approach to theory development. The third is the subject of the study of artificial intelligence or AI.

CRUCIAL CONCEPT

Artificial intelligence (AI) is the study of how to make machines do the sorts of things that humans do. Many different types of AI program have been developed, from playing chess to filtering out background noise (as in the human ability of selective attention).

Many computer models of psychological processes have been developed and commonly these are written as computer programs. There are a number of advantages of using this approach (as opposed to expressing a theory as a handful of general statements), but there are a number of problems with the approach too.

Strengths

The greatest strengths of the computer metaphor are:

- **Precision**. Theories that describe mental processes or behaviour can be expressed in a number of ways. They can be expressed as a series of statements, as a diagram (such as a box-and-arrow diagram), or as an algorithm with an accompanying computer program. The latter method requires greater precision in determining how the theory can be put together (since one has to develop a computer simulation of it), and it also generates more precise predictions. Very often when transposing a theory from a series of statements into a computer program one finds that some features either do not work as expected or they are incompatible with other features. In this way, computer simulation is a very good way of testing the internal consistency of a theory.

- **Explicitness of assumptions**. Tied in with precision of the inner workings of the model is the need to make one's assumptions explicit. This means that when developing a computer simulation, one has to make decisions about basic assumptions in cognitive psychology. These assumptions become apparent in the description of the model.

- **Novel experimental predictions**. One can quite easily generate a theory as a series of statements and overlook interesting predictions of the theory. Computer models have the advantage that when they are running their behaviour can be quite unexpected and hence lead to testable predictions.

These positive features make computer models of cognition much easier to evaluate and test than other types of theories. For example, one criticism of box-and-arrow theories is that it might not be clear what an arrow represents. It might represent passing information from one module to another, or it might represent a particular process. That process may or may not be compatible with other processes.

Weaknesses

Several weaknesses of the computer metaphor are the following:

- **Algorithms are serial**. The algorithm may be only one way of describing how mental processes operate. Because of its design, the computer can only do one thing at a time. Although it can carry out calculations at an enormous speed, it only has one processor. Hence algorithms are descriptions of serial processes. The brain, on the other hand, has something like 10^{13} processors or neurons. Each neuron can be understood as carrying out a simple calculation, but their combined operation can lead to a different kind of process, namely, **parallel processing**. Algorithms follow a sequence of logical steps. In analysing a visual input, for example, (which is encoded as thousands of dots or 'pixels'), the traditional method is to examine the input dot by dot; the processing of each dot is carried out serially. What might be required is a computer that processed information in parallel (i.e. one that could carry out many computations at any one time). In this example, this would mean that the computer analyses each pixel of an image in parallel, and this would speed up the process significantly. The implication is that the serial nature of the algorithm makes it inappropriate as a metaphor for mental processing.

- **Algorithms are difficult to devise**. A second problem with the algorithmic approach is that in order to design a computer to do the sorts of things that people can do, one first needs to know what the algorithm is, and this will be based on the underlying theory. However, algorithms for doing things we find easy, such as selectively attending to information in the environment, understanding speech, perceiving depth and so on, are not well understood. Imagine how easy it is for us to understand speech even when it is spoken with an accent, or at different rates, or in a noisy environment. An algorithm for speech recognition cannot be just written down;

it requires extensive research. The quest for algorithms that may describe some aspect of human ability or intelligence is the main goal of AI. So, while the technology of computer modelling is available, progress in this area is slowed by the fact that our theories are too underdeveloped and the complexity of many human abilities has been underestimated.

- **Human knowledge is acquired, not built in**. Having developed a theory and designed an algorithm the next task is to program the computer. In programming the computer model, the knowledge the model needs to simulate the cognitive process has to be built-in by the programmer. A criticism here of this approach is that human ability isn't just built-in or **hardwired**, it is acquired through **learning**.

- **Human brains look nothing like computers**. Another problem with the computer metaphor concerns its similarities (or lack thereof) with the brain. Indeed, there seems to be no clear idea how a program could be represented in the brain. Cognitive psychologists and AI researchers have tended to ignore or avoid any serious attempt to specify how their models might be implemented in the brain. The algorithm or program (the software) is thought of as a metaphor of the mind, and the hardware (the computer's nuts and bolts) as the equivalent of the brain. An implication of this is that memory has been viewed as a filing cabinet or as a library, passively storing information in individual compartments which are searched during recall. As Rumelhart and Norman (1981) record:

Of course we have always realised that someday our theories of memory would have to be brought into line with our knowledge of brain function, but we assumed that the hardware of the brain was general enough to support almost any proposal that we found useful to postulate. (p. 2)

Despite such problems, many AI researchers still view the algorithm as a valid metaphor of mind, yet others are severely critical. In considering these kinds of problems we see that the conventional computer is not a good metaphor of the brain or of human information processing in general, the point being that computers are often laboriously slow and inefficient at doing those things that humans find so easy.

CRUCIAL CONCEPT

To the lay person a researcher in AI might conjure up the image of a Dr Frankenstein sort of character who is attempting to create a machine so intelligent that it threatens human existence. Popular cinema often ascribes to this picture: it depicts a computer or a group of androids as machines with human-like intelligence, emotions and intentions. In reality, however, current achievements in AI are significantly inferior to their fictional counterpart. The question here is why? Is it because the algorithms underlying human skills and intelligence are too complex and that we simply do not know at present what they are, or is it because the computer analogy is inappropriate and we can never build serial computers to behave in human-like ways?

Quick test

1. Write down the algorithm for doing a three-point turn in a car or going into a restaurant and ordering a meal (being as explicit as you can).
2. What are the strengths of the computer metaphor and computer modelling?
3. What are the weaknesses of the computer metaphor?

Section 2

Foundations of connectionism

The connectionist metaphor has, to a large extent, taken the place of the computer metaphor. Here you will learn about why this is so and the principles of connectionist models.

One idea is that the brain is a massively **parallel,** richly interconnected set of processors. Neurons, it is argued, may act as simple processors, with each neuron making a very small contribution to the overall storage of memory. This sharing of information gives the brain a **distributed representation**: a single memory may involve thousands of neurons (and a single neuron may be involved in many memories). In addition, neural networks in the brain acquire knowledge through **learning** – they do not embody pre-programmed knowledge. This is extremely powerful because it implies that we may no longer need to search for an appropriate algorithm, but rather get the neural network to 'discover' one. This approach has been referred to as **parallel distributed processing**, as **artificial neural networks**, and as **connectionism** (the latter term being most used by psychologists). The properties that emerge from this kind of processing may be more cognitive-like than the algorithms designed for the conventional computer. Indeed, such an approach has shown great promise, and has initiated a trend towards modelling human intelligence based on the theory of neural networks.

CRUCIAL CONCEPT

Unlike the traditional computer metaphor, connectionist models are said to have **emergent properties**. These are useful features of the behaviour of the model that have not been built-in explicitly. So, while the behaviour of the traditional computer model is predicted by the algorithms that have been programmed in, the behaviour of the connectionist model is not. The list below describes some of these emergent properties, and it is intriguing that these properties are not explicitly built into the model. they emerge from the combined behaviour of the set of units in the model.

Properties of connectionist models

Connectionist models are mathematical models of the computations and activities thought to be occurring in the brain. They exploit the notion that the brain achieves parallel processing with distributed representational properties. They are also systems that **learn** about the environment they are exposed to. The kinds of properties that emerge from a connectionist network are **generalisation, optimisation** and **fault tolerance.**

Generalisation

- **Heteroassociation**. Generalisation is the ability to correctly categorise, identify or retrieve information for stimuli that are novel or incomplete in some way. Classifying objects or concepts into distinct categories may be viewed as a problem of pattern recognition. This includes identifying a pattern as a member of a class or set of patterns (such as handwritten letters, spoken words, etc.). Classification is the grouping of a set of objects on the basis of similarity. Such groupings may be found in much of human information processing, such as in speech recognition and concept formation. Objects of a group share a common label and are assumed to have many other common attributes. Once a network has been trained on the a set of examples, it is able to correctly classify new items.

- **Autoassociation**. Conventional computers store information by assigning a random location in memory – the computer simply records the location of the memory for future reference. Neural networks, on the other hand, store new information in 'locations' according to its relationship with existing information (i.e., it stores information through its **meaning**). Human memory is also said to have this **content-addressable** nature. For example, when cued with a fragment of a particular memory, we can recall its whole. We know that a person's identity (name) can be discovered when only a small amount of information is given. Also we can visually recognise an object even though it may be partially hidden. Human speech is often poorly articulated, frequently occurs among much background noise, is occasionally spoken in unfamiliar accents; the message, too, may be delivered in an ungrammatical form, yet it may still be correctly perceived. This means that information may be imprecise, incomplete or 'noisy' yet still be understood. Neural networks performing this type of association may be said to act as 'clean-up' systems, where distorted or 'dirty' input patterns activate their errorless, 'clean' prototypes. A major attraction of neural networks is their content-addressability.

Optimisation

All processing is ultimately dependent upon selecting an output (response) for a particular input (stimulus) in a given context. It is desirable for a system to respond with the optimal output. For conventional methods this means searching among a vast number of options, which may take an impractical amount of time. Rather than selecting an output through serial search, neural networks can achieve a **parallel search** for the optimal output. Some neural network approaches have been shown to be highly likely to settle into an optimum response, although near optimal responses may be common.

Fault tolerance

The human and animal brain is noted for its tolerance to damage. If neurons in a particular region are damaged the whole region does not stop functioning, except in cases of extreme damage. Modern digital computers generally do not have this capacity. Neural networks, on the other hand, have been shown to be resistant to the removal of some of their units (Hinton and Sejnowski, 1986; Hinton and Shallice, 1990), showing a **graceful degradation** (a gradual decrease of efficiency) as the amount of damage increases. This is something that is known to occur in the brain, e.g., as in the case of Alzheimer's disease.

Principles of a connectionist network

A connectionist network consists of a set of 'artificial neurons'; these are processing units that do very simple calculations and are said to mimic (albeit in highly simplified form) the activity of real neurons. Neurons in the brain are connected to many other neurons. A neuron will have many inputs from other neurons and will also output to many other neurons. When a neuron receives its input from other neurons it makes a decision: to fire or not to fire (thus it is an all-or-none affair). If the neuron fires then it delivers a signal (the same signal) to other neurons with which it is connected. Firing patterns go in one direction – thus a connection may either be an input to the neuron or an output from the neuron. The decision whether to fire or not is dependent upon the particular **pattern** of signals it receives in its inputs. Some connections are **excitatory** in that they try to force other neurons to fire and some are **inhibitory** in that they try to prevent other neurons from firing. In addition, some neurons may have a greater (excitatory or inhibitory) influence over a particular neuron than others. The **degree** of excitation or inhibition of one neuron upon another is known as a **weight**. It is the **strength of a connection between neurons**.

Connection weights

Learning in a connectionist network takes place on the connection weights. These are increased and decreased when the network is exposed to stimuli. How are appropriate weight values chosen? What is required is a simple rule that will help determine these values. We consider first the **Hebb rule**. This rule is named after the psychologist Donald Hebb who had a number of ideas about how real neurons learn:

When an axon of cell A is near enough to excite a cell B and repeatedly or persistently takes part in firing it, some growth process or metabolic change takes place in one or both cells, such that A's efficiency, as one of the cells firing B, is increased. (Hebb, 1949, p. 62)

Put simply, this states that when two neurons are firing the connection weight between them is increased. In addition, a modification to the Hebb rule is that when one unit fires and the other unit does not fire then the weight between them is decreased. Consider the network in Figure 9.1. This is a simple network that has to learn to discriminate between men and women. The bottom row of units represents inputs, features of people such as things that they do or other features that they have. The top row of units represents the output units. These are the units that make the final decision about whether the features correspond to those of a **man** or those of a **woman**. The lines between the two rows represent the weights and the arrows indicate the direction of the signals (from input units to output units). Suppose that the network is presented with the features of one particular woman (e.g., she has **long hair**, is not a **soccer fan**, **reads Cosmo**politan magazine, does not **drink beer**, **wears trousers**, and **drives a hatchback**). The features present are represented by filled circles, and these units are said to be excitatory. Unfilled circles are features not present in the input and are inhibitory.

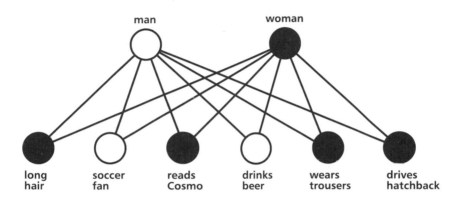

Figure 9.1 An example of a classification network

According to the Hebb rule, weights between the active inputs (excitatory units) and the active output unit (**woman**) are increased, and weights between inhibitory units (unfilled circles) and the active output unit are decreased. One can view the connection weights as being correlational: when they are both active they are highly correlated. If many more examples were presented to the network, some connection weights would become large and positive (e.g. that between **long hair** and **woman**, presumably), some would be close to zero because some women do and some women don't have these features (e.g. that between **drives hatchback** and **woman**), and some weights would be large and negative (e.g. that between **reads Cosmo** and **man**).

As the network begins to learn, it develops the power to generalise. So, if we presented the details of someone new, the network would make a good guess at whether it was a man or a woman. Furthermore, if one input unit was made inoperable then the network could still produce a decent guess. This is the property of fault tolerance.

Other types of networks have been designed, such as the Perceptron, the Adaline, the Multi-Layered Perceptron, and the weightless network (Kan and Aleksander, 1987). Other rules for changing the connection weights have also been devised, such as the **Delta rule** (Widrow, 1962) and **error back propagation** (Rumelhart et al., 1986). Some networks, such as the Perceptron, are limited in terms of the kinds of patterns they can discriminate between (Minsky and Papert, 1969). However, many of these problems have been overcome by the application of more sophisticated learning rules, such as error back propagation.

The physicist and Nobel Prize winner John Hopfield investigated another type of network (Hopfield, 1982). This work also gave the field a major impetus. The model analysed by Hopfield is a fully interconnected, **dynamic system** in which each unit receives input from all other units (feedback), except from itself (see Figure 9.2). The weight between each unit can be modified according to the Hebb rule or Delta rule. This type of system has a **distributed representation** of memory, i.e. each unit is involved in the storage of many memories, and each memory involves many units.

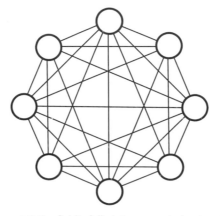

Figure 9.2 Hopfield's fully interconnected network

The pattern of activation of the set of units at any time is the **state** of the network. On presentation of an input, each node makes the decision whether to excite or inhibit other units. They then pass their signals to each of the other units and the process is repeated. Through this **iterative process**, the activation of each unit, and hence the state of the system, may continually change, moving over time until it reaches a **stable limit point** (a process known as **relaxation**) – this is a point at which the activity of the set of units is **unchanging.** Each stable point has a region known as the **basin of attraction**, which a stable system will aim towards, usually finding the 'nearest'. One can think of basins of attraction as valleys at various distances apart and the state of the system as a ball (Figure 9.3). The ball moves in time towards one of the valleys (the nearest or the deepest) whereupon it settles and moves no more. A system with a number of stable states can be viewed as a **content-addressable memory,** a memory accessed by **content** (as in the brain).

Deepest basin

Figure 9.3 The basins of attraction metaphor. The valleys represent the stable states of the system (memories) and the ball represents the current state of the system. The surrounding 'terrain' conveys the areas from which each basin will attract the ball. The arrow indicates the direction the ball will follow (i.e. to the nearest or deepest basin)

The Hopfield model epitomises the connectionist metaphor of memory. Memories are accessed by their content: partial information, processed in parallel, is used to reinstate a memory whole. This is in stark contrast to the previous view where memories are accessed by physical location (which gives rise to the library metaphor of memory, with individual memories or **books** being retrieved through the process of serial search). With this new approach some questions concerning human memory can be addressed with fresh insight. If connectionist models are to be of any value to psychology, they must explain phenomena in the literature on various aspects of human memory, and they must also add to our understanding.

Connectionist models have been applied to a range of cognitive phenomena, including dream sleep (Crick and Mitchison, 1983), grammar acquisition (McClelland and Rumelhart, 1986), synthetic grammar acquisition (Cleeremans and McClelland, 1991), neuropsychological modelling (Hinton and Shallice, 1990), classical conditioning (Grossberg and Levine, 1987), and models of emotion (Fulcher, 2002). Here we will only consider models of reading to give a flavour of the approach.

Connectionist models of reading

One of the earliest connectionist models of reading was that of McClelland and Rumelhart (1981). Their network simulated reading by converting visual letter features into word units through a hierarchical process. Letters are presented to the network, which first analyses the features of each letter and representations of individual letters become active when sufficient features are recognised. Representations of words then become active when certain patterns of letter representations are activated. The network determines its output through a 'winner-takes-all' process, in which the response (word naming) corresponds to the most active word unit, which will be the one with the best fit to letter patterns. The weights in the network are pre-programmed and equate to knowledge of the relationships between letter features, letters and words. The model can account for a broad array of observations on reading performance. However, it cannot account for certain 'migration errors' that result from the spatial representation of text, and this is because the input is not spatially represented. An example of a migration error (from Ellis and Humphreys, 1999):

PSYCHMENT

DEPARTOLOGY

This can be read as PSYCHOLOGY DEPARTMENT before the reader realises what the text actually says. This shows that reading errors can be based on the relative positions of words.

To overcome this and a few other problems, McClelland (1986) developed **PABLO** (Programmable Blackboard Model), which has position-specific input and output units, a knowledge store, and modifiable (programmable) connections between the knowledge store and the position-specific information of words. Another model that takes positional information into account is **BLIRNET** (Mozer, 1987), which is also a hierarchical scheme. Position-coded units are activated by visual letter features to combination units that process several recognised features in parallel. Word recognition occurs when the activity of letter cluster units of a particular word reaches a threshold. BLIRNET can account for many reading errors, including migration errors.

Connectionist models of reading have also been designed around theories of the processing routes involved in reading (see Chapter 6, Section 2). For example, **NETtalk** (Sejnowski and Rosenberg, 1987) models the direct-access route. Inputs are letters and spaces between words, and the output is a phonemic representation of the words. The network uses a 'moving window' that corresponds to perceptual span and the reading of one letter at a time, and from left to right. The network was trained on 20,000 words and was correct about 75 per cent of the time. Although quoted successful in its performance, there is little evidence that the moving window approach is psychologically plausible. Rather, letters may be read in parallel (see also Chapter 6, Section 2). Furthermore, the training set designed for this simulation was not broken down into different word types, such as high and low frequency words.

Seidenberg and McClelland (1989) used a network where the letters of words were presented in parallel. The network has orthographic units for visual word recognition, which then activate their phonological representations. The model was tested on high and low frequency words, and is able to account for much of the evidence on reading, such as regularity effects in word naming times (words that have an irregular correspondence between their pronunciation and spelling take longer to name). There is some data that is difficult for the model, such as human data on reading nonwords (the model performs much worse than humans).

Plaut et al. (1996) developed the above model further. Their approach is a modular one, in which separate networks, or modules, carry out different functions. According to Plaut et al. (1996) both humans and an adequate model of reading 'gradually learn to be sensitive to the statistical structure among orthographic, phonological, and semantic representations and in which these representations simultaneously constrain each other in interpreting a given input' (p. 429). In other words, learning to read involves identifying regularities in the way words are spelled, in the way they are pronounced and in the way they are used within a sentence to convey meaning. Furthermore, the different kinds of learned regularities each inform the reader about the identity of the word. Some learned regularities will instantly rule out certain phonological outputs thereby speeding up the 'search' for the correct output. Networks that are able to utilise information from more than one source may need to be modular in structure.

Simulating acquired dyslexia by 'lesioning' a connectionist network

Recall that one advantage of the connectionist approach is that a connectionist network is tolerant to a degree of damage. In other words, unlike the computer metaphor where damage to one component might bring the machine to a halt, a connectionist network will still be able to produce an output event though a number of its units are damaged. More interestingly, the output it produces, although it may be in error, is likely to be a near miss. One way of testing connectionist models of reading is to **mimic brain damage** (for example, acquired dyslexia) and compare the resulting performances with those of individuals with various forms of dyslexia.

Mozer (1991) attempted to model neglect dyslexia by lesioning a modified version of BLIRNET, known as **MORSEL**. This model has two modules, one for word recognition and one for attention. The word recognition module is sensitive to spatial information (word and letter order), while the attention module controls attention to individual spatial locations. This attention serves to avoid mixing up letters and making errors (miscombinations of letters). When the attention module is lesioned by making the left side of the module less likely to become activated by its inputs, a certain pattern of errors is produced that mimics those made in neglect dyslexia. For example, it made errors of the form **hand** being read as **sand**. This error occurred more often with non-words, e.g. **tand** being read as **sand**, and this, and other errors made by the model, are consistent with those made in neglect dyslexia.

The model developed by Plaut et al. (1996), discussed earlier, has been tested on neuropsychological data from surface dyslexia. Lesions were simulated by removing a portion of units and connections, and by adding noise to some of the weights (changing the values of some weights by small amounts). Lesions affected performance on exception words, which accords with the data on surface dyslexia. However, the increase in regularisation errors observed in surface dyslexia were not mirrored by the model's behaviour. Plaut et al. argue that this type of error is likely to occur during semantic processing (which this model does not simulate in an adequate form).

Finally, Hinton and Shallice (1990) have modelled deep dyslexia. Their model consists of a layer of grapheme units (position-specific letter units) that feed a layer of sememe units (attractor units that contain semantic information), which in turn interact with a set of 'clean-up' units (these units reduce the errors made in the semantic units and enable generalisation of meaning). The sememe and clean-up units act together to form an attractor network. Recall that an attractor network represents information as basins of attraction or 'attractor states' in a network. Attractor states represent the stimuli the network has been trained to recognise. This means that when an incomplete pattern (e.g. a word with one letter missing) is presented to the network, the state of the network will move towards the nearest attractor state. So, for example, when presented with the word B*OK, the network will output BOOK. However, Hinton and Shallice (1990) employ the attractor analogy to semantic information. This means that attractors such as CAT and DOG are nearby attractors but CAT and MUG are distant attractors.

After training on a set of words the network was lesioned. Several types of error emerged:

- visual errors: CAT – COT (caused by lesions within the grapheme units);
- semantic errors: CAT – DOG (caused by lesions between sememe and clean up units);
- mixed errors: CAT – RAT (caused by both types of lesions);
- unrelated errors: CAT – MUG (caused by both types of lesions).

Visual, semantic and mixed errors were more common than unrelated errors, and indeed these errors match those found in deep dyslexia.

Evaluation: the problem domain of connectionism

Learning in a connectionist network appears to be of an **implicit nature**, that is to say learning is through 'mere exposure' to material rather than through direct efforts to learn a set of rules. Connectionist networks are useful at (1) modelling the process by which memory wholes are automatically activated by their parts, and (2) inferring the rules of category membership from a set of exemplars the system has been exposed to. These are behaviours that appear to be rule governed, and although they may be described by rules, they may not be produced on the basis of explicitly stored rules.

The common feature of these forms of learning is that they involve the **association** of a **stimulus** (a verb, an exemplar, a representation of time, a particular date, the visual form of a word, the vocalised form of a word, etc.) with a **response** (past tense form of a verb, a category label, a choice of two alternatives, the name of a particular day, or a word label, and so on). Such associations may involve skills in which the way a response is computed is difficult or impossible to verbalise. Thus we may not be aware of the process by which we transform an irregular verb into its past tense form, but we certainly are aware of utterances that contain erroneous transformations (e.g. 'I goed shopping').

If neural networks merely involve the learning of stimulus–response associations, are they anything more than sophisticated behaviourist models? Lachter and Bever (1988), critics of connectionism, argue that they are models of the Hullian (behaviourist) tradition that implement learning through many S–R associations. Lachter and Bever mockingly rename the collective units of a connectionist network as '**massively parallel rodents**' (MPRs), where each processing unit could be replaced by rat! Each rat receives a pinch on its tail (an input) and either freezes or lunges at the tail of the rat in the next layer (outputs 0 or 1). Performance feedback of the network of MPRs is a conditioning schedule of the Skinnerian variety, where the reinforcement (error signal) is specific to each rat. If Lachter and Bever are correct then neural networks might be, at best, limited to describing forms of animal learning rather than human linguistic mechanisms (and indeed, there are several connectionist models of classical conditioning).

Behind Lachter and Bever's critique of connectionist networks might be a concern that connectionism signifies a return to behaviourism. However, such a view is without foundation. According to behaviourist philosophy, internal representations were inferred and not directly observable; they were therefore unacceptable as phenomena of study.

Only the response (R) to the stimulus (S) was observable and hence worthy of study. Connectionist networks are intrinsically concerned with internal representations and cannot, therefore, be compatible with behaviourism (see also Pinker and Prince, 1988).

Connectionism is clearly a lively area of research and is having ever more impact in psychology, and **theoretical psychology** is the major benefactor. Connectionist networks help us to better model aspects of human behaviour. These models provide detailed accounts of specific behaviours and may be used to test other hypotheses. In addition, they inspire experiments that might not otherwise have been thought of and the results of which could enhance ideas in applied areas. In short, 'The neural network of the future can be to the psychologist what a row of test tubes is to the chemist: a test-bed for new conjectures' (Aleksander and Burnett, 1987). Another advantage of developing connectionist models is that important links are made between aspects of behaviour, cognition and neurophysiology. The bridging of these areas is, perhaps, something long overdue. Until recently, cognitive psychologists had been ignoring the work in neuro-psychology. Clearly, there is much to gain from this kind of enterprise.

Quick test

1. Outline two applications of connectionism.
2. What are the strengths of the connectionist approach?
3. What is Lachter and Bever's main criticism of connectionist models?
4. What is the link between connectionism and learning theory?

Section 3

Thinking machines

If we take the computer metaphor to its extreme, or consider the computer not as a metaphor but as closely corresponding to human mental processes, then the question that arises is whether machines can think. The answer to this question may have major implications for the validity of the approach. Here you will study the views of the most outspoken supporters and critics of the view that machines can think or will be able to think at some point in the future.

Many cognitive researchers in the 1960s were of the view that such machines would be developed in the near future. Despite several major advances in the processing power of the modern computer, the desktop PC sitting in front of me is no closer to being able to think than the radio sitting next to it. Yet could a combination of even better computing power and some sophisticated programming yield a thinking machine? For example, what about Pearl, the chess program that beat the world champion Kasparov in 1997 – can it be said to think?

The Turing test

If a researcher in AI claimed to have created a thinking machine how could we put that claim to the test? Alan Turing, a British mathematician, devised a test for answering this question (Turing, 1950). The test, which later became known as the **Turing test**, is designed to discover whether a human observer can tell whether the person or thing it is interacting with is a human or a computer.

The test is set up as a game, which Turing called the imitation game. There are three players, a person, a machine and an interrogator. The person and the machine are hidden from the view of the interrogator, and all communication between players is typewritten.

The aim of the interrogator is to identify which player is the machine and which player is the person. The aim of the machine is to convince the interrogator that it is the person and that the person is a machine, and it is the aim of the person to convince the interrogator that the machine is a machine and he or she is the person.

The point of the exercise was to show that in order to make the claim that a machine can think, it must be able to understand and must be able to generate germane responses that could fool a person into thinking it was human. But if a computer were able to perform in such a way that an expert could not discriminate between its performance and that of a human, to what extent does this mean that the machine can think?

The '**strong AI**' view is that if a machine passed the Turing test it 'would not merely be a model of the mind; it would literally be a mind, in the same sense that a human mind is a mind' (Searle, 1990, p. 26). The '**weak AI**' view, which Searle (1980, 1990) adheres to, is that such a machine could not be considered as having a mind. He argues that it is more realistic to 'think of computer models as being useful in studying the mind in the same way that they are useful in studying the weather, economics, or molecular biology' (Searle, 1990, p. 26). Searle takes us through the '**Chinese room thought experiment**' to explain how he arrives at the position that conventional computing machines cannot, and will never be able to, think.

The Chinese room

Searle (1980) asks us to consider a language that we do not understand. In his case (and in mine) it is Chinese. To Searle (and to me), Chinese writing looks like 'meaningless squiggles'. He then asks us to imagine that we are placed in a room containing hundreds of Chinese symbols and a rule book in English for matching Chinese symbols with other Chinese symbols. People outside the room **do** understand Chinese and these people submit Chinese symbols into the room and wait for us to hand them back another Chinese symbol. Our task is to use the rule book to identify which symbol to return based on the symbol we have been given.

This scenario is Searle's analogy of the modern computer. The people outside the room are the programmers, the person inside the room is the computer, the rule book is the computer program, the Chinese symbols posted into the room are queries, and the symbols returned are the answers. Suppose that the symbols posted to the room represent the question 'What is your favourite colour?' and the symbols handed back represent the statement 'My favourite colour is blue but I also like green a lot.' To the person outside of the room it appears as though the person inside the room has understood the question, yet to the person inside the room the symbols are meaningless. Remember in our earlier discussion about algorithms we noted that the computer follows a strict set of rules when doing something. It matters not whether the task is to search a database for a particular author or to carry out a t-test in a statistics package. The computer does not process any meaning: it just follows a set of instructions. Just as the person in the Chinese room does not understand Chinese, so the computer does not understand the information it is processing.

Searle argues, then, that computers are essentially **syntactic** (rule-based systems) but human minds deal with meaning. Since syntax alone cannot produce meaning (see Chapter 6 on language) then computer programs cannot create minds. Searle (1990) concludes with an amusing but salient point:

> ... one can imagine a computer simulation of the oxidation of hydrocarbons in a car engine or the action of digestive processes in a stomach when it is digesting pizza. And the simulation is no more the real thing in the case of the brain than it is in the case of the car or the stomach. Barring miracles, you could not run your car by doing a computer simulation of the oxidation of gasoline, and you could not digest pizza by running the program that stimulates such digestion. It seems obvious that a simulation

of cognition will similarly not produce the effects of the neurobiology of cognition. (p. 29)

Simulating angst: I am suffering the angst of postindustrial society under late capitalism

For Searle, one could write a computer program to print out sentences such as 'I am suffering the angst of postindustrial society under late capitalism', thereby simulating the feeling of angst, but simulation is not the same thing as duplication.

AI programs have been successful at solving complex mathematical problems, solving tactical problems, playing chess, proving theorems and engaging in some forms of dialogue. Yet what computers lack is the vast store of **background knowledge** that people bring to problems as well as their **commonsense ability** to use their knowledge as the situation demands (Dreyfus, 1972). Another problem with computers of the 1970s and 1980s was that computer systems designed to process visual information took an enormous amount of time to recognise simple objects. A feat that takes biological visual systems just seconds. Yet the processors of the computer are about a million times faster than those of the brain.

CRUCIAL TIP

If this topic is covered in your course then try to get hold of a copy of Searle's original article – it is a very accessible read.

Churchland and Churchland (1990) argue that machines may be able to think, and that computers based on connectionist networks are more likely to achieve this than the conventional (rule-based) digital computer. They argue that the brain has the ability to think because of the following:

- The nervous system processes in **parallel** rather than in serial. For example, the retina sends information to the brain in the form of about a million distinct signals. The largest number of parallel signals the computer processes at any one time is a meagre 16 or 32, depending upon whether it is a 16- or 32-bit machine.
- Neural processes are **dynamic**. Neurons that project to another area of the brain receive signals back from the same area. These 'recurrent' signals allow the system to modulate its own sensory processing.

Connectionist networks share more of these features with the brain than does the modern computer. Furthermore, connectionist systems are not rule governed, they do not process symbols. The Churchlands argue, therefore, that Searle's Chinese room does not apply to computers based on connectionist principles.

The Chinese gym

Searle's reply to the Churchlands' argument was to suppose the Chinese room was replaced by a **Chinese gym** in which there are lots of people all arranged to work on the symbols in parallel (thereby mimicking a connectionist network). The people in the gym could still send back messages that have meaning to the people outside the gym, yet to those inside the symbols are still meaningless. The Churchlands reply that the same is true of the brain – no single neuron in a Chinese speaker's brain understands Chinese, although their whole brain does. To the Churchlands the brain is a computer but in a radically different style, and it is still not known how the brain deals with meaning. They conclude that there is no principled reason why science could not construct an artificial system capable of thought by using what is known about the nervous system.

Quick test

1. What is the Turing test?
2. Explain the Chinese room thought experiment.
3. State two criticisms of Searle's view.
4. State the view of the Churchlands on whether machines can, or could in principle, be said to think.

Section 4

End of chapter assessment

Questions

1. Evaluate the traditional computer metaphor of cognition.
2. What is a connectionist network?
3. Can a machine think?

Answers

1. You can begin by stating that all sorts of metaphors have been used to describe human cognitive processes, especially memory. Describe the computer metaphor briefly, by drawing on the perceived similarities of the computer and cognition, such as temporary storage registers being similar to short-term memory, the computer algorithm being similar to sequential thought and the software/hardware analogy of the mind/brain dichotomy. Go on to discuss the strengths of this metaphor and how artificial intelligence workers and cognitive psychologists at times work on very similar problems. Then highlight the weaknesses of the computer metaphor, focusing on as many of these as you can because it is here you can gain many marks. Although not directly asked for in the question, you can briefly say how the connectionist metaphor (often referred to as the 'brain metaphor') addresses some of these problems and shows much promise.

2. Question 2 takes off where question 1 ended, but what you need to do here is the reverse of question 1. Begin with a brief discussion of the computer metaphor highlighting its many problems. Signpost to your reader that connectionist systems address these problems, and then go on to describe the connectionist approach. Outline the 'feedforward' network (as illustrated by the man/woman example) and the Hopfield network. Draw your reader's attention to the important emergent properties such as generalisation and fault tolerance. The key point here is that these properties are not directly programmed into the model, as they would need to be in the traditional algorithmic approach. Mention a few applications of connectionism. This provides your positive evaluation of connectionist networks, and you can now mention some of the weaknesses, such as their behaviourist-like behaviour. You can also mention that although they are thought to be more brain-like than the traditional computer metaphor, the behaviour of the units is not like that of neurons in the brain.

3. For this question you can simply lay bare Searle's argument and then follow it up with that of the Churchlands. Discuss the Chinese room thought experiment, making the point that the thrust of Searle's argument is that computers do not process semantics (meaning), they only follow rules (deal with syntax). Since thinking and understanding involves semantics then computers cannot think. The Churchlands approach this by arguing that machines developed on connectionist principles and given more meaningful interactions with the environment have the potential to think. You can then outline the Chinese gym analogy. Finally, you can draw on the works of other authors

who have commented on this question, and you can offer your own view (provided it is clearly thought out).

Section 5

Further reading

The original collection of papers that inspired many psychologists to become interested in connectionism is quite an accessible read:

McClelland, J. and Rumelhart, D. E. (1986) *Parallel Distributed Processing: Explorations in the Microstructure of Cognition. Volume 2. Psychological and Biological Models.* Cambridge, MA: MIT Press.

See also:

Churchland, P. S. and Churchland, P.N. (1990) 'Could a machine think?' Recent arguments and new prospects', *Scientific American*, *262*, 32–7.

Ellis, R. and Humphreys, G. W. (1999) *Connectionist Psychology: A Text with Reading.* Hove: Psychology Press.

Searle, J. R. (1990) 'Is the brain's mind a computer program?', *Scientific American*, *262(1)*, 26–37.

Questions and answers

In this final chapter you will be provided with fuller answers to a couple of essay or exam questions, and one laboratory report. The purpose is to guide you through the essay writing processes and to highlight some important features of writing good essays. The lab report will illustrate how to construct each subsection of a report. Question 1 concerns the material covered in Chapter 3, Section 1. Question 2 provides new material (research on recovered memories and false memories) but shows how material from Chapter 5 can be drawn on. Question 3 is a research report on a hypothetical practical that brings together material from Chapter 4 and Chapter 5.

Question 1: Discuss two theories of focused attention

[For your first few sentences, state what the problem is and what behaviour needs to be explained. Give an everyday example, if relevant.]

The study of focused attention is concerned with how we are able to selectively attend to some information in the environment, ignoring other information. An example of this problem was described by Cherry (1953) and is known as the 'cocktail party effect'. When we are at a party, we are able to focus on what someone is saying to us, despite a lot of background noise (other people talking and loud music). We can effectively ignore this background noise. However, should someone, other than the person we are talking to, mention our name then we are likely to hear it immediately. This effect highlights the difficult question of how we can ignore something, yet still be attending to it.

[Tell your reader which approaches your essay will focus on. State what the main theoretical approaches are in attempting to explain the behaviour.]

Several theories have been proposed that attempt to explain this and other attentional phenomena, and this essay will discuss two theories of focused auditory attention, namely Treisman's attenuation model (Treisman, 1964) and the late selection theory of Deutsch and Deutsch (1963).

[Take a historical approach, if there is much research on the topic (e.g. as in focused auditory attention); otherwise take each theory in turn beginning with the weakest.]

Both the attenuation model and the late selection theory use variations of the dichotic listening task in conjunction with the shadowing task. Participants are presented with two auditory messages, one to each ear via a set of headphones. They are required to attend to one message while ignoring the other message. To be sure that participants are attending to the message they are asked to repeat aloud the message they hear (the task known as 'shadowing'). Typically, the messages presented are of spoken words or sentences. Researchers wish to know how much and what type of information the participant can hear from the non-attended message (the 'unshadowed' message).

Early studies using this method suggested that little information is attended to in the unshadowed message. These led theorists such as Broadbent (1958) to suggest that in focused auditory attention, we filter out the ignored message so that we can focus on the relevant message. In the sensory channels, too much information creates a bottleneck and this problem is solved through the process of filtering. However, other findings suggested that some information, such as one's own name, the gender of the speaker and other features could be detected in the unshadowed message. This led Treisman to develop her attenuation model of attention (Treisman, 1964).

[Describe the approaches with some evaluative statements. Describe the theory and any evidence that supports it. Next, describe any research that does not support the theory or any behavioural observations that the theory cannot account for.]

According to Treisman, the unattended message is not entirely filtered out but just 'tuned' down. Physical (shallow) features of the stimulus are processed first, followed by stimulus meaning (deep features). The more processing capacity that is available, the deeper the unattended message can be processed. This fits in with Cherry's (1953) observation that the physical characteristics of unattended inputs, such as the sex of the speaker, can be noticed more often than their meaning, since usually there is sufficient processing capacity for this. Research that supports the model comes from Treisman (1960) in which bilingual speakers of French and English heard an English message in one ear and a French translation in the other ear. When the messages were presented at about the same time, participants recognised that the two messages had the same meaning. However, they did not recognise this when there was a time delay between the two messages. In another study, Treisman (1964), it was found that the participants' ability to shadow the attended message was affected by the degree of similarity between the attended and unattended ear. The more similar the passages were (e.g. different passages from the same novel), the harder it was to shadow the attended message. These studies suggest that the unattended message is processed for meaning to some extent.

There may be problems with the Treisman model. However, the model of Deutsch and Deutsch (1963) needs to be discussed next before the research evidence can be evaluated.

[Next, describe a second theory, saying in what ways it is similar to and different from the first theory. Provide evidence that supports it and evidence or observations that do not support it. Do the same for a third theory, if appropriate.]

Deutsch and Deutsch (1963) proposed a model in which all stimuli are fully analysed, with the most important message determining the response. While this theory has the notion of a bottleneck as in Treisman's model, it places its location closer to the response end of the system. It is therefore known as a late-selection theory. As the decision is made late, it assumes that most processing is parallel up to that point.

The model predicts that since selection is made much later than in the Treisman model, then some information in the unattended channel may be processed at least non-consciously. The study by Von Wright *et al.* (1975) supports this prediction, since in that study a physiological response was recorded during the presentation of significant stimuli to the participant in the unattended channel. The main difference between this model and that of Treisman's is essentially that in the former all stimuli are processed for meaning, while in the latter the available resources determine the amount and depth of processing.

[Provide a critical evaluation of the approaches. Finally, highlight the strength and weaknesses of each theory. Then provide an overall evaluation of which theory accounts for the behaviour, outlining its main strengths.]

Determining which model accounts for the available research evidence better may be difficult. For example, in Treisman and Geffen (1967), the participants shadowed one of two auditory messages, and were told to tap whenever they detected a target word in either message. Attenuation theory predicts that participants will be less able to detect the target in the unattended channel since most attention is directed at the attended channel and the unattended channel is attenuated. However, the Deutsch and Deutsch model predicts that detection of the target should be the same regardless of whether it is presented in the attended or unattended channel. Results indicated that detection rates were significantly better in the attended channel (87 per cent versus only 8 per cent in the unattended channel), therefore supporting Treisman's model. However, Deutsch and Deutsch argued that participants had to shadow the message and be vigilant for targets in the attended channel, but only had to listen out for targets in the unattended channel, and therefore the processing priorities were not matched. In response to this criticism, Treisman and Riley (1969) replicated the study but required that participants stop shadowing when they heard the target. In this way the demands made on both channels were more equal. Once again, though, significantly more targets were detected in the attended channel than in the unattended channel, providing support for Treisman's model.

The study by Johnstone and Wilson (1980) provides some evidence that both models may be partly correct. Pairs of words were presented and the task was to identify target words (e.g. sock) that were members of a given category (e.g. articles of clothing). Each target word was presented with another word (e.g. smelly or punches) that would bias its meaning. When participants did not know which ear the target would be presented in, target detection was improved by appropriate other words that biased its meaning. Therefore, participants were processing both channels for meaning. However, when participants were told to attend to the words in one ear only, target detection was unaffected by the other word that was supposed to bias its meaning. This suggests that non-target words presented in the unattended ear were not processed for meaning. These findings indicate that the amount and depth of processing of non-attended channels is more than is necessary to perform the main task. In sum, it suggests that more information in the unattended channel is processed than is suggested by Treisman, but less than is suggested by Deutsch and Deutsch.

In conclusion, neither of the models suggested by Treisman (1964) and Deutsch and Deutsch (1963) may represent the final word on focused auditory attention. These models mainly differ in terms of the point at which selection is made, rather than on what basis selection is made. The work of Johnston and colleagues (Johnstone and Heinz, 1978; Johnstone and Wilson, 1980) may provide a more plausible account of the process of focused attention. It offers a new, but subtle, account of the way in which psychologists think about focused attention, which is that attention may 'switch' between signals, rather than actively or prematurely selecting one signal and ignoring another. In addition, recent research on divided attention has put doubt on the notion that there is an attention bottleneck in the first place. Attention may be dependent upon the particular task being carried out and the amount of skilled behaviour involved. As such, attention seems to be more flexible than proposed by the two models discussed here.

[Ideally, the answer would include descriptions of a handful of additional studies, or more details of the models presented – see Chapter 3, Section 1.]

Question 2: Is it possible to remember something that did not happen?
Evaluate some of the evidence that has been gathered to answer this question

[This question concerns an ongoing debate about whether 'false memories' can exist and some of the material covered in Chapter 5 will be useful in answering it].

A false memory can be defined as a 'memory' of something that did not happen (Neath, 1998). Although there is substantial evidence in memory research of the inaccuracies of memory, the current debate about the existence of false memory was instigated by the controversy surrounding recovered memories. [*Note the essay begins by applying and defining a psychological term (false memory) that is used for the phenomenon of remembering something that did not happen.*]

There are a number of famous cases where the recovery of long lost memories has led to a conviction (Loftus and Ketchum, 1994). Many of these cases involved adults who recovered lost memories of being sexually abused as children. These memories may reflect events which actually occurred, but they are often difficult to verify by others. Why they have been forgotten for many years is often explained by the psychoanalytic construct of repression. Painful memories of being abused by parents or relatives get pushed into the unconscious because they are difficult to deal with. At some point in the future, the memory may re-emerge, cued either by something in the person's environment or by a therapist. [*The next paragraph lays out a little bit of history behind the research and outlines one claim, that recovered memories are of events that actually happened.*]

Some memory researchers, familiar with the research on the inaccuracies of memory, suggest that claims of recovered memories should not be accepted without an element of doubt. For example, Loftus (1993) points out that in an effort to help their clients, therapists may unintentionally mislead the client into believing that a traumatic event must have occurred in the client's childhood. Furthermore, although people who report recovered memories also report being very confident in them, there is much evidence that confidence in the accuracy of a memory and actual accuracy can often be weakly correlated. Several studies have shown that people can be misled into recalling something when they are first provided with misleading information. [*This paragraph presents an alternative claim that recovered memories might not be accurate, or worse, they may be false memories. The next paragraph provides some evidence for this alternative claim concerning whether it is possible to remember something that did not happen. I have lifted the phrase from the question here to remind you that in a topic such as this it is all too easy to stray from the question.*]

Strong evidence that misleading information can yield a false memory comes from Loftus (1993) where people were misled into believing that a traumatic event had occurred in their childhood. In one case, Chris was asked to recall events from his childhood after reading a log of his childhood compiled by his brother. The brother was asked to include a event that did not occur, that of being lost in a shopping mall. Not only did Chris (falsely) recall being lost in a shopping mall, he also reported the event in detail, citing how fearful he had felt and also the physical features of the stranger who came to his aid. Chris reported the event as though it was a real memory, when it was an experimental manipulation and hence a false memory. Evidence like this raises the possibility that recovered memories may be wrong or may have been implanted in some way. [*You could add description of the Crucial Study: Eyewitness testimony from Chapter 5, Section 2: Memory in the long term.*]

Earlier research on reality monitoring provides an interesting way of showing how memory for an event can become confused. Participants were presented with a list of words, some of which were read aloud by the experimenter and some of which the participant was asked to imagine being read aloud by the experimenter. In this case, the source of each word was either externally or internally generated. A reasonable assumption is that externally generated information is associated with a broad set of attributes linked to sensory properties, while for internally generated information this is less so. One should expect, therefore, that participants could easily discriminate between external events and internal events when required to identify the source of each word in the list. However, when participants were instructed to do this there were a significant number of errors or confusions (Johnson *et al.*, 1988). This research suggests that discriminating between real and imaginary events can sometimes be difficult. [*This paragraph introduced research from another type of study and shows a breadth of knowledge and also adds weight to the argument.*]

Monitoring the source of an event may involve an inferential process: qualities of a memory are used to infer its source, and richer qualities are associated with external rather than internal sources. There is much evidence from research in episodic memory to suggest that when individuals attempt to date an event, they also make inferences when reaching a decision. [*You could add a discussion of episodic memory here – see Chapter 5, Section 2: Memory in the long term.*]

Other laboratory research has shown that people can create a false memory for words they have not been shown. Roediger and McDermott (1995) presented a long list of words (e.g. table, sit, legs, butter, sandwich). Each word was associated with a target word, such as chair or bread, which was not shown. After the list was presented, participants had to rate how confident they were that each word from a second list had been shown earlier. The second list contained words from the original list but also non-presented words. There were two types of non-presented words, target words (such as chair and bread) and non-target words that were semantically unrelated (e.g. boy). They found that 86 per cent of presented words were rated as being shown in the original list, and remarkably 84 per cent of non-presented target words were rated as being shown in the original list. Participants had then created false memories of words that had not been shown. These intrusions have been found with a variety of stimuli (Robinson and Roediger, 1997; Brainerd and Reyna, 1998). One could conclude that similar intrusions occur with childhood memories: the details recalled may be similar to actual experiences but never occurred. [*It is important to give details of important studies like this one. Note that I have not mentioned the percentage of non-presented non-target words in this paragraph. I want to use this to make a point about schematic memory in the next paragraph.*]

Whether false memories such as those demonstrated by Roediger and McDermott (1995) result from the same processes as those arising from episodic memory has been questioned by Freyd and Gleaves (1996). They argue that there is little similarity between a false memory of a word that did not appear on a list and a false memory of childhood sexual abuse. [*Note that we have come full circle here. We set out what the debate was and offered two viewpoints. Having examined one in detail we have returned to the other.*] Furthermore, while it is possible to create a false memory of being lost in a shopping mall, a false memory of having had a rectal enema is difficult to achieve (Pezdek et al., 1997). This may be because this type of event is too dissimilar from existing real memories. Support for this explanation is from the fact that in the Roediger and McDermott (1995) study, only 2 per cent of non-presented unrelated words were falsely recognised. Since these words were semantically unrelated, the processes involved in false memory may be based on semantic content. Thus a false memory for a non-presented word in the lab may occur because semantic information may be organised schematically. Indeed, a false memory may be the result of schematic memory and inferential processes. In other words, a false memory may only occur when it is first related to an actual experience and second whether it is plausible or not. [*The discussion has now moved on to how false memory could be explained using our knowledge of models of semantic memory. So, you could extend this discussion by examining several theories of semantic memory and asking whether each or any can account for these findings – see Chapter 5, Section 3: Semantic Memory. The next paragraph is one example of how to do this*].

Much of the data from false memory experiments can be interpreted as examples of schema-driven errors in memory rather than the creation of false memories in the sense of recalling an episode or event in life that did not happen. [*Insert a brief description of what schema theory is here.*] For example, in a study by French and Richards (1993), participants were asked to draw a clock with numbers represented by Roman numerals. Some were asked to draw the clock after having been shown the clock for six minutes, and others copied from a drawing of the clock in front of them. They found that only participants in the copy condition drew the clock without any errors. That is, they drew the numeral representing four as IIII and not as IV. [*The Roman numeral for four is nearly always written as IV, except on a clock face where it is drawn as IIII for aesthetic reasons.*] This demonstrates that a schema in memory can under certain conditions overwrite what one

137

sees. However, this would not be regarded as a false memory but results when information is schematically organised in memory. Hence experiments like Roediger and McDermott's may be better understood within the framework of schema theory.

[All that is left now is a coherent conclusion, and a correctly constructed References section].

Many people claim to have recalled a so-called long-lost memory. It may be that it is an accurate memory of a real event. However, research has shown that false memories can be created whereby the individual believes the memory to be true but it is false. In addition, research shows that confidence and the reality of the memory do not correlate. Therefore, the recovered memory and the false memory may both be partially correct. The research on this topic has shown that human memory is flexible and malleable, and it is open to making errors. These errors are not just about how information can be forgotten but also about the construction of events that never happened.

Question 3: Hypothetical student report on a form of implicit learning

TITLE: Evaluative learning: affective stimuli and the occurrence of implicit learning

ABSTRACT
Evidence suggests that evaluative learning (a procedure for changing the feelings towards stimuli) can occur independently of conscious awareness (when the participant is unaware of the change). In this experiment, liked and disliked stimuli were presented subliminally (too brief to be consciously detected) and immediately before neutral stimuli. Participants were told about the expected influence of the affective stimuli on the neutral stimuli in terms of how they would rate them. They were further instructed to resist the effect of the subliminal stimuli when rating the neutral stimuli. The findings provide further support for implicit evaluation learning.

[**Notes:** *The first sentence introduces the topic area and the main research question. The abstract then describes a complex procedure in a couple of well-structured sentences. It ends with an unambiguous conclusion. The indented paragraph is visually pleasing but not necessary. A sentence about the actual results is missing, such as 'The main result was that participants were unable to resist evaluative learning when instructed to do so.' Check with your tutors about writing abstracts, as some colleges now expect you to use structured abstracts.*]

INTRODUCTION

Understanding our emotional responses to everyday objects and situations enables us to appreciate the ways in which we acquire our attitudes (Zajonc, 1984; De Houwer *et al.*, 1994). According to Osgood *et al.* (1957) we attach a value to all such experiences, thus forming our preferences. It has further been argued that our preferences may be made without our cognitive awareness (Zajonc, 1980; Murphy and Zajonc, 1993). Understanding this phenomenon is of great importance to our knowledge of human behaviour.

[**Notes:** *The introduction begins with the issue of preferences. There are no general and really obvious statements like 'Memory is really important, without it we would not be able to remember anything'. Next, the issue of awareness is introduced immediately. This way the reader is told straightaway what the research concerns. A definition of evaluative learning follows. It is important to begin to define very important terms as soon as possible.*]

Much evidence has been put forward to support the theory that we may develop our preferences through evaluative learning (Levey and Martin, 1975; De Houwer et al., 1994; De Houwer et al., 1997; Johnsrude et al., 1999; Fulcher and Hammerl, 2001). This behavioural paradigm proposes that when a neutral stimulus is paired with an affective stimulus, a shift in valence (change in liking or disliking) will occur towards the neutral stimulus. An everyday example might be disliking the name Peter because of previous bad experiences with someone of that name. Levey and Martin (1975) demonstrated this by presenting participants with a number of pictures and requesting they be sorted into three categories; liked, disliked and neutral. A neutral picture (conditioned stimulus) was paired with either a liked or a disliked picture (unconditioned stimulus). When the valence toward the neutral picture was measured, a neutral picture paired with a liked picture was also liked. In contrast, a neutral picture was disliked if it had previously been paired with a disliked picture, thus supporting the theory that we acquire such preferences through evaluative learning.

[*Next, the author introduces the main opposition to this theory.*]

A growing body of evidence suggests that evaluative learning can occur independently of our conscious awareness (Lewicki et al., 1992; Hammerl and Grabitz, 1996; Fulcher and Cocks, 1997; Fulcher et al., 2001). For example, one might still dislike the name Peter even though one has forgotten about that person and the associated bad experiences. The modern approach to investigating this phenomenon has extended the initial work of Martin and Levey (1975). Recent evidence confirms the occurrence of evaluative learning when liked and disliked stimuli are presented subliminally (too briefly to be consciously detected) and, therefore, outside the realms of consciousness (Krosnick et al., 1992; De Houwer et al., 1997; Fulcher and Hammerl, 2001). In contrast, other researchers reject this proposal and suggest that the concept of learning is only related to awareness (Cohen, 1964; Holender, 1986). Further evidence in support of this argument has been presented by Klein and Wiener (1966) who confirmed that lowered awareness levels did not result in learning. Recent evidence (Field, 2000a; Field, 2000b) also disputes the concept that learning can occur without awareness and more specifically critiques the methods of data collection employed by those researchers who support this claim.

[*Next, we are told how proponents of the main theory have responded to such criticisms. Note that this response is the first hint of the actual method to be used in the current study.*]

In response to such criticism, Fulcher and Hammerl (2001) varied the length of time affective stimuli were presented. In this instance, pictures of faces expressing emotions of anger or happiness were presented subliminally (for 12.5 ms) or overtly (for 125 ms). Immediately afterwards, Chinese ideographs (Chinese symbols) were presented. Participants were asked to rate whether each ideograph was 'liked' or 'disliked'. The results confirmed that subliminal presentation of stimuli had resulted in implicit evaluative learning because those ideographs presented with a happy face were rated as 'liked' and ideographs were 'disliked' if they had previously been paired with an angry face.

[*Having described the published study that is closest to the current experiment, and in some detail, the next paragraph (a clear statement of the rationale for the current experiment) is easy to write.*]

The purpose of this experiment was to replicate the method of Fulcher and Hammerl's (2002) study but by revealing the nature of evaluative learning to participants in advance of the experiment and by including the instruction to resist the effect when subsequently rating the neutral pictures. It was predicted that participants would not be able to resist evaluative learning as indicated by their ratings of the neutral stimuli.

[*Note the way the hypotheses are presented. They are not presented as 'Hypothesis 1: There will be ...', but rather in the form 'It was predicted that ...'. The former style is acceptable, but if you read academic journals you would know that the latter style is most commonly used (but check the advice from your department as they may insist on a particular style for stating the hypothesis or null-hypothesis). Other important points to note about this introduction:*

- *it does not waffle on about studies that are tangential (not absolutely essential) to the current study;*
- *it is brief and written without ambiguity, in good English, and to the point;*
- *there is evidence that the student **has read the recommended reading**;*
- *students who do not read the recommended reading for an assignment can't possibly hope to write well on the subject – and they certainly do not fool the tutor when they try to change the debate or talk about issues not directly related to the subject.*]

METHOD

Design:

The experiment employed a between subjects, repeated measures design. The independent variable was whether the affective stimulus was of a smiling or an angry face. The dependent variable was the ratings of the ideographs.

[**Note**: *The design of the study is clearly stated, as are the independent and dependent variables. Always begin the Method with a word about the design. State what type of design it is, what the IV is, and what the DV is. State these **accurately**.*]

Participants

Sixty-eight participants took part in this experiment, 80 per cent of whom were female. The overall calculated mean age was 24.28. Equal numbers of participants were assigned to each condition (n=34).

[**Note**: *Don't provide unnecessary details about the participants. You could add that they were psychology undergraduates enrolled on a cognitive psychology module, but not much more is needed.*]

Apparatus:

The experiment took place on the computer. All experimental instructions were presented to the participants on the computer screen and the experimenter confirmed that these had been fully understood. Participants were requested to select the 'A' key on the computer keypad if they considered an angry face had been presented and the '5' key on the numeric keypad if they considered a smiling face had appeared.

[*Note that the author does not provide a list or a bullet pointed list. The apparatus or materials need to be discussed using complete, grammatically correct sentences. The author could have mentioned that digitised ideographs, and digitised images of smiling and angry faces were used.*]

Procedure:

Individuals were requested to pose for photographs exhibiting either a smiling or an angry face. At random, the photographs were paired with Chinese ideographs. The photographs appeared on the computer screen for 12.5 ms. Immediately afterwards, an ideograph was presented and remained on the computer screen for two seconds. Participants were told that subliminal faces would be presented and the possible effects of this.

[**Note:** *It is important to mention randomised presentations and counterbalancing where they occur. This is hinted at above but not discussed in enough detail.*]

The experiment comprised three phases. Phases one and two requested participants to simply rate whether they had seen an 'angry' or a 'smiling' face. Phase three asked participants to resist this effect, while they rated them on the scale −10 to +10.

[**Note**: *The procedure is quite well written: it is clear, logically structured and to the point. The author could state that −10 is the highest dislike rating and +10 is the highest like rating, and that the values increase from −10 in units of 1. The instructions are summarised rather than printed in full (with severe word limits, you have to summarise them, but without such limits you can print them in full if you think it would help the reader understand the procedure, which it often can. Again, seek advice from your tutors on this issue as they may disagree.*]

RESULTS

The mean ratings for ideographs paired with smiling faces and ideographs paired with angry faces were calculated, and can be viewed in Table 1.

[**Note**: *When you create a table **always** refer to it in the text, as here. Don't let it 'speak for itself'.*]

The data was analysed using a related t-test. The results confirmed that there was a significant difference between mean ratings for ideographs paired with smiling faces and ideographs paired with angry faces (t (66) = 5.255, p <0.01, computed p = 0.0034). The effect size was calculated as 0.87, which means that this procedure produced a strong effect.

[**Note**: *The results are reported within a meaningful sentence. Don't have it printed on a line by itself nor should you say something like: 'The results were significant, t(66) = 5.255, P < 0.05' without saying where the difference lies. Remember you are not reporting the results of a football match. Tottenham 5 Manchester Utd 0 speaks for itself but t(66) = 5.255, P < 0.05 does not. It is the difference between the means that is statistically significant. The effect size tells us that there is a strong effect and that statistical significance would have still been reached with much fewer participants.*]

Table 1 Mean ratings of ideographs paired with smiling or angry faces

Mean ratings of ideographs paired with smiling faces	Mean ratings of ideographs paired with angry faces
6.2794 (1.94)	4.4559 (2.15)

[*Note the table is **numbered** and has a **title**. The title should mean something to a reader who is just scanning the report. Two decimal places would suffice for data like this. The student could have also stated that the standard deviations for each condition are in brackets.*]

DISCUSSION

The results of this study support the prediction that there would be a significant difference between the mean ratings of ideographs paired with smiling faces and that of ideographs paired with angry faces. Thus first confirming that learning can occur without our conscious awareness, since the faces were presented outside of conscious awareness.

[**Note:** *The first thing you do in the discussion is to relate the results to the hypothesis.*]

Second, these results occurred in participants aware of the evaluative learning effect and who were trying to resist it. More specifically, the results conclude that evaluative learning is independent of contingency awareness and is impervious to conscious control.

[**Note:** *The author takes the first step in identifying the implications of the results. Note that the term 'the results conclude' is inaccurate, and should say something like 'from* *these results it is possible to conclude'. Next, the author discusses the results with respect to the main theory.*]

The conclusions of this report replicate the recent findings of Fulcher and Hammerl (2002), thus providing further evidence for their argument. Arguably such conclusions confirm the occurrence of implicit evaluative learning.

In other studies, before the pictures are presented as pairs, the participants rate how much they like or dislike each neutral picture and again after the pairings. It is found that neutral pictures paired with pleasant pictures show an increase in their rating, while neutral pictures paired with unpleasant pictures show a decrease in their rating (Levey and Martin, 1975). In this study, ratings were taken at the end only, and a comparison of the ratings of ideographs paired with smiling faces against the ratings of ideographs paired with angry faces taken. Although such differences may have occurred through evaluative learning there may be an unlikely, but still possible, alternative explanation, such as poor counterbalancing.

[**Note:** *Next, the author discusses the wider implications of the results and adds some caution.*]

In a wider context, the finding reported here is an important contribution to our understanding of the ways in which we acquire our preferences. It has been suggested, however, that generalising conclusions, such as those presented in this study, outside the laboratory must be done with caution (Rozin, *et al.*, 1998). It is, therefore, proposed that future research could focus on the study of preferences in the real world, thus increasing the ecological validity of evaluative learning.

[**Note:** *There is a discussion of a possible future study but more details are required to take this suggestion seriously. The author could provide an outline of such an experiment. There aren't many criticisms of the method. Always think about the materials used and why they may have been chosen. Are they representative of materials found in everyday life? Is the procedure tightly controlled? A positive feature is that the author does not make trivial criticisms or unsupported statements, such as 'all Ps were psychology students, therefore we cannot generalise to the population' – why not? Or 'there were too few Ps to draw any firm conclusions' – how many should we have then? How many is too few? To make comments like these we need some supportive evidence. For example, if you are to consider the issue of the number of participants, you need to discuss the issues of 'statistical power' and 'effect sizes'. When you have calculated these you can then say whether you needed more Ps or not.*]

Overall, the student has adhered to the conventions of report writing, but has done so in a way that provides clear evidence that she is familiar with the format of journal articles. This correct formatting, her level of understanding of the central issues and the quality of her writing style is clear evidence that she has read the recommended reading and shows a good level of understanding. She also demonstrates the ability to critically evaluate arguments and understands the limits of empirical research. Note that the references should follow but I have not included them here separately to save space, but they are included in the general references section of this book.]

References

Adeyemo, S. (1994) 'Individual differences in thinking and problem solving', *Personality and Individual Differences*, 17(1), 117-24.

Aleksander, I. and Burnett, P. (1987) *Thinking Machines: The Search for Artificial Intelligence*. New York: Alfred A. Knopf.

Allard, F. and Starkes, J. L. (1991) 'Motor-skill experts in sports, dance, and other domains', in K. A. Ericsson and J. Smith (eds), *Toward a General Theory of Expertise*. Cambridge: Cambridge University Press, pp. 126-52.

Allport, D. A., Antonis, B. and Reynolds, P. (1972) 'On the division of attention: a disproof of the single channel hypothesis', *Quarterly Journal of Experimental Psychology*, 24, 225-35.

Anderson, J. R. (1987) 'Skill acquisition: compilation of weak-method problem situations', *Psychological Review*, 94(2), 192-210.

Anderson, J. R. (1993) *Rules of the Mind*. Hillsdale, NJ: Erlbaum.

Anderson, J. R., Corbett, A. T., Koedinger, K. and Pelletier, R. (1995) 'Cognitive tutors: lessons learned', *Journal of Learning Sciences*, 4, 167-207.

Annis, R. C. and Frost, B. J. (1973) 'Human visual ecology and orientation anisotropies in acuity', *Science*, 182, 729-31.

Arterberry, M. E., Yonas, A. and Bensen, A. (1989) 'Self-produced locomotion and the development of responsiveness to linear perspective and texture gradients', *Developmental Psychology*, 25, 976-82.

Atkinson, R. C. and Shiffrin, R. M. (1968) 'Human memory: a proposed system and its control processes', in K. W. Spence and J. T. Spence (eds), *The Psychology of Learning and Motivation*, Vol. II. Oxford: Academic Press.

Baddeley, A. D. (1966) 'Short-term memory for word sequences as a function of acoustic, semantic and formal similarity', *Quarterly Journal of Experimental Psychology*, 18(4), 362-5.

Baddeley, A. D. (1986) *Working Memory*. New York: Clarendon Press/Oxford University Press.

Baddeley, A. D. (1992) 'Working memory: the interface between memory and cognition', *Journal of Cognitive Neuroscience*, 4(3), 281-8.

Baddeley, A. D. and Hitch, G. J. (1974) 'Working memory', in G. H. Bower (ed.), *The Psychology of Motivation and Learning*, Vol. 8. New York: Academic Press.

Baddeley, A. D. and Hitch, G. J. (2000) 'Development of working memory: should the Pascual-Leone and the Baddeley and Hitch models be merged?', *Journal of Experimental Child Psychology*, 77(2), 128-37.

Baddeley, A. D., Lewis, V. and Nimmo-Smith, I. (1978) 'When did you last …?', in M. M. Gruneberg, P. E. Morris and R. N. Sykes (eds), *Practical Aspects of Memory*. New York: Academic Press.

Baddeley, A. D., Lewis, V. and Vallar, G. (1984) 'Exploring the articulatory loop', *Quarterly Journal of Experimental Psychology: Human Experimental Psychology*, 36A(2), 233-52.

Baddeley, A. D., Thomson, N. and Buchanan, M. (1975) 'Word length and the structure of short-term memory', *Journal of Verbal Learning and Verbal Behavior*, 14(6), 575-89.

Baeyens, F., Eelen, P. and Van den Bergh, O. (1990) 'Contingency awareness in evaluative conditioning: a case for unaware affective-evaluative learning', *Cognition and Emotion*, 4, 31-8.

Baker, A. G. and Mackintosh, N. J. (1977) 'Excitatory and inhibitory conditioning following uncorrelated presentations of CS and UCS', *Animal Learning and Behavior*, 5, 135-319.

Ball, W. and Tronick, F. (1971) 'Infant responses to impending collision: optical and real', *Science*, 171, 818-20.

Baluch, B. and Besner, D. (1991) 'Visual word recognition: evidence for strategic control of lexical and nonlexical routines in oral reading', *Journal of Experimental Psychology: Learning, Memory, and Cognition*, 17, 644-52.

Barker, M. (2003) *History and Perspectives in Psychology*. Exeter: Learning Matters.

Bartlett, J. C. and Santrock, J. W. (1979) 'Affect-dependent episodic memory in young children', *Child Development*, 50(2), 513-18.

Bell, B. E and Loftus, E. F. (1989) 'Trivial persuasion in the courtroom: the power of (a few) minor details', *Journal of Personality and Social Psychology*, 56(5), 669-79.

Bernstein, B. (1961) 'Aspects of language and learning in the genesis of the social process', *Journal of Child Psychology and Psychiatry*, 1, 313-24.

Bierwisch, M. (1975) 'Psycholinguistics: independent cognitive processes and linguistic structures', *Zeitschrift für Psychologie*, 183(1), 1-52.

Bishop, D. V. M. (1990) *Handedness and Developmental Disorders*, Clinics in Developmental Medicine 110. Oxford: Blackwell Scientific and Philadelphia: J. B. Lippinscott.

Bjork, R. A. and Whitten, W. B. (1974) 'Recency-sensitive retrieval processes in long-term free recall', *Cognitive Psychology*, 6(2), 173-89.

Blakemore, C. and Cooper, G. P. (1970) 'Development of the brain depends on the visual environment', *Nature*, 228, 477.

Boas, F. (1911) *Handbook of American Indian Languages* (Bur. of Amer. Ethnol., Bull. 40, Part I.) Washington, DC: Gov. Print. Office.

Bower, G. H. (1981) 'Mood and memory', *American Psychologist*, 36(2), 129-48.

Bower, G. H. (1987) 'Commentary on mood and memory', *Behavior Research Therapy*, 25, 443-55.

Bower, T. G., Broughton, J. M. and Moore, M. K. (1970) 'The coordination of visual and tactual input in infants', *Perception and Psychophysics*, 8(1), 51-3.

Bower, G. H., Gilligan, S. G. and Monteiro, K. P. (1981) 'Selective learning caused by affective states', *Journal of Experimental Psychology: General*, 110, 451-73.

Bradshaw, J. L.. and Nettleton, N. C. (1974) 'Articulatory inference and the MOWN-DOWN heterophone effect', *Journal of Experimental Psychology*, 102, 88-94.

Brainerd, C. J. and Reyna, V. F. (1998) 'Fuzzy-trace theory and children's false memories', *Journal of Experimental Child Psychology*, 71, 81-129.

Bransford, J. D., Johnson, M. K. (1972) 'Contextual prerequisites for understanding: some investigations of comprehension and recall', *Journal of Verbal Learning and Verbal Behavior*, 11(6), 717-26.

Brewer, W. F. (1977) 'Memory for the pragmatic implications of sentences', *Memory and Cognition*, 5, 673-8.

Broadbent, D. E. (1958) *Perception and Communication*. New York: Pergamon.

Broadbent, D. E. and Broadbent, M. H. P. (1987) 'From detection to identification: response to multiple targets in rapid serial visual presentation', *Perception and Psychophysics*, 42(2), 105-13.

Brown, R. (1973) 'Development of the first language in the human species', *American Psychologist*, 28(2), 97-106.

Brown, R. and Kulik, J. (1977) 'Flashbulb memories', *Cognition*, 5(1), 73-99.

Brown, R., Cazden, C. and Bellugi, U. (1969) 'The child's grammar from I to III', in J. P. Hill (ed.), *Minnesota Symposium on Child Psychology*, Vol. 2. Minneapolis, MI: University of Minnesota Press.

Bruce, V. and Valentine, T. (1985) 'Identity priming in the recognition of familiar faces', *British Journal of Psychology*, 76, 373-83.

Bruce, V. and Young, A. (1986) 'Understanding face recognition', *British Journal of Psychology*, 77, 305-27.

Bruner, J. S. (1964) 'The course of cognitive growth', *American Psychologist*, 19, 1-15.

Bruner, J. S. and Minturn, A. L. (1955) 'Perceptual identification and perceptual organization', *Journal of General Psychology*, 53, 21-8.

Bruyer, R., Laterre, C. and Seron, X. (1983) 'A case of prosopagnosia with some preserved covert remembrance of familiar faces', *Brain and Cognition*, 2, 257-84.

Burgess, N. and Hitch, G. J. (1992) 'Toward a network model of the articulatory loop', *Journal of Memory and Language*, 31, 429-60.

Bushnell, I. W. (1979) 'Modification of the externality effect in young infants', *Journal of Experimental Child Psychology*, 28, 211-29.

Byrne, B. and Fielding-Barnsley, R. (1991) 'Evaluation of a program to teach phonemic awareness to young children', *Journal of Educational Psychology*, 83(3), 451-5.

Campos, J. J., Langer, A. and Krowitz, A. (1970) 'Cardiac responses on the visual cliff in prelocomotor human infants', *Science*, 170, 196-7.

Carpenter, P. A., Miyake, A. and Just, M. A. (1994) 'Working memory constraints in comprehension: evidence from individual differences, aphasia, and ageing', in M. Gernsbacher (ed.), *Handbook of Psycholinguistics*. San Diego, CA: Academic Press, pp. 1075-122.

Carpenter, P. A., Miyake, A. and Just, M. A. (1995) 'Language comprehension: sentence and discourse processing', *Annual Review of Psychology*, 46U, 91-120.

Chase, W. G. and Simon, H. A. (1973) 'The mind's eye in chess', in W. G. Chase (ed.), *Visual Information Processing*. New York: Academic Press.

Cherry, E. C. (1953) 'Some experiments on the recognition of speech with one and two ears', *Journal of the Acoustical Society of America*, 25, 975-9.

Cheyne, J. A., Goyeche, J. R. and Walters, R. H. (1969) 'Attention, anxiety, and rules in resistance-to-deviation in children', *Journal of Experimental Child Psychology*, 8(1), 127-39.

Chi, M. T. H., Feltovich, P. J. and Glaser, R. (1981) 'Categorization and representation of physics problems by experts and novices', *Cognitive Science*, 5, 121-52.

Chomsky, N. (1965) *Aspects of the Theory of Syntax*. Cambridge, MA: MIT Press.

Churchland, P. S. and Churchland, P. M. (1990) 'Could a machine think? Recent arguments and new prospects', *Scientific American*, 262, 32-7.

Cleeremans, A. and McClelland, J. L. (1991) 'Learning the structure of event sequences', *Journal of Experimental Psychology: General*, 120(3), 235-53.

Cohen, B. H. (1964) 'Role of awareness in meaning established by classical conditioning', *Journal of Experimental Psychology*, 67(4), 373-8.

Colle, H. A. and Welsh, A. (1976) 'Acoustic masking in primary memory', *Journal of Verbal Learning and Verbal Behavior* 15(1), 17-31.

Collins, A. M. and Loftus, E. F. A. (1975) 'Spreading-activation theory of semantic processing', *Psychological Review*, 82(6), 407-28.

Coltheart, M. and Rastle, K. (1994) 'Serial processing in reading aloud: evidence for dual-route models of reading', *Journal of Experimental Psychology: Human Perception and Performance*, 20, 1197-211.

Conrad, R. (1964) 'Acoustic confusions in immediate memory', *British Journal of Psychology*, 55(1), 75-84.

Corteen, R. S. and Wood, B. (1972) 'Autonomic responses to shock associated words in an unattended channel', *Journal of Experimental Psychology*, 94, 308-13.

Cowan, N. (1993) 'Activation, attention, and short-term memory', *Memory and Cognition*, 21(2), 162-7.

Crick, F. and Mitchison, G. (1983) 'The function of dream sleep', *Nature*, 304(5922), 111-14.

Crowder, R. G. and Wagner, R. K. (1992) *The Psychology of Reading: An Introduction*, 2nd edn. London: Oxford University Press.

Damasio, A. R (1994) *Descartes' Error: Emotion, Reason and the Human Brain*. New York: Grosset/Putnam Books.

Daneman, M. and Green, I. (1986) 'Individual differences in comprehending and producing words in context', *Journal of Memory and Language*, 25, 1-18.

Davey, G. C. (1992) 'Classical conditioning and the acquisition of human fears and phobias: a review and synthesis of the literature', *Advances in Behaviour Research and Therapy*, 14(1), 29-66.

De Houwer, J., Baeyens, F. and Eelen, P. (1994) 'Verbal evaluative conditioning with undetected US presentations', *Behaviour Research and Therapy*, 32(6), 629-33.

De Houwer, J., Hendrickx, H. and Baeyens, F. (1997) 'Evaluative learning with "subliminally" presented stimuli', *Consciousness and Cognition*, 6, 87-107.

De Valois, R. L., Abramov, I. and Jacobs, G. H. (1966) 'Analysis of response patterns of LGN cells', *Journal of the Optical Society of America*, 56, 966-77.

de Villiers, J. G. and de Villiers, P. A. (1973) 'A cross-sectional study of the acquisition of grammatical morphemes in child speech', *Journal of Psycholinguistic Research*, 2(3), 267-78.

Deutsch, J. A. and Deutsch, D. (1963) 'Attention: some theoretical considerations', *Psychological Review*, 70, 80-90.

Dodson, C. and Reisberg, D. (1991) 'Indirect testing of eyewitness memory: the (non)effect of misinformation', *Bulletin of the Psychonomic Society*, 29(4), 333-6.

Doleys, D. M. (1977) 'Behavior treatments for nocturnal enuresis in children: a review of the recent literature', *Psychological Bulletin*, 84(1), 30-54.

Dreyfus, H. L. (1972) What Computers Can't Do: A Critique of Artificial Reason. New York: Harper & Row.

Dunbar, G. L. (2000) 'Traces of reasoning with pragmatic schemas', *Thinking and Reasoning*, 6(2), 173-81.

Duncker, K. (1945) 'On problem-solving', *Psychological Monographs*, 58, 113.

Eden, G., VanMeter, J., Rumsey, J., Maisog, J., Woods, R. and Zeffiro, T. (1996) 'Abnormal processing of visual motion in dyslexia revealed by functional brain imaging', *Nature*, 382, 66-9.

Edwards, J. R. (1979) 'Social class differences and the identification of sex in children's speech', *Journal of Child Language*, 6(1), 121-7.

Eich, J. E., Weingartner, H., Stillman, R. C. and Gillin, C. (1975) 'State-dependent accessibility of retrieval cues in the retention of a categorized list', *Journal of Verbal Learning and Verbal Behavior*, 14(4), 408-17.

Ellis, R. and Humphreys, G. (1999) *Connectionist Psychology*. Hove: Psychology Press.

Estes, W. K. (1972) 'An associative basis for coding and organization in memory', in A. W. Melton and E. Martin (eds), *Coding Processes in Human Memory*. Washington, DC: V. H. Winston & Sons.

Farb, P. (1974) *Word Play: What Happens When People Talk*. Oxford: Alfred A. Knopf.

Field, A. P. (2000a) 'I like it, but I'm not sure why: can evaluative conditioning occur without conscious awareness?', *Consciousness and Cognition*, 9, 13-36.

Field, A. P. (2000b) 'Evaluative conditioning is Pavlovian conditioning: issues of definition, measurement, and the theoretical importance of contingency awareness', *Consciousness and Cognition*, 9, 41-9.

Fischer, B. and Boch, R. (1983) 'Saccadic eye movements after extremely short reaction times in the monkey', *Brain Research*, 260, 21-6.

Fischer, B. and Ramsperger, E. (1984) 'Human express saccades: extremely short reaction times of goal directed eye movements', *Experimental Brain Research*, 57, 191-5.

Fox, D. K., Hopkins, B. L. and Anger, W. K. (1987) 'The long-term effects of a token economy on safety performance in open-pit mining', *Journal of Applied Behavior Analysis*, 20(3), 215-24.

French, C. C. and Richards, A. R. (1993) 'Clock this! An everyday example of schema-driven error in memory', *British Journal of Psychology*, 84, 249-53.

Freyd, J. J. and Gleaves, D. H. (1996) '"Remembering" words not presented in lists: relevance to the current recovered/false memory controversy', *Journal of Experimental Psychology: Learning, Memory and Cognition*, 22, 811-13.

Friedman, W. J. (1993) 'Memory for the time of past events', *Psychological Bulletin*, 113(1), 44-66.

Friedman, W. J. and Wilkins, A. J. (1985) 'Scale effects in memory for the time of events', *Memory and Cognition*, 13(2), 168-75.

Fulcher, E. P. (2002) 'Neurons with attitude: a connectionist account of evaluative learning', in S. Moore and M. Oaksford (eds), *Emotional Cognition*. Amsterdam: John Benjamins.

Fulcher, E. P. and Cocks, R. P. (1997) 'Dissociative storage systems in human evaluative conditioning', *Behaviour Research and Therapy*, 35, 1-10.

Fulcher, E. P. and Hammerl, M. (2001) 'When all is revealed: a dissociation between evaluative learning and contingency awareness', *Consciousness and Cognition*, 10, 524-49.

Fulcher, E. P., Mathews, A., Mackintosh, B. and Law, S. (2001) 'Evaluative learning and the allocation of attention in anxiety', *Cognitive Therapy and Research*, 25, 261-80.

Gardner, R. and Gardner. B. (1969) 'Teaching sign language to a chimpanzee', *Science*, 165, 664-72.

Gibson, E. J. and Walk, R. D. (1960) 'The "visual cliff"', *Scientific American*, 202(4), 64-71.

Gibson, J. J. (1979) *The Ecological Approach to Visual Perception*. Boston, MA: Houghton Mifflin.

Gibson, J. J. (1986) *The Ecological Approach to Visual Perception*. Hillsdale, NJ: Lawrence Erlbaum Associates.

Gilchrist, J. C. and Nesberg, L. S. (1952) 'Need and perceptual change in need-related objects', *Journal of Experimental Psychology*, 44, 369-76.

Giles, H. (1973) 'Communicative effectiveness as a function of accented speech', *Speech Monographs*, 40(4), 330-1.

Glanzer, M. and Cunitz, A. R. (1966) 'Two storage mechanisms in free recall', *Journal of Verbal Learning and Verbal Behavior*, 5(4), 351-60.

Gleason, J. B. and Ratner, N. B. (1993) *Psycholinguistics*. Fort Worth, TX: Harcourt Brace Jovanovich.

Godden, D. R. and Baddeley, A. D. (1975) 'Context-dependent memory in two natural environments: on land and underwater', *British Journal of Psychology*, 66(3), 325-31.

Goodwin, D. W., Powell, B., Bremer, D., Hoine, H. and Stern, J. (1969) 'Alcohol and recall: state dependent effects in man', *Science*, 163(3873), 1358-60.

Gorn, G. J. (1982) 'The effects of music in advertising on choice behavior: a classical conditioning approach', *Journal of Marketing*, 46(1), 94-101.

Gray, J. A. and Wedderburn, A. A. I. (1960) 'Grouping strategies with simultaneous stimuli', *Quarterly Journal of Experimental Psychology*, 12, 180-4.

Greene, J. (1975) *Thinking and Language*. London: Methuen.

Greeno, J. G. (1974) 'Hobbits and orcs: acquisition of a sequential concept', *Cognitive Psychology*, 6(2), 270-92.

Greeno, J. (1991) 'A view of mathematical problem solving in school', in M. U. Smith (ed.), *Toward a Unified Theory of Problem Solving*. Hillsdale, NJ: Lawrence Erlbaum Associates, pp. 69-98.

Gregor, A. J. and McPherson, A. (1965) 'A study of susceptibility to geometric illusion among cultural subgroups of Australian Aborigines', *Psychologia Africana*, 11, 1-13.

Gregory, R. L. (1963) 'Distortion of visual space as inappropriate constancy scaling', *Nature*, 199, 678-80.

Gregory, R. L. and Wallace, J. (1963) 'Recovery from early blindness: a case study', reprinted in R. L. Gregory (1974), *Concepts and Mechanisms of Perception*. London: Duckworth Books.

Grice, H. P. (1975) 'Logic and conversation', in P. Cole and J. Morgan (eds), *Syntax and Semantics*, Vol. 3. New York: Academic Press.

Grossberg, S. and Levine, D. S. (1987) 'Neural dynamics of attentionally modulated Pavlovian conditioning: blocking, interstimulus interval, and secondary reinforcement', *Applied Optics*, 26(23), 5015-30.

Guilford, J. P. (1959) 'Three faces of intellect', *American Psychologist*, 14, 469-79.

Haig, N. D. (1984) The effect of feature displacement on face recognition', *Perception*, 13, 505-12.

Hall, R. V., Lund, D. and Jackson, D. (1968) 'Effects of teacher attention on study behavior', *Journal of Applied Behavior Analysis*, 1, 1-12.

Hall, R. V., Panyan, M., Rabon, D. and Broden, M. (1968) 'Instructing beginning teachers in reinforcement procedures which improve classroom control', *Journal of Applied Behavior Analysis*, 1(4), 315-22.

Hammerl, M. and Grabitz, H. (1996) 'Human evaluative conditioning without experiencing a valued event', *Learning and Motivation*, 27, 278-93.

Harley, T. A. (1995) *The Psychology of Language: From Data to Theory*. Hove: Psychology Press.

Hasher, L. and Zacks, R. T. (1979) 'Automatic and effortful processes in memory', *Journal of Experimental Psychology: General*, 108(3), 356-88.

Haugen, E. (1966) 'Dialect, language, nation', *American Psychologist*, 68, 922-35.

Hearst, E. Y. and Franklin, S. R. (1977) 'Positive and negative relations between a signal and food: approach-withdrawal behavior to the signal', *Journal of the Experimental Analysis of Behavior*, 3, 37-52.

Hebb, D. O. (1949) *The Organization of Behavior: A Neuropsychological Theory*. New York: John Wiley & Sons.

Hebb, D. O. (1961) 'Distinctive features of learning in the higher animal', in J. F. Delafresnaye (ed.), *Brain Mechanisms and Learning*. Oxford: Oxford University Press, pp. 37-46.

Hess, E. H. (1956) 'Space perception in the chick', *Scientific American*, 195, 71-80.

Hinton, G. E. and Sejnowski, T. J. (1986) 'Learning and relearning in Boltzmann machines', in D. E. Rumelhart and J. L. McClelland (eds), *Parallel Distributed Processing: Explorations in the Microstructure of Cognition*, Vol. I. Cambridge, MA: Bradford Books.

Hinton, G. E. and Shallice, T. (1990) 'Lesioning an attractor network: investigations of acquired dyslexia', *Psychological Review*, 98, 74-95.

Hirst, W., Spelke, E. S., Reaves, C. C., Caharack, G. and Neisser, U. (1980) 'Dividing attention without alternation or automaticity', *Journal of Experimental Psychology: General*, 109, 98-117.

Hocket, C. F. (1966) *The Origin of Speech, Human Communication: Language and Its Psychobiological Base*. San Francisco: Freeman.

Holender, D. (1986) 'Semantic activation without conscious identification in dichotic listening, parafoveal vision, and visual masking', *Behavioural and Brain Sciences*, 9, 1-66.

Hopfield, J. (1982) 'Neural networks and physical systems with emergent collective computational abilities', *Proceedings of the National Academy of Sciences of the USA*, 9(2554).

Hubel, D. H. and Wiesel, T. N. (1968) 'Receptive fields and functional architecture of monkey striate cortex', *Journal of Physiology* (London), 195, 215-43.

Huitema, J. S., Dopkins, S., Klin, C. M. and Myers, J. L. (1993) 'Connecting goals and actions during reading', *Journal of Experimental Psychology: Learning, Memory and Cognition*, 19, 1053-60.

Hull, C. L. (1932) 'The goal-gradient hypothesis and maze learning', *Psychological Review*, 39, 25-43.

Hull, C. L. (1943) *Principles of Behavior: An Introduction to Behavior Theory*. New York: Appleton-Century-Crofts.

Humphrey, G. (1951) *Thinking: An Introduction to Its Experimental Psychology*. Oxford: Wiley.

Jacoby, L. L. (1991) 'A process dissociation framework: separating automatic from intentional uses of memory', *Journal of Memory and Language*, 30, 513-41.

James, W. (1890) *The Principles of Psychology*. Oxford: Holt.

Johnson, M. K., Foley, M. A. and Leach, K (1988) 'The consequences for memory of imagining in another person's voice', *Memory and Cognition*, 16(4), 337-42.

Johnsrude, I. S., Owen, A. M., Zhao, W. V. and White, N. M. (1999) 'Conditioned preference in humans: a novel experimental approach', *Learning and Motivation*, 30 (3), 250-64.

Johnstone, W. A. and Heinz, S. P. (1978) 'Flexibility and capacity demands on attention', *Journal of Experimental Psychology: General*, 107, 420-35.

Johnstone, W. A. and Wilson, J. (1980) 'Perceptual processing of non-targets in an attention task', *Memory and Cognition*, 8, 372-7.

Jones, D. M. and Macken, W. J. (1993) 'Irrelevant tones produce an irrelevant speech effect: implications for phonological coding in working memory', *Journal of Experimental Psychology: Learning, Memory, and Cognition*, 19(2), 369-81.

Jones, M. C. (1924) 'The elimination of children's fears', *Journal of Experimental Psychology*, 7, 382-90.

Kahneman, D. (1973) *Attention and Effort*. Englewood Cliffs, NJ: Prentice-Hall.

Kamin, L. (1969) 'Predictability, surprise, attention, and conditioning', in B. Campbell and R. Church (eds), *Punishment and Aversive Behavior*. New York: Appleton-Century-Crofts.

Kan, W. K. and Aleksander, I. (1987) 'A probabilistic logic neuron network for associative learning', in *Proceedings of the IEEE International Conference on Neural Networks*, Vol. II, San Diego, California, pp. 541-8.

Kandel, H. J., Ayllon, T. and Roberts, M. D. (1976) 'Rapid educational rehabilitation for prison inmates', *Behaviour Research and Therapy*, 14(5), 323-31.

Kintsch, W. (1994) 'The psychology of discourse processing', in M. A. Gernsbacher (ed.), *Handbook of Psycholinguistics*. San Diego, CA: Academic Press.

Klein, B. and Wiener, M. (1966) 'Awareness in the "learning without awareness" paradigm', *Journal of Experimental Research in Personality*, 1 (3), 145-52.

Klin, C. M., Guzman, A. E. and Levine, W. H. (1999) 'Prevalence and persistence of predictive inferences', *Journal of Memory and Language*, 40, 593-604.

Koestler, A. (1964) *The Act of Creation*. London: Hutchinson.

Koppenaal, L. and Glanzer, M. (1990) 'An examination of the continuous distracter task and the "long-term recency effect" ', *Memory and Cognition*, 18(2), 183-95.

Kowler, E. and Blaser, E. (1995) 'The accuracy and precision of saccades to small and large targets', *Vision Research*, 35, 1741-54.

Kristofferson, M. W. (1972) 'When item recognition and visual search functions are similar', *Perception and Psychophysics*, 12, 379-84.

Krosnick, J. A., Betz, A. L., Jussim, L. J. and Lynn, A. R. (1992) 'Subliminal conditioning of attitudes', *Personality and Social Psychology Bulletin*, 18, 152-62.

Kuffler, S. (1984) *From Neuron to Brain*, 2nd edn. Cambridge, MA: Sinauer Associates.

Labov, W. (1970) *On the Adequacy of Natural Languages: The Development of Tense*, Linguistic Agency University of Trier Paper No. 23, Series B.

Labov, W. (1972) *Language in the Inner City: Studies in the Black English Vernacular*. Oxford: University of Pennsylvania Press.

Lachter, J. and Bever, T. G. (1988) 'The relation between linguistic structure and associative theories of language learning: a constructive critique of some connectionist learning models', *Cognition*, 28(1-2), 195-247.

Lashley, K. S. (1950) 'In search of the engram', *Proceedings from Social Experimental Biology*, 4, 454-82.

Lazarus, R. S. (1982) 'Thoughts on the relations between emotion and cognition', *American Psychologist*, 37(9), 1019-24.

Lazarus, R. S. and McCleary, R. A. (1951) 'Autonomic discrimination without awareness: a study of subception', *Psychological Review*, 58, 113-22.

LeDoux, J. E. (1989) 'Cognitive-emotional interactions in the brain', *Cognition and Emotion*, 3(4), 267-89.

Lenneberg, G. H. (1967) *Biological Foundations of Language*. New York: Wiley.

Lesgold, A., Rubinson, H., Feltovich, P., Glaser, R., Klopfer, D. and Wang, Y. (1988) 'Expertise in a complex skill: diagnosing X-ray pictures', in M. Chi, R. Glaser and M. J. Farr (eds), *The Nature of Expertise*. Hillsdale, NJ: Erlbaum, pp. 311-42.

Levey, A. B. and Martin, I. (1975) 'Classical conditioning of human "evaluative" responses', *Behaviour Research and Therapy*, 13, 221-6.

Lewicki, P., Hill, T. and Czyzewska, M. (1992) 'Nonconscious acquisition of information', *American Psychologist*, 47 (6), 796-801.

Lewis, D. J. and Duncan, C. P. (1956) 'The effect of partial reinforcement and length of acquisition-series upon resistance to extinction of a motor and a verbal response', *American Journal of Psychology*, 69, 644-6.

Lieberman, D. A. (2000) *Learning: Behavior and Cognition*, 3rd edn. Belmont, CA: Wadsworth/Thomson Learning.

Light, L. L. and Carter-Sobell, L. (1970) 'Effects of changed semantic context on recognition memory', *Journal of Verbal Learning and Verbal Behavior*, 9(1), 1-11.

Lloyd, G. G. and Lishman, W. A. (1975) 'Effect of depression on the speed of recall of pleasant and unpleasant experiences', *Psychological Medicine*, 5, 173-80.

Loftus, E. F. (1979) 'The malleability of human memory', *American Scientist*, 67(3), 312-20.

Loftus, E. F. (1993) 'The reality of repressed memories', *American Psychologist*, 49, 518-37.

Loftus, E. F. and Ketcham, K. (1994) *The Myth of Repressed Memory*. New York: St. Martin's Press.

Luo, C. R., Johnson, R. A. and Gallo, D. A. (1998) 'Automatic activation of phonological information in reading: evidence from the semantic relatedness decision task', *Memory and Cognition*, 26(4), 833-43.

Lyons, J. (1981) 'Language and speech', *Philosophical Transactions of the Royal Society of London*, 295 (1077, Series B), 215-22.

McClelland, J. L. (1986) 'The programmable blackboard model of reading', in J. L. McClelland and D. E. Rumelhart (eds), *Parallel Distributed Processing: Explorations in the Microstructure of Cognition*, Vol. II. Cambridge, MA: MIT Press.

McClelland, J. L. and Rumelhart, D. E. (1981) 'An interactive activation model of context effects in letter perception: Part 1. An account of basic findings', *Psychological Review*, 88, 375-407.

McClelland, J. L. and Rumelhart, D. E. (1986) *Parallel Distributed Processing: Explorations in the Microstructure of Cognition*, Vol. II. Cambridge, MA:

McClelland, J. L., Rumelhart, D. E. and Hinton, G. E. (1988) 'The appeal of parallel distributed processing', in A. M. Collins and E. E. Smith (eds), *Readings in Cognitive Science: A Perspective from Psychology and Artificial Intelligence*. San Mateo, CA: Morgan Kaufmann, pp. 52-72.

McCutchen, D., Bell, L. C., France, I. M. and Perfetti, C. A. (1991) 'Phoneme-specific interference in reading: the visual tongue-twister effect revisited', *Reading Research Quarterly*, 26, 87-103.

McGurk, H. and MacDonald, J. (1976) 'Hearing lips and seeing voices', *Nature*, 264, 746-8.

MacKay, D. G. (1973) 'Aspects of the theory of comprehension, memory and attention', *Quarterly Journal of Experimental Psychology*, 25, 22-40.

McKoon, G. and Ratcliff, R. (1992) 'Inference during reading', *Psychological Review*, 99, 440-66.

McKoon, G. and Ratcliff, R. (1998) 'Memory-based language processing: psycholinguistic research in the 1990s', *Annual Review of Psychology*, 49, 25-42.

McLaughlin, B. (1984) *Second-language Acquisition in Childhood, Vol. 1: Preschool Children*, 2nd edn. Hillsdale, NJ: Lawrence Erlbaum Associates.

MacLeod, C. M. (1996) 'How priming affects two speeded implicit tests of remembering: naming colors versus reading words', *Consciousness and Cognition: An International Journal*, 5(1-2), 73-90.

MacLeod, C. and Mathews, A. (1988) 'Anxiety and the allocation of attention to threat', *Quarterly Journal of Experimental Psychology: Human Experimental Psychology*, 40(4-A), 653-70.

MacLeod, C., Mathews, A. and Tata, (1986) 'Attentional bias in emotional disorder', *Journal of Abnormal Psychology*, 95(1), 15-20.

MacNichol, E. F., Jr (1986) 'A unifying presentation of photopigment spectra', *Vision Research*, 29, 543-6.

Martin, J. A. (1977) 'Effects of positive and negative adult–child interactions on children's task performance and task preferences', *Journal of Experimental Child Psychology*, 23, 493-502.

Martin, L. (1986) ' "Eskimo words for snow": a case study in the genesis and decay of an anthropological example', *American Anthropologist*, 88, 418-23.

Mathews, A. (1994) 'Cognitive approaches to emotion and emotional disorders', *Annual Review of Psychology*, 45, 25-50.

Mathews, A. and MacLeod, C. (1994) 'Cognitive approaches to emotion and emotional disorders', *Annual Review of Psychology*, 45, 25-50.

Matlin, M. W. (2002) *Cognition*, 5th edn. Fort Worth, TX: Harcourt.

Medin, D. L., Ross, B. H. and Markman, A. B. (2001) *Cognitive Psychology*, 3rd edn. Orlando, FL: Harcourt.

Miller, G. A. (1956) 'The magical number seven, plus or minus two: some limits on our capacity for processing information', reprinted in *Psychological Review*, 101(2), 343-52.

Miller, G. A. and McNeill, D. (1969) *Linguistics. The Handbook of Social Psychology*, Vol. 3. Reading, MA: Addison-Wesley.

Minsky, M. and Papert, S. (1969) *Perceptrons*. Oxford: MIT Press.

Miyake, A., Carpenter, P. A. and Just, M. A. (1994) 'A capacity approach to syntactic comprehension disorders: making normal adults perform like aphasic patients', *Cognitive Neuropsychology*, 11(6), 671-717.

Miyawaki, K. *et al.* (1975) 'An effect of linguistic experience: the discrimination of (r) and (l) by native speakers of Japanese and English', *Perception and Psychophysics*, 18(5), 331-40.

Mogg, K., Bradley, B. P., Williams, R. and Mathews, A. (1993) 'Subliminal processing of emotional information in anxiety and depression', *Journal of Abnormal Psychology*, 102(2), 304-11.

Moray, N. (1959) 'Attention in dichotic listening: affective cues and the influence of instructions', *Quarterly Journal of Experimental Psychology*, 11, 56-60.

Morris, R., Garrud, P., Rawlins, J. and O'Keefe, J. (1982) 'Place navigation impaired in rats with hippocampal lesions', *Nature*, 297, 681-3.

Mowrer, W. M. (1938) 'Enuresis: a method for its study and treatment', *American Journal of Orthopsychiatry*, 8, 436-59.

Mozer, M. C. (1991) *The Perception of Multiple Objects: A Connectionist Approach*. Cambridge, MA: MIT Press.

Mozer, M. C. (1987) 'Early parallel processing in reading: a connectionist approach', in M. Coltheart (ed.), *Attention and Performance, Vol. XII: The Psychology of Reading*. Hove: Lawrence Earlbaum Associates, pp. 83-104.

Murdock, B. B. Jr (1962) 'Direction of recall in short term memory', *Journal of Verbal Learning and Verbal Behavior*, 1(2), 119-24.

Murphy, S. T. and Zajonc, R. B. (1993) 'Affect, cognition, and awareness: affective priming with optimal and suboptimal stimulus exposures', *Journal of Personality and Social Psychology*, 64, 723-39.

Murray, D. J. (1967) 'The role of speech responses in short-term memory', *Canadian Journal of Psychology*, 21(3), 263-76.

Nairne, J. S. (1990) 'A feature model of immediate memory', *Memory and Cognition*, 18, 251-69.

Navon, D. and Gopher, D. (1979) 'On the economy of the human processing system', *Psychological Review*, 86, 214-55.

Neath, I. (1998) *Human Memory: An Introduction to Research, Data, and Theory*. Belmont, CA: Brooks/Cole Publishing.

Neisser, U. (1964) 'Visual search', *Scientific American*, 210(6), 941-02.

Neisser, U. (1967) *Cognitive Psychology*. New York: Meredith.

Neisser, U. and Harsch, N. (1992) 'Phantom flashbulbs: false recollections of hearing the news about Challenger', in E. Winogrand and U. Neisser (eds), *Affect and Accuracy in Recall: Studies of 'Flashbulb' Memories*. New York: Cambridge University Press, pp. 9-31.

Newell, A. and Simon, H. A. (1972) *Human Problem Solving*. Oxford: Prentice Hall.

Newport, E. L. (1994) 'Maturational constraints on language learning', *Cognitive Science*, 14, 11-28.

Norma, D. A. (1968) 'Toward a theory of memory and attention', *Psychological Review*, 75, 522-36.

Norman, D. A. and Bobrow, D. G. (1975) 'On data limited and resource limited processes', *Cognitive Psychology*, 7, 44-64.

Norman, D. A and Rumelhart, D. E. (1981) 'The LNR approach to human information processing', *Cognition*, 10, 235-40.

Norton, D. and Stark, L. W. (1971) 'Scanpaths in saccadic eye movements while viewing and recognizing patterns', *Vision Research*, 11, 929-42.

O'Brien, E. J. and Myers, J. L. (1999) 'Text comprehension: a view from the bottom up', in S. Goldman *et al.* (eds), *Narrative Comprehension, Causality, and Coherence: Essays in Honor of Tom Trabasso*. Mahwah, NJ: Erlbaum.

Öhman, A., Erixon, G. and Lofberg, I. (1975) 'Phobias and preparedness: phobic versus neutral pictures as conditioned stimuli for human autonomic responses', *Journal of Abnormal Psychology*, 1975, 84, 41-5.

O'Leary, S. G. (1995) 'Parental discipline mistakes', *Current Directions in Psychological Science*, 4(1), 11-13.

O'Neill, H. (2000) 'How DNA became a perfect witness', *Toronto Star*, 21 September; available online: http://www.deathpenaltyinfo.org/Toronto-DNA.html.

Osgood, C. E., Suci, G. J. and Tannenbaum, P. H. (1957) *The Measurement of Meaning*. Urbana, IL: University of Illinois Press.

Owen, E. and Sweller, J. (1985) 'What do students learn while solving mathematics problems?', *Journal of Educational Psychology*, 77(3), 272-84.

Palmer, S. E. (1975) *Structural Aspects of Perceptual Organization*. Department of Psychology, University of California, San Diego.

Parrot, W. G. and Schulkin, J. (1993) 'Neuropsychology and the cognitive nature of the emotions', *Cognition and Emotion*, 7, 43-59.

Patterson, K. and Kay, J. (1982) 'Letter-by-letter reading: psychological descriptions of a neurological syndrome', *Quarterly Journal of Experimental Psychology*, 34A, 411-41.

Patterson, K., Coltheart, M. and Marshall, J. C. (eds) (1985) *Surface Dyslexia*. Hillsdale, NJ: Erlbaum.

Pavlov, I. P. (1927) *Conditioned Reflexes*. London: Oxford.

Pearce J. M. (1987) *An Introduction to Animal Cognition*. Hove: Erlbaum.

Perfetti, C. A. and Bell, L. (1991) 'Phonemic activation during the first 40 ms of word identification: evidence from backward masking and masked priming', *Journal of Memory and Language*, 30, 473-85.

Peters, R. and McGee, R. (1982) 'Cigarette smoking and state-dependent memory', *Psychopharmacology*, 76(3), 232-5.

Pezdek, W., Finger, K. and Hodge, D. (1997) 'Planting false childhood memories: the role of event plausibility', *Psychological Science*, 8, 437-41.

Phillips, E. L. (1968) 'Achievement place: token reinforcement procedures in a home-style rehabilitation setting for "pre-delinquent" boys', *Journal of Applied Behavior Analysis*, 1(3), 213-23.

Piaget, J. (1952) *The Origins of Intelligence in Children*, trans. Margaret Cook. New York: International Universities Press.

Pinker, S. (1994) *The Language Instinct*. New York: William Morrow.

Pinker, S. and Prince, A. (1988) 'On language and connectionism: analysis of a parallel distributed model of language acquisition', *Cognition*, 28, 73-194.

Plaut, D. C., McClelland, J. L., Seidenberg, M. S. and Patterson, K. (1996) 'Understanding normal and impaired word reading: computational principles in quasi-regular domains', *Psychological Review*, 103, 56-115.

Pollatsek, A. and Rayner, K. (1990) 'Eye movements and lexical access in reading', in D. A. Balota, G. B. Flores d'Arcais and K. Rayner (eds), *Comprehension Processes in Reading*. Hillsdale, NJ: Lawrence Erlbaum Associates.

Postman, L. and Phillips, L. W. (1965) 'Short-term temporal changes in free recall', *Quarterly Journal of Experimental Psychology*, 17(2), 132-8.

Pressley, M., Rankin, J. and Yokoi, L. (1996) 'A survey of instructional practices of outstanding primary-level literacy teachers', *Elementary School Journal*, 96, 363-84.

Ratner, N. B. and Gleason, J. B. (1993) 'An introduction to psycholinguistics: what do language users know?', in J. B. Gleason and N. B. Ratner (eds), *Psycholinguistics*. Fort Worth, TX: Harcourt Brace Jovanovich.

Raymond, M. J. (1964) 'The treatment of addiction by aversion conditioning with apomorphine', *Behavior Research and Therapy*, 1, 287-91.

Rayner, K. (1988) 'Word recognition cues in children: the relative use of graphemic cues, orthographic cues, and grapheme-phoneme correspondence rules', *Journal of Educational Psychology*, 80, 473-9.

Rayner, K. (1998) 'Eye movements in reading and information processing: 20 years of research', *Psychological Bulletin*, 124, 372-422.

Reitman, W. R. (1965) *Cognition and Thought: An Information Processing Approach*. Oxford: Wiley.

Rescorla, R. A. (1968) 'Probability of shock in the presence and absence of CS in fear conditioning', *Journal of Comparative and Physiological Psychology*, 66(1), 1-5.

Rescorla, R. A. and Wagner, A. R. (1972) 'A theory of Pavlovian conditioning: variations in the effectiveness of reinforcement and nonreinforcement', in A. H. Black and W. F. Prokasy (eds), *Classical Conditioning II: Current Research and Theory*. New York: Appleton-Century-Crofts, pp. 64-99.

Riddoch, J., Humphreys, G., Cleton, P. and Fery, P. (1990) 'Interaction of attentional and lexical processes in neglect dyslexia', *Cognitive Neuropsychology*, 7, 369-89.

Riesen, A. A. (1950) 'Arrested vision', *Scientific American*, 186, 107-8.

Riesen, A. H. and Kinder, E. F. (1952) *Postural Development of Infant Chimpanzees: A Comparative and Normative Study Based on the Gesell Behavioral Examination*. New Haven, CT: Yale University Press.

Robinson, K. J. and Roediger, H. L. (1997) 'Associative processes in false recall and false recognition', *Psychological Science*, 8, 231-7.

Roediger, H. L. and McDermott, K. B. (1995) 'Creating false memories: remembering words not presented in lists', *Journal of Experimental Psychology: Learning, Memory, and Cognition*, 21(4), 803-14.

Roediger, H. L. and Payne, D. G. (1983) 'Superiority of free recall to cued recall with "strong" cues', *Psychological Research*, 45(3), 275-86.

Rozin, P., Wrzesniewski, A. and Byrnes, D. (1998) 'The elusiveness of evaluative conditioning', *Learning and Motivation*, 29, 397-415.

Rumelhart, D. E. and McClelland, J. L. (1985) 'Levels indeed: a response to Broadbent', *Journal of Experimental Psychology: General*, 114(2), 193-7.

Rumelhart, D. E. and Norman, D. (1981) 'Analogical processes in learning', in J. R. Anderson (ed.), *Cognitive Skills and Their Acquisition*. Hillsdale, NJ: Erlbaum.

Rumelhart, D. E., Hinton, G. E. and Williams, R. J. (1986) 'Learning representations by back-propagating errors', *Nature*, 323, 533-6.

Sachs, J., Bard, B. and Johnson, M. L. (1981) 'Language learning with restricted input: case studies of two hearing children of deaf parents', *Applied Psycholinguistics*, 2(1), 33-54.

Saffran, E. M., Bogyo, L. C., Schwartz, M. F. and Marin, O. S. M. (1980) 'Does deep dyslexia reflect right-hemisphere reading?', in M. Coltheart, K. Patterson, and J. C. Marshall (eds), *Deep Dyslexia*. London: Routledge & Kegan Paul, pp. 381-406.

Salamé, P. and Baddeley, A. D. (1982) 'Disruption of short-term memory by unattended speech: implications for the structure of working memory', *Journal of Verbal Learning and Verbal Behavior*, 21(2), 150-64.

Salapatek, P. (1975) 'Pattern perception in early infancy', in L. Cohen and P. Salapatek (eds), *Infant Perception: From Sensation to* Cognition, Vol. 1. New York: Academic Press, pp. 133-249.

Sandford, (1936) 'The effects of abstinence from food on imaginal processes', *Journal of Psychology*, 2, 129-36.

Saslow, M. G. (1967) 'Saccade latency and warning signals: stimulus onset, offset and change as warning events', *Journal of the Optical Society of America*, 57, 102-49.

Savage-Rumbaugh, E. S. (1986) *Ape Language: From Conditioned Response to Symbol*. New York: Columbia University Press.

Schiller, P. H., Logothetis, N. K. and Charles, E. R. (1990) 'Functions of the color-opponent and broad-band channels of the visual system', *Nature*, 343, 68-72.

Schneider, W. and Shiffrin, R. M. (1977) 'Controlled and automatic human information processing: 1. Detection, search, and attention', *Psychological Review*, 84, 1-66.

Schoenfeld, A. (1985) *Mathematical Problem Solving*. New York: Academic Press.

Schoenfeld, A. H. and Herrmann, D. J. (1982) 'Problem perception and knowledge structure in expert and novice mathematical problem solvers', *Journal of Experimental Psychology: Learning, Memory, and Cognition*, 8(5), 484-94.

Schwartz, A., Campos, J. and Baisel, E. (1973) 'The visual cliff: cardiac and behavioral responses on the deep and shallow sides at five and nine months of age', *Journal of Experimental Child Psychology*, 15, 86-99.

Schwartz, S. H. (1971) 'Modes of representation and problem solving: well evolved is half solved', *Journal of Experimental Psychology*, 91, 347-50.

Searle, J. R. (1979) *Expressions and Meaning*. Cambridge: Cambridge University Press.

Searle, J. R. (1980) 'Minds, brains, and programs', *Behavioral and Brain Sciences*, 1, 417-24.

Searle, J. R. (1990) 'Is the brain's mind a computer program?', *Scientific American*, 262(1), 26-37.

Segall, M. H, Campbell, D. T. and Herskovits, M. J. (1966) *The Influence of Culture on Visual Perception*. Indianapolis, IN: Bobbs-Merrill.

Seidenberg, M. (1995) 'Visual word recognition: an overview', in P. Eimas and J. L. Miller (eds), *Handbook of Perception and Cognition: Language*. New York: Academic Press.

Seidenberg, M. S. and McClelland, J. L. (1989) 'A distributed, developmental model of word recognition and naming', *Psychological Review*, 96, 523-68.

Sejnowski, T. J. and Rosenberg, C. R. (1987) 'Parallel networks that learn to pronounce English text', *Complex Systems*, 1, 145-68.

Sekular, R. and Blake, R. (1985) *Perception*. New York: Knopf.

Seligman, M. E. and Maeir, S. F. (1967) 'Failure to escape traumatic shock', *Journal of Experimental Psychology*, 74(1), 1-9.

Shaffer, D. R. (1993) *Developmental Psychology: Childhood and Adolescence*, 3rd edn. Pacific Grove, CA: Brooks/Cole.

Shatz, M. and Gelman, R. (1973) *The development of communication skills: modifications in the speech of young children as a function of listener*, Monographs of the Society for Research in Child Development No. 38, 1-37.

Shiffrin, R. M. and Schneider, W. (1977) 'Controlled and automatic human information processing: II. Perceptual learning, automatic attending, and a general theory', *Psychological Review*, 84, 127-90.

Simon, H. A. (1988) 'Creativity and motivation: a response to Csikszentmihalyi', *New Ideas in Psychology*, 6(2), 177-81.

Simon, H. A. (1980) 'Problem solving and education', in D. T. Tuma and F. Reif (eds), *Problem Solving and Education: Issues in Teaching and Research*. Hillsdale, NJ: Erlbaum, pp. 81-96.

Simon, H. A. (1995) 'Problem forming, problem finding, and problem solving in design', in A. Collen and W. W. Gasparski (eds), *Design Systems: General Applications of Methodology*, Vol. 3. New Brunswick, NJ: Transaction Publishers, pp. 245-57.

Simon, H. A. and Chase, W. G. (1973) 'Skill in chess', *American Scientist*, 61(4), 394-403.

Singley, M. K. and Anderson, J. R. (1989) *Transfer of Cognitive Skill*. Cambridge, MA: Harvard University Press.

Skinner, B. F. (1957) *Verbal Behavior*. East Norwalk, CT: Appleton-Century-Crofts.

Skinner, B. F. (1969) *Contingencies of Reinforcement*. New York: Appleton-Century-Crofts.

Smith, G. H. and Engel, R. (1968) 'Influence of a female model on perceived characteristics of an automobile', *Proceedings of the 7th Annual Convention of the American Psychological Association*, 3, 681-2.

Smith, S. M. and Blankenship, S. E. (1991) 'Incubation and the persistence of fixation in problem solving', *American Journal of Psychology*, 104(1), 61-87.

Smith, S. M., Glenberg, A. and Bjork, R. A. (1978) 'Environmental context and human memory', *Memory and Cognition*, 6(4), 342-53.

Speisman, J. C., Lazarus, R. S., Davison, L. and Mordkoff, A. M. (1964) 'Experimental analysis of a film used as a threatening stimulus', *Journal of Consulting Psychology*, 28(1), 23-33.

Spelke, E., Hirst, W. and Neisser, U. (1976) 'Skills of divided attention', *Cognition*, 4, 215-30.

Spence, K. W. (1969) *Behavior and Conditioning*. Oxford: Yale University Press.

Stroop, J. R. (1935) 'Studies of interference in serial verbal reactions', *Journal of Experimental Psychology*, 18, 643-62.

Sweller, J. and Chandler, P. (1994) 'Why some material is difficult to learn', *Cognition and Instruction*, 12(3), 185-233.

Teasdale, J. D. and Fogarty, S. J. (1979) 'Differential effects of induced mood on retrieval of pleasant and unpleasant events from episodic memory', *Journal of Abnormal Psychology*, 88(3), 248-57.

Thompson, C. P., Skowronski, J.J. and Lee, J. (1988) 'Telescoping in dating naturally occurring events', *Memory and Cognition*, 16(5), 461-8.

Thorndike, E. L. (1911) *Animal Intelligence. Experimental Studies*. Oxford: Macmillan.

Tolman, E. C. (1936) 'Operational behaviorism and current trends in psychology', reprinted in E. C. Tolman (ed.) (1966), *Behavior and Psychological Man: Essays in Motivation and Learning*. Berkeley, CA: University of California Press.

Torrance, E. P and Witt, G. (1966) 'Experimental grouping on the basis of creative abilities and motivations', *Gifted Child Quarterly*, 10(1), 9-14.

Trabasso, T. T. and Bower, G. H. (1968) *Attention in Learning: Theory and Research*. New York: Wiley & Sons.

Treisman, A. M. (1960) 'Verbal cues in selective listening', *Quarterly Journal of Experimental Psychology*, 12, 242-8.

Treisman, A. (1964) 'Verbal cues, language and meaning in attention', *American Journal of Psychology*, 77, 206-14.

Treisman, A. M. and Geffen, G. (1967) 'Selective attention: perception or response?', *Quarterly Journal of Experimental Psychology*, 19, 1-18.

Treisman, A. M. and Riley, J. G. A. (1969) 'Is selective attention selective perception or selective response: a further test', *Journal of Experimental Psychology*, 79, 27-43.

Tulving, E. (1986) 'What kind of a hypothesis is the distinction between episodic and semantic memory?', *Journal of Experimental Psychology: Learning, Memory, and Cognition*, 12(2), 307-11.

Tulving, E. and Thomson, D. M. (1973) 'Encoding specificity and retrieval processes in episodic memory', *Psychological Review*, 80(5), 359-80.

Tulving, E., Mandler, G. and Baumal, R. (1964) 'Interaction of two sources of information in tachistoscopic word', *Journal of Verbal Learning and Verbal Behavior*, 1, 321-34.

Turing, A. M. (1950) 'Computing machinery and intelligence', *Mind*, 59, 433-60.

Turkkan, J. S. (1989) 'Classical conditioning: the new hegemony', *Brain and Behaviour Sciences*, 12, 121-79.

Ullman, S. (1989) 'Aligning pictorial descriptions: an approach to object recognition', *Cognition*, 32, 193-254.

Underwood, B. J. (1977) *Temporal Codes for Memories: Issues and Problems*. Oxford: Lawrence Erlbaum.

van den Broek, P. (1994) 'Comprehension and memory of narrative texts', in M. A. Gernsbacher (ed.), *Handbook of Psycholinguistics*. San Diego, CA: Academic Press.

Von Senden, M. (1932) *Form- und Gestaltauffassung bei operierten Blindgeborenen vor und nach der Operation* (Shape and gestalt comprehension in operated on congenitally blind people before and after the surgery). Leipzig.

Von Wright, J. M., Anderson, K. and Stenman, U. (1975) 'Generalisation of conditioned GSR's in dichotic listening', in P. M. A. Rabbitt and S. Dornic (eds), *Attention and Performance*, V. London: Academic Press.

Wallas, G . (1926) *The Art of Thought*. London: Cape.

Ward, G. and Allport, A. (1997) 'Planning and problem-solving using five-disc tower of London task', *Quarterly Journal of Experimental Psychology: Human Experimental Psychology*, 50A(1), 49-78.

Ward, T. B. (1994) 'Structured imagination: the role of category structure in exemplar generation', *Cognitive Psychology*, 27, 1-40.

Ward, T. B., Smith, S. M. and Finke, R. A. (1999) 'Creative cognition', in R. J. Sternberg (ed.), *Handbook of Creativity*. Cambridge: Cambridge University Press.

Warrington, E. K. and Shallice, T. (1980) 'Word-from dyslexia', *Brain*, 103, 99-112.

Waters, G. S., Rochon, E. and Caplan, D. (1992) 'The role of high-level speech planning in rehearsal: evidence from patients with apraxia of speech', *Journal of Memory and Language*, 31(1), 54-73.

Watkins, M. J. (1972) 'Locus of the modality effect in free recall', *Journal of Verbal Learning and Verbal Behavior*, 11(5), 644-8.

Watkins, M. J. and Watkins, O. C. (1973) 'The postcategorical status of the modality effect in serial recall', *Journal of Experimental Psychology*, 99(2), 226-30.

Waugh, N. C. and Norman, D. A. (1965) 'Primary memory', *Psychological Review*, 72(2), 89-104.

Weaver, C. A. (1993) 'Do you need a "flash" to form a flashbulb memory?', *Journal of Experimental Psychology: General*, 122(1), 39-46.

Weber, R. J. and Dixon, S. (1989) 'Invention and gain analysis', *Cognitive Psychology*, 21(3), 283-302.

Weisberg, R. (1986) *Creativity: Genius and Other Myths*. New York: W. H. Freeman.

White, A. G. and Bailey, J. S. (1990) 'Reducing disruptive behaviors of elementary physical education students with Sit and Watch', *Journal of Applied Behavior Analysis*, 23(3), 353-9.

Whorf, B. L. (1956) *Language, Thought, and Reality: Selected Writings*. Cambridge, MA: Technology Press of MIT.

Wickens, C. D. (1987) 'Attention', in P. A. Hancock (ed.), *Human Factors Psychology*. Amsterdam: North Holland.

Widrow, B. (1962) 'Generalization and storage in networks of ADALINE neurons', in G. T. Yovits (ed.), *Self-Organizing Systems*. New York: Spartan Books, pp. 435-61.

Wierson, M. and Forehand, R. (1994) 'Parent behavioral training for child noncompliance: rationale, concepts, and effectiveness', *Current Directions in Psychological Science*, 3(5), 146-50.

Wiesel, T. (1982) 'Postnatal development of the visual cortex and the influences of environment', *Nature*, 299, 583-91.

Wolf, M., Braukmann, C. and Ramp, K. (1987) 'Serious delinquent behavior as part of a significantly handicapping condition. Cures and supportive environment', *Journal of Applied Behavior Analysis*, 20, 347-59.

Wolpe, J. (1958) *Psychotherapy by Reciprocal Inhibition*. Stanford, CA: Stanford University Press.

Wydell, T. N., Patterson, K. E. and Humphreys, G. W. (1993) 'Phonologically mediated access to meaning for Kanji: is a *rows* still a *rose* in Japanese Kanji?', *Journal of Experimental Psychology: Learning, Memory, and Cognition*, 19, 491-54.

Zajonc, R. B. (1980) 'Feeling and thinking: preferences need no inferences', *American Psychologist*, 35, 151-75.

Zajonc, R. B. (1984) 'On the primacy of affect', *American Psychologist*, 39(2), 117-23.

Zeki, S. M. (1992) 'The functional organization of projections from striate to prestriate visual cortex in the rhesus monkey', *Cold Spring Harbor Symposia on Quantitative Biology*, 15, 591-600.

Zimmer-Hart, C. L. and Rescorla, R. A. (1974) 'Extinction of a Pavlovian conditioned inhibitor', *Journal of Comparative and Physiological Psychology*, 86, 837-45.

Index